Richard Francis Burton

Wanderings in West Africa from Liverpool to Fernando Po

In Two Volumes. Vol. II

Richard Francis Burton

Wanderings in West Africa from Liverpool to Fernando Po
In Two Volumes. Vol. II

ISBN/EAN: 9783744751285

Printed in Europe, USA, Canada, Australia, Japan

Cover: Foto ©Andreas Hilbeck / pixelio.de

More available books at **www.hansebooks.com**

WANDERINGS IN WEST AFRICA

FROM

LIVERPOOL TO FERNANDO PO.

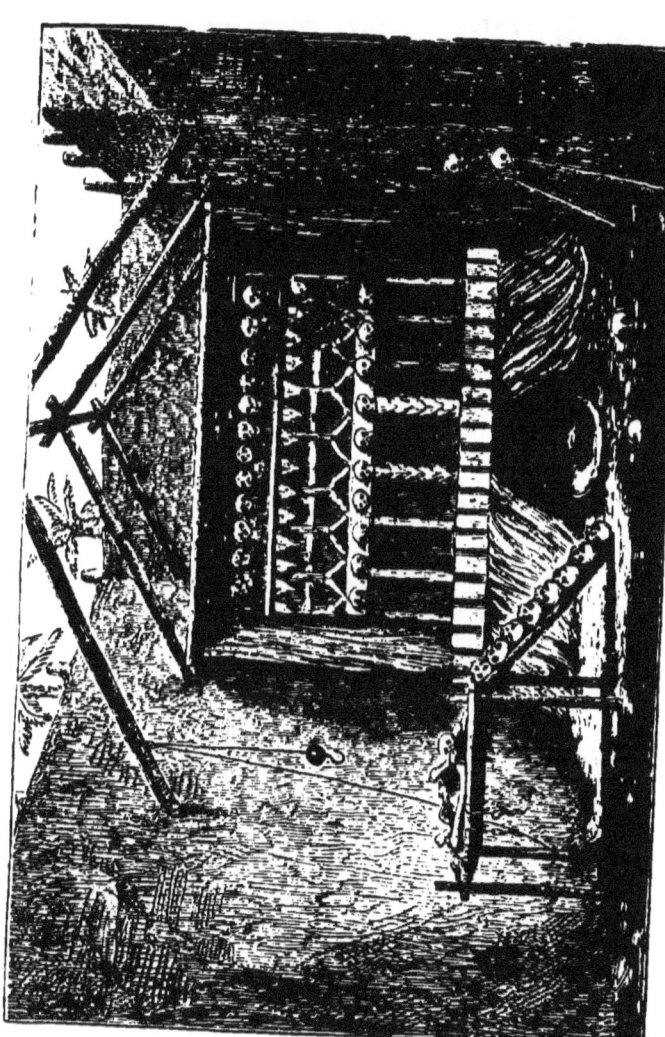

THE JUJU, OR SACRIFICE HOUSE, GRAND BONNY RIVER.

(From a Sketch by the Author.)

WANDERINGS IN WEST AFRICA

FROM

LIVERPOOL TO FERNANDO PO.

By A F.R.G.S.

With Map and Illustration.

IN TWO VOLUMES.
VOL. II.

LONDON:
TINSLEY BROTHERS, 18, CATHERINE ST., STRAND.
1863.

LONDON:
BRADBURY AND EVANS, PRINTERS, WHITEFRIARS.

CONTENTS.

	PAGE
CHAPTER VI. *(continued)*.	
SIX HOURS AT THE CAPE OF COCOA PALMS	1
CHAPTER VII.	
TWENTY-FOUR HOURS AT CAPE COAST CASTLE	39
CHAPTER VIII.	
GOLD IN AFRICA	104
CHAPTER IX.	
A PLEASANT DAY IN THE LAND OF ANTS	132
CHAPTER X.	
A DAY AT LAGOS.	186
CHAPTER XI.	
BENIN—NUN—BONNY RIVER TO FERNANDO PO	242

CHAPTER VI. (*continued.*)

SIX HOURS AT THE CAPE OF COCOA PALMS.

"Cape de las Palmas, a fair high land; but having on the eastern side some low places by the shore which look like red cliffs, with white streaks resembling highways, reaching the length of a cable."
Capt. JOHN LAKE, *the first English visitor at this place in* 1554.

16TH SEPTEMBER, 186—.

AFTER subscribing to the Cavalla Messenger,* and taking leave of Mr. Hoffman, with gratitude for his kindness, indeed highly pleased with the civility of all after our short but sharp experience at S'a Leone, we walked back to the Hotel, where we found a luncheon provided for us by Mr. John Marshall. Our leave of absence was soon ended; we unfolded umbrellas—a pre-

---

* It is published monthly at Cavalla, the head-quarters of Bishop Payne. The printing, which is tolerable, is "done" by two native youths. The subscription, payable in advance, is fifty cents (two shillings) per annum; or, including postage per steamer, seventy-five cents.

caution never to be disregarded in these latitudes, where the more you know of the sun the more you respect him —and took our way to the boats. On the steps a document was handed to me: it bore the novel direction:

For Nanpopo (Fernando Po),
Mr. Friday,
In the care of one* Crewman (Kruman).

The Consul had failed in recruiting men. "Nanny Po," was a word of fear to the Krumen; they had been made to work in gardens and on the roads, and they complained—most falsely, I afterwards found—of "*puoco comer, mucho trabajo.*" Some of them had been engaged for one year, not two, and had been kept for three—the usual time—to the great sorrow of their mammies and to the abiding resentment of themselves. Hearing the Consul speak a few words of Spanish, they decided him to be "a 'Panyer," and resolutely refused, with characteristic independence, to accompany him. One man came down to the wharf and expressed willingness to engage; he asked, besides passage to and from his country, and food, clothes, and lodging, $4 and 2 pezetas *per mensem*—$2 being the usual wages. His terms were agreed to, but he forgot to come on board. We also failed in buying Kru canoes, which are useful for fishing and for sending notes to ships in harbour. They are usually plentiful, and sell for 1*l.* each; the people, however, in actual sight of "siller," declared that they

---

* The African language has no indefinite article: hence *one* is always used for our *a*.

wanted all their craft, and I know the African too well to waste time when he urges that plea and takes that stand.

Cape Palmas, called Bàmnepo by the natives, is in the county of Maryland, the easternmost of the five into which the Liberian Republic is divided, beginning from the east Sinoe, Bassa, Mesurado, in which the capital stands, and Kassa, the northernmost which contains the much-vexed Gallinhas River. It was begun in 1834 by the Maryland State Colonization Society, which granted to it an annual sum of 2000*l.* from the treasury. The Governor, or, as he is here called, the Superintendent of Public Affairs at Cape Palmas Station, is Hon. J. C. Gibson, who is under the present President of Liberia, Hon. S. A. Benson,—who succeeded ex-President Roberts,—a good working man, but as arbitrary as democrats when in power are apt to be. There are two senators—Hon. J. Marshall, and Hon. J. Moulton. Whenever a dispute arises between the colonists and the natives, a council, composed of the Superintendent and the Senators, together with the African Headman, holds "palaver" upon the subject. The Krumen have as yet shown a rooted aversion to all taxation; they prefer to be plundered wholesale, at uncertain periods, by their own people, than pay a certain and invariable, though trifling assessment, for law, order, and protection. Consequently Harper is rather depressed for want of means. The principal income is from ships entering the harbour; they are charged 3*l.* 1*s.* for anchorage and lighthouse dues. Another tax might be put upon water, of which there are good, but not abundant, springs at the Cape. The number of Krumen who flock to this station for employment seldom falls below 1500, and of course it is made a source of profit to individual colonists. The Republic desires that trade be restricted to six ports of entry, of which Harper is one.*

The Methodists who, about eight years ago, established themselves in these lands, number the largest body of Christians in Liberia—their annals, however, are a necrology. The reader may see below the state of the Protestant Episcopal Mission at the time of my visit.† In the

* Of these six, three are in one county, and one in each of the others, viz. :—

Roberts Port, ⎫
Monrovia, ⎬ Mesurad County.
Marshall, ⎭
Buchanan, Bassa County.
Greenhill, Sinoe County.
Harper, Maryland County.

† "*The Mission Field about Cape Palmas.*

"It was a wise and merciful Providence which first directed the Protestant Episcopal Mission, and others, to Cape Palmas and parts adjacent. It was the healthiest of the settlements then made on the coast. Unlike some other portions of the Liberian coast, the tribes around had not been thinned or broken up by the slave trade and domestic wars which it ever excites. While the Cavalla River, alive with an active trade, opened a highway eighty miles into the interior.

"These favourable circumstances, made known by Dr. James Hall, then Governor at Cape Palmas, and Rev. Dr. Wilson, who accompanied him on his expedition to purchase land for the colony, determined the Foreign Committee of the Protestant Episcopal Church to commence their missionary work at Cape Palmas.

"In the autumn of 1836, Rev. Dr. Savage arrived at Cape Palmas, Mr. James M. Thomson, a Liberian, had been employed by the Foreign Committee to make preliminary arrangements, and had so well

several settlements of Rocktown, Fishtown, and Springhill there are about 130 catechumens, who are instructed by

occupied his time that when Dr. Savage arrived, the lot at Mount Vaughan was partially cleared, and Mr. Thomson had gathered a small native school in a thatched house on the premises.

"On July 4th, 1837, Rev. Messrs. Minor and Payne joined Dr. Savage. By this time the first Mission House at Mount Vaughan was so far completed that, by putting up curtains, we managed to make out three rooms for the Mission family.

"In the Mission field they found Rev. Dr. Wilson and associates of the American Board occupying Cape Palmas, Rocktown, Fishtown, and Half Cavalla ; and Rev. F. Burns, of the Methodist Mission, regularly in the colony.

"The field immediately about the Cape being so well occupied, the Protestant Episcopal Mission at once directed its efforts towards the interior. Accordingly, while Mr. Payne officiated for a small colonist congregation, and occasionally at 'Joe War's Town' (not Hoffman station), Grahway and Perebo, Mr. Minor was sent to make arrangements to open a station at Dihně (Dinnah), on the Cavalla, thirty miles from its mouth.

"The lot had been selected for the building and the plan of the house decided upon when the people of Bărěkě, a larger town midway between Mount Vaughan and Dihně, insisted upon our having a Mission station at their place before going beyond them.

"As they commanded the road, we could do no better than fall back on Bărěkě. Here, again, Mr. Minor had gone and selected a Mission lot ; and King Tedi Bliâ had visited Mount Vaughan to complete arrangements for building, when suddenly war broke out between Bărěkě and the colony, and our progress was again arrested. Soon after this, Dr. Wilson, of the American Board, and associates determined to remove their Mission to the Gaboon River, and their stations about Cape Palmas were gradually transferred to the Protestant Episcopal Mission."

"*General Statistics of the Protestant Episcopal Mission at Capes Palmas and Parts adjacent.*

"We give this month the general statistics of our Mission. We shall be most happy to receive from our brethren the coast statistics of their Mission, and any items of intelligence connected therewith.

three Anglo-Americans and their families. With excellent sense the missionaries employ their pupils for a short time in reading and writing, ciphering, and psalmody, and for a long time in learning trades and handicraft. Education is cheap; the poor pay but 2 cents, the rich $5, a year. They thus form a Civilization Society; whilst others, neglecting all things save the cure of souls, are successful in producing, as the phrase is, more convicts than converts. They possess however a great advantage in the collaboration of a coloured population, not from Jamaica, or from what

"Stations.—Colonists, 6 ; natives, 15. Total, 21.

"These Stations extend 270 miles along the coast, from Monrovia to Taboo ; and seventy-five miles interior, from Cavalla to Bohlen.

"Missionaries.—Foreign, 4 ; colonists, 4. Total, 8.

"Catechists, Teachers, and Assistants.—Foreign, 5 ; colonial, 8 ; and native, 18. Total, 31.

"Baptisms (past year returns imperfect).—Infant, 13 ; adult, 21. Total, 34.

"Confirmations (past year), 37.

"Communicants.—Foreign and colonists, 211 ; native, 158. Total, 369.

"Boarding Scholars.—Colonists, 37 ; natives, 104. Total, 140.

"Day Scholars.—Colonists, 133 ; natives, 250. Total, 383.

"Sunday Scholars.—Colonists, 334 ; natives, 150. Total, 484.

"Candidates for Orders.—Foreign, 1 ; colonists, 4 ; natives, 2. Total, 7.

"Field of labour of Liberia.—Three counties, eight native tribes—aggregate population, 16,000.

"The Grebo language reduced to writing: Genesis, four Gospels, Acts, Common Prayer Book (in part), Bible History, Life of Christ, Hymn Book, Primer, Grebo History and Dictionary—published in the language. Also, printing press ; paper—the 'Cavalla Messenger'—published monthly."

may perhaps be worse, Barbadoes, but from the United States. Civilized and perfectly capable of managing and utilizing their wild congeners, the colonists appear in a most favourable light after the semi-reclaimed Akus and Ibos, their northern neighbours. They have even proposed to take charge of S'a Leone; and I doubt not that, if permitted, they would soon effect important changes. Liberia is a Republic, that is to say, she is pretty far gone in the ways of despotism—the only fit government for "Africa and the Africans." "*Morte alla constituzione!*" (in these lands) I exclaim with the unhappy Florentines, when they marched in arms through their streets and put a forcible end to a system which imposed upon them by an ambitious and unscrupulous *medio ceto*, a dynasty of doctors, lawyers, professors, and professional politic-mongers, enslaved them to 1000 rogues *in esse*, instead of to—possibly—one.

Liberia is at present in trouble; we heard many rumours of wars, and saw martial preparations when on shore. The Spanish vice-consul of Accra, who was on board, did not disembark at Cape Palmas. At S'a Leone our Frenchman—there is always one on board in these steamers—had blurted out something which might not have pleased H.I.M.S.S. La Ceres. According to him this gun-boat had sailed from Fernando Po to settle a dispute touching the Gallinhas River. She had entered the harbour and had attacked the "Quail," generally known as the "Lively Quail," in the harbour of Monrovia, and had sunk her and her crew, receiving but a single shot through her cabin door. The "Quail" is an old schooner, now carrying three guns—one 32-pounder and two 12-pounder carronades. She was presented by the British Government to assist in the suppression of the slave trade. She is one of the two that compose the "Liberian Navy;" the other vessel, a gift from the United States, never puts out to sea.

Now all this was a *canard*. The facts proved to be as follows. Of course there are two versions of the affair: that of the Spaniards, and that of the Liberians. I will give precedence to the former.

The Spaniards assert that a small vessel named the "Buenaventura Cubano," touched, on her way from Tenerife to Fernando Po, at the Gallinhas River, and was cast upon rocks inside the bar. That the master, seeing an opportunity, began to trade for palm-oil, when the "Quail" of Liberia attacked her, hauled down the Spanish flag, plundered the cargo, and compelled the master and men to fly from assassination. That the goëlette "La Ceres" was sent for the purpose of demanding satisfaction at Liberia, where, finding batteries and ships prepared to attack her, she fired into the "Quail" and retired. They deny the right of Liberia to the Gallinhas waters, and they assert that were the contrary the case, as they have neither treaties nor established usages with Liberia, that the latter cannot be allowed to molest their subjects. Finally, they demand suitable reparation for the offence, and indemnification for the loss of the cause of dispute.

The Liberians, on the other hand, declare that Prince

Mannah, the Chief of Gallinhas, reported to head-quarters that a Spanish ship was in the river with slave gear on board, and collecting her live cargo. That the "Quail," having ascertained these facts, captured her on the 30th May, 1861, and was about to tow her to Monrovia for judgment at the Admiralty Court, when the officer commanding Her Majesty's ship "Torch" sent the prize crew away, and hauled down the (single) star-spangled banner of the Republic, and on the 13th June, 1861, burned the Liberian prize. That, so far from injuring the Spanish subjects, they had been permitted to go to S'a Leone, where there is a Spanish consul-general, and to take with them all necessary supplies; moreover, that Prince Mannah had provided them with a large canoe. That the "Ceres," having reconnoitered the harbour of Monrovia, returned about fourteen days afterwards, and steamed in under pretext of visiting the President. That without any warning she began firing, on the 11th September, 1861, into the "Quail," when the batteries gave her such a dose that she was glad to make her escape.* That the Gallinhas is within the Republic's jurisdiction, and she is bound by treaties with Great Britain to suppress slavery within her dominions. Finally, that her weakness is her strength quoad the great Powers of Europe; that one of them has weakened her authority with the aborigines, and that she is entitled

---

* The "Cavalla Messenger" confirms this:—"The 'Ceres' received so spirited a response from the 'Quail,' which was anchored under the fort's guns, that she withdrew, having suffered, it is said, considerably."

to reparation for the attack of the "Ceres" and remuneration for the legal prize burned by the British officer.

This great question evidently turns upon the ownership of the Gallinhas waters. In 1842, block-houses were recommended to the British Government for the suppression of slave trade—evidently showing that in those days it was not Liberian territory. In 1848 took place the after-dinner conversation between Lord Ashley and Mr. Gurney with Mr. President Roberts, and the wily negro persuaded them that by paying 2000*l.*, slavery would be eradicated from the Gallinhas River and,— 700 miles annexed to the Republic. In 1849, H.M.S. "Albert," Commander Dunlop, broke up the slave factories—they had been previously injured by Captain Denham, R.N.—and carried off European traders and 1200 slaves to S'a Leone. The Republicans, however, insist that the land and the several points known as the Gallinhas were bought on the 13th April, 1850, from Prince Mannah and the other chiefs. On the other hand, it is believed that the Prince totally denies the transaction. As has already been said, Africans have no idea of permanently alienating land which is common property, not that of the king or chiefs; even a written contract implies, according to their ideas, only that the stranger has the rights of citizenship and of personal occupancy.* A joint commission is, I believe, in orders

* Of course our popular writers in "Chambers" and so forth assert that the native chiefs transferred the sovereignty of their country to the Liberian Government, and general readers believe them. It is thus that history is written. Evidently the natives should be consulted,

to settle the north-western limits of Liberia. Should the Gallinhas fall to them, they purpose to establish another port of entry either on that river or on the Shebar, and where it would not be too near Roberts Port, and to name it Gurney, after their late benefactor.

It would hardly be fair to leave Cape Palmas without saying something touching its peculiar population. The theme has been treated by every writer upon the subject of this coast, Owen, Boteler, Smith, Wilson, Hutchinson, and Durrant, not to mention dozens of others. Yet there is more to say than has been said.*

The word Kru—written Croo, Kroo, Krou, and, by other writers, Carow and Crew, upon the principle that Sipahi became Sepoy, or Seapie—is a corruption of the name by which the people call themselves "Kráo." It is a small tribe, living about half-way between Cape Mesurado and Cape Palmas, about seventy-five miles above or to the north-west of the latter. The district extends from twenty to thirty miles along the coast, and

and if the sale be *bond fide* it should be confirmed to Liberia, and *vice versâ*. At present, uncertainty causes much irritation, and the merchants of Sierra Leone are preparing to assert their joint rights to the Gallinhas by force if necessary.

* The following remarks concerning the origin of the Kru are derived from information received from Bishop Payne, and from the Introduction to his Dictionary of the Grebo Language. New York: Jenkins, Frankfort Street, 1860.

The little volume contains about 2500 words, or nearly half the language. It is to be hoped that this excellent Minister of the Gospel will soon publish his expected Grammar of the Grebo tongue.

perhaps, as much into the interior. They had originally five chief settlements, which, beginning from the north-west, are Little Kru; Settra Kru the chief town, Krubah, Nanna Kru, or Kru Settra, and King Will's Town. They were the first to go to sea, and, as some twenty other tribes, numbering, perhaps, 150,000 souls, followed their example, all are now known by the common name Krumen. As Mr. M'Queen says, they never enslave one another; yet they were the life and soul of the Spanish and Portuguese slavers, and they proved themselves probably the greatest kidnappers on the coast. They first began the peculiar tattoo, which the adjoining tribes soon imitated, and now they are in the habit of buying bushmen and boy-slaves, and marking them like themselves, thus transforming them to "Krumen," that they may be engaged as seamen. When the slave-trade began to decline, they preferred the service of ships of war and merchantmen, they visited S'a Leone in considerable numbers, and they became the Coolies and Lascars of West Africa. They seem to be created purposely for the oil trade.

The chief tribes that followed their example were the people of Niffu, or Piccaninny Sess; the Bwidabe, or Fishmen; the Mcnawe of Grand Sess, the Wiábo of Garoway, the Babo below Cavalla River, the Plabo,* and

---

* On this part of the coast, all the places and tribes have double names. The Cavalla River is called Dokrinyun; Cape Monrovia, Trubo; Cape Mount, Chepe; Drewin, Wayra; St. Andrew's, Nisonti; and Settra Kru, Wete. Of individual names, more hereafter.

others, extending to Cape St. Andrew's, and about forty miles into the interior. Of these tribes, who are all cognate, as their language and physique prove, the most influential are the Grebos of Cape Palmas: the total number, however, probably does not exceed 40,000. Like the peoples generally upon the African coast, they have lately come from the interior. Their own tradition is, that a Kobo Kui, or foreign house—no doubt some European slave factory—was found by them on arrival at Cape Palmas. Their earliest settlements near the sea were behind Berebi, sixty miles to the eastward. After becoming too numerous for their narrow limits, a portion of them determined, Irish-like, upon a kind of exodus to the west. The movement was secretly managed, because it was opposed to the wishes of the majority. Whilst embarking, a number of canoes were capsized, and those in them were left behind. They were called Woríbo, or the Capsized, from the verb Wore. The others, who succeeded in bounding over the waves, took the name of Grebo, from the jumping grey monkey, Gré or Grí.

Proceeding up the coast, the Grebos landed detached parties in the country now inhabited by the Bubos, at Cavalla and at Cape Palmas, where they built small temporary settlements. They continued their migration as far as Grand Sesters, forty miles above Cape Palmas: at length, directed by an oracle, they all gathered together and built on the Cape of Cocoas a large town, called Bwini, or Bwimli. These wanderings account for the close analogy of the Grebo tongue and that of Sino (written Sinori, or Sinoe), in N. lat. 5° 1′, or about ninety miles to the north-west of Harper. At Grand Sesters there are still large branches of the Grebo family, and many merchant-ships prefer them as being the best-conducted men. After them are the people of Niffu, or Piccaninny Sesters. For fishing, the Fishmen are the best servants.

Strictly speaking, it is incorrect to call the Grebo "Krumen." As, however, the people of this coast readily converse together, hold constant intercourse, and are remarkably like one another in physique, as in *morale*, they may be described as one, and the best name for them is that which custom sanctions— Krumen.

The peculiar contrast of feature and figure which distinguishes this people has already been described. The features are distinctly African, without an admixture of Arab; the conjunctiva is brown, yellow, or tarnished, a Hamitic peculiarity; and some paint white goggle-like ovals round the orbits, producing the effect of a "loup." This is sometimes done for sickness, and invalids are rubbed over with various light and dark coloured powders. The skin is very dark, often lamp-black; others are of a deep rich brown or bronze tint, but a light-complexioned man is generally called Tom Coffee; and people put waggish questions touching his paternity. They wear the hair, which is short and kinky, in crops, which look like Buddha's skull-cap:

and they shave when mourning for their relations: a favourite "fash." is to scrape off a parallelogram behind the head, from the poll to the cerebellum; and others are decorated in that landscape or parterre style which wilder Africa and Germany love. The back of the cranium is often remarkably flat, and I have seen many heads of the pyramidal shape, rising narrow and pointed high to the apex. The beard is seldom thick, and never long; the moustachio is removed, and the pile, like the hair, often grows in tufts. The tattoo has been described: there seems to be something attractive in this process— the English sailor can seldom resist the temptation. They also chip, sharpen, and extract the teeth. Most men cut out an inverted V between the two middle incisors of the upper jaw; others draw one or two of the central and lower incisors; others, especially the St. Andrew's men, tip or sharpen the incisors, like the Wahiao, and several Central African tribes. Odontology has its mysteries. Dentists seem, or rather seemed to hold as a theory, that destruction of enamel involves the loss of the tooth; the Krumen hack their masticators with a knife, or a rough piece of hoop iron, and find that the sharpening, instead of producing caries, acts as a preservative, by facilitating the laniatory process. Similarly there are physiologists who attribute the preservation of the negro's teeth to his not drinking anything hotter than blood heat. This is mere empiricism. The Arabs swallow their coffee nearly boiling, and the East African will devour his agali, or porridge, when the temperature would scald the hand. Yet both these races have pearls of teeth, except when they chew lime or tobacco.* The Krumen, like most other wild people, always wash the teeth after eating. A cleanly race, and never passing a day—unless it be very cold—without bathing, the African fetor is not always perceptible, but it exists.† The hands and feet are large and coarse, but not such outrages to proportion as the races further south.

The Krumen show all that propensity to ape Europeans which characterizes the African generally. A noble savage enough in his semi-nudity, when a single shukkeh covers his middle—the women wear even less—with a bead necklace, and coarse iron, ivory, or brass rings round his wrists and ankles; he is fond of making himself grotesque, as an old-clo' man. The hat is borrowed from the sailor; it is of every form—chimney-pot, Kossuth, skull-cap, naval casquette, red nightcap, straw or broad-brimmed wide-awake; not unfrequently it surmounts a bandanna, or some gaudy kerchief. A tooth-stick is in every mouth, and not a few snuff or chew. The neck is variously decorated, from the band of hairy skin to the Popo, or Aggri bead,‡ which, on the Gold Coast,

---

* On the other hand, it is said of the Guanches at Tenerife that "they drank nothing but water, and that only at a certain pèriod after eating anything heated, for fear of destroying their teeth."

† The Persians find a similar fetor in the Jewish race, and call it by a peculiar name—"bui shimit." This, however, arises probably not so much from the conformation of the skin, as from the extreme impurity of the race.

‡ Much has been written touching these beads, which are dug from

is more valuable than gold. The favourite ornaments are strings of leopards' teeth, small chains of brass and iron, and beads of every form and substance—glass and porcelain, white and black, blue, green, and yellow; the necklace is used to hold the clay dudheen, of European make. The wrists bear from one to half a dozen ivory bracelets, rings painfully cut out with a knife, and turned with a wet cord rubbed to and fro; the most pretentious of these decorations have the wearer's name engraved upon the ivory in coloured letters, or upon a brass-plate, or expressed in metal tacks forming the words; they are at once passports and characters for future service. On the arm, also, is the Gri, or Fetish, leopards' teeth, or the smallest deer-horns, with cowries and other "medicine" bound on by a bit of string. Ligatures round the ankles are similarly fetished, and some are drawn so tight that the cord leaves a deep mark upon the skin. I presume that, like the tribes of the Arab Bedouins, these are intended for ligatures in case of snake bites; they are certainly the only alleviation when suffering from cramp, a painful nervous disease in these lands, ever liable to be induced by cold, wet, or confined positions. They are fond of finger-rings, but care little whether they are gold, silver, or brass. The pagne, or loin cloth, is generally a cheque of white and pink or blue; it is tied round the waist, or tucked into a cord: and only great swells have cricket, military, or elastic belts. Some

the ground. Many are found upon the Liberian coast, and cannot be imitated in Europe. Some travellers have derived them from Egypt.

carry sticks of peculiar shape, edged and notched like certain Hindostani swordblades. The few women whom we saw were shaven-pated and nude to their loins, which were covered with the scantiest cloth: they showed a decided steatopyga and the pulpy African development. Their principal ornaments were massive brass anklets; and all were at work, carrying upon their heads rice-bags in wicker cradles, and freshly-caught fish in the bark bandboxes described by Central African travellers. The children are attired *secundum naturam*, except the mission boys, who are decently clad in loose jackets and pantaloons: they have all two "given names," *è. g.*, A. B. Smith; and the negrillons about the house are also promoted to shirt and loin-cloth.

The Rev. Mr. Wilson, late of the Gaboon Mission, who, some thirty years ago, took so active a part in purchasing land for the colony, has well and accurately described in a book to which the reader is referred,[*] the curious polity of this people. Like the Guanches of Tenerife, and indeed most primitive people from Etruria to India, the Kru Republic is divided into four classes, which can hardly, however, be called castes. These are the elders, the middle-aged men who form the soldiery; the youth who aspire to become warriors; and the demon doctors, priests, and physicians. As amongst

[*] Western Africa; its History, Condition, and Prospects. New York: Harper and Brothers, 1856. Chap. 6 is the best treatise on the Kru Republic that I know. Generally the work abounds in flaws, but if properly edited it would form a good handbook of Western Africa.

the Wanyika of the Eastern Coast, there appears to be a regular initiation to each step in rank.* The two first classes meet in deliberative assembly when any measure touching the public interests is proposed; the juveniles, however, are expected to be seen and not heard, except when the subject discussed has special reference to their own body. Oratory, as amongst all African tribes, is greatly cultivated, and to judge from its effects upon the audience, with success. A highly aristocratic form is secured by the preponderance of the first class in the commonwealth. The youths are hardly permitted to hold property; if they return wealthy from beyond the sea their gains are systematically appropriated. Nay, more: even an elder who presumes to excel his fellows in riches or importance is at once reduced, for "too much sass," to the general level. The "saucewood," or red wood of the giddu tree, ordeal is fearfully prevalent amongst them, killing its thousands; the only check is, that if the defendant survives the poisonous draught, the plaintiff must drink it in his turn. Capital punishment is rare, except in cases of murder or witchcraft, where the criminal is beaten to death or drowned. As usual amongst uncivilized people, even the Chinese, little difference is made between wilful murder and justifiable homicide: the object seems to teach the value of human life. Adultery and theft are punished by fine,

---

* "Among the Wanyika the orders are three in number: Nyene, the young; Khánbi, the middle-aged; and Nfaya, the old."—Zanzibar, and Two Months in East Africa. Blackwood's Magazine, Feb., 1858.

and the informer is regarded with general contempt. Another check upon crime is the system of headmen. The eldest male member of the several families into which the tribes are divided, is at once their representative in palavers, and their security for good behaviour. Property is held as a kind of joint-stock, and from it fines and other penalties for misdemeanors must be paid.

The *morale* of this people appears to the European exceedingly contradictory, not to say unintelligible. The same, however, may be affirmed of all barbarous tribes, where viewed with purely civilized eyes. For instance, the Krumen have, for the last two centuries, been a race of sailors; they have chosen what is by no means an undangerous profession, and they are accustomed to cross the perilous bars, and to trust themselves to the mercy of the sharks and the breakers. Yet they are arrant cowards. When real firing begins on board ship, they will run and hide themselves in the coal bunkers. During the descent of the Niger, in 1859, when the hostile villages below Abo shot at the Government Contract Steamer "Rainbow," Captain Creen, it was necessary to drive the Krumen from their retreat behind the paddle-boxes. They will desert their master upon the least appearance of danger. It is impossible to mistake their state of panic: if a roller strikes a boat unexpectedly, they will lay oars by, gaze with a blank face, and if the stick be not used, rise to spring overboard. The least corporal punishment makes them scream like women, and, unlike most Africans, they are exceedingly sensitive to pain. Sickness afflicts them mentally as well as bodily; and if one of a boat's crew be lost off a bar, or devoured by sharks, it is found advisable to send the others home. The canoe men or Guinea men on the other hand, if supplied with a gallon of rum, will forget the mishaps by the next day. Kru poltroonery is open and unaffected; other African tribes appear ashamed to show it; the Kruman, however, boasts of it. If you ask him to fight, he replies unblushingly that he has but one life, and wishes again to see "we country." I have no doubt that excessive affection for their own land and for their parents—especially for the mother—partly causes this loathing to face danger. But though there are exceptions amongst them, and some few are brave, even to ferocity, as a rule there is no mistaking their timidity. During the Indian mutiny, it was proposed to levy a Kru battalion, and officers were selected for that purpose. The project suddenly fell to the ground, owing, it is said, to the contradictory statements of the best authorities; some recommending the Krus as excellent food for powder, others reporting them as far readier to run away than to do battle. I made many inquiries upon the subject, and after seeing much of the Krumen, and learning something of their language, I satisfied myself that they would be quite useless as soldiers; they would not fight, they prefer ship-work to shore-work, and as their women never travel, they would not willingly engage themselves for any length of time. "*Un des plus grands malheurs des honnêtes gens*," says a French author, with great truth, "*c'est qu'ils sont des lâches;*" this, however, cannot be applied to Krumen. Besides cowardice, their principal fault is thieving, a disposition which they never fail to evince; and nothing comes amiss to them, from wholesale robbery to petty prigging. Like the true coward, too, they are bullies when they meet those more timid than themselves. Some years ago they seized the north-west part of Fernando Po, from the feeble Bubes, plundered the people, carried off the women, and were defeated only by the combined action of the natives by land, and Governor Beecroft who attacked them from the sea. When the Niger expedition was encamped at Jeba, in 1857-58, the Kru seamen stole from them about 140*l*. worth of cloth, cowries, mirrors, and small ware. The robbery was discovered by the natives firing the grass, and the whole was consumed. Fanaticism ruined the unfortunate Niger expedition of 1841—Philanthropy and disputes that of 1857-62: these rascally Krumen were actually allowed to remain unflogged. Their favourite style of thieving, however, is on the smallest scale: knives, penknives, and scissors, will be taken out of the master's room, turnscrews and brass-tipped ramrods will disappear most inexplicably. They have no hesitation in robbing from one another's boxes, arms, and ammunition, wire, padlocks, and similar articles. When a crew is dismissed, the master usually insists upon the large chests in which they have stowed away their goods, being examined, and finds nothing: the cunning villains have either trusted their spoils to a comrade, or they have sent them on by another ship. They never, except when soundly flogged, "peach" upon one another; and if one of a gang commits a robbery, all expect to benefit by it. Similarly, if rations be given to one out of twenty, he will share it with the other score. Provisions are never safe from them. Goats hungrily browsing will be brought in dead by them an hour or two afterwards, strangled secretly, and made to appear as if bitten by snakes. When this is done, the only way is to throw the body into the sea; if buried they will exhume and devour it. My plan was to dig a hole, and after heaping the earth up, write upon it in large letters, "Thou shalt not steal!" Poultry cannot be preserved from them. They are fond of drink, and will suffer even bodily pain to obtain it. In various journeys I have never drunk my own last bottle of cognac: that operation has been performed by some Kruboy of the party. The greatest robbers are the St. Andrew's men; they are hard-working fellows; honesty, however, never seems to suggest itself to them. I have no belief in punishment as regards the individual punished, not a shade of faith in its ever doing him good. As an intimidation to others, if properly managed, it may possibly have its uses. Its real objects, however, should be to repay society for the loss that it has sustained, and to defend the body social from further attacks by the same hand. But to manage it properly, it must everywhere be modified. In England we still practise the barbarous and useless system of capital punishment in case of murder, and we make the penalty lighter for theft. In most parts of Africa I would treat the robber much more severely than the assassin.

As regards morality, in its limited sense, the Krumen are not bright in the scale of creation. Adultery is punished, it is true, by a fine, and in the case of a wealthy or powerful man, there may be a "great palaver." The European stranger, however, travelling in their country is expected to patronise their wives and daughters, and these unconscious followers of Lycurgus and Cato feel hurt, as if dishonoured, by his refusing to gratify them. The custom is very prevalent along this coast. At Gaboon, perhaps it reaches the acme; there a man will in one breath offer the choice between his wife, sister, and daughter. The women of course do as they are bid by the men, and they consider all familiarity with a white man a high honour.*

The Kruman believes in the "education of travel." He leaves home early, learns a little waiting, and perhaps makes a voyage to England; he never, however, returns there, dreading the cold. At the age of puberty he ships under some headman, who began life in the same

* Dr. Livingstone, chap. 25, asserts, "I have heard women speaking in admiration of a white man, because he was pure and never was guilty of any secret immorality." This is amongst the Makololos: he would have heard them speak in anything but an admiring way about continence in these regions.

way, and who having learned a little English, and the handling of a rope, engages a gang of youngsters. A good headman takes as much from his dependents as possible, stopping their pay on all occasions; he is expected to defend the master's property from them—which often he does not do—and to punish them severely with his own hand. It is this comparative energy and willingness to do work, which together with their independent bearing, has given the Krumen such a name on the coast;—bad as they are, all the rest are worse. We are rapidly, however, spoiling these men. About ten years ago they were happy to receive 5*s.* per month, in goods, which reduced it to 3*s.* As in India, however, so here, servants' wages are increasing, till they threaten to become exorbitant. Now, on board H.M.'s ships they are paid the wages of ordinary able seamen, 1*l.* 10*s.* per month, or 18*l.* per annum. Besides which, they are entitled to the rations of a white man, and their compensation money will probably run up to another 12*l.* per annum. The pay might be reduced to $5 per month, and rice rations, with beef every two days; thus the cruisers would not injure the trade. There is for them an inexplicable charm on board a man-of-war. They are very proud of their uniform; which, however, renders them effeminate and more subject to disease, than those who are less clothed; they would, I think, look much better with shaven heads, red caps, and short blue drawers. They treat with a certain contempt the "river boys." Yet, African like, they must desert at times, especially after a good flogging from the headman, for not keeping a bright look out. On the other hand, a vessel of war wanting Krumen, has only to give a hint to those of the nearest merchantman, and they will be smuggled on board presently; this has been done by fellows, who wrapped up in navy shirts, and with caps pulled over their faces, have passed out unrecognised, even by captains of the mail steamers. But a Kruman who has once served on board a ship of war, is like a foreign domestic in an English family, useless for all other purposes. When shipped at S'a Leone for merchant service, their wages are more than those who embark at Cape Palmas; nominally the former now receive 30s., the latter $2 per month in goods, which reduce it to $1. Some picked gig-crews in the Oil Rivers, receive $5, besides additional clothes and caps; the average pay, however, is from $3 to $4. A crew, well picked out of a number of men, is wonderful to look at; their muscles stand out almost like those of that caricature, the Farnese Hercules; they row at a stretch 40 miles, pulling as if for dear life, and at the end they seem as little fatigued as white ants. Generally the headman's pay is double that of his boys, and coin is never given. Their rations are 1½ lb. of rice or yams a day, with salt meat or fresh steak once or twice a week; they usually eat three times, breakfast at 9, dine at 2, and sup at 7 P.M.; when working hard, they are allowed a liberal allowance of rum. Tobacco depends greatly on the master; it is, however, a favour, not a right; they expect to receive a clean cloth worth, say 18*d*., every Sunday; it is more general, however, to give them the Sunday cloth, as they call it, every three weeks. They will ship for long voyages, but scarcely ever engage themselves for more than three years. On the other hand they dislike all shore work, and will not act as servants for more than two years. Their favourite period of engagement—here, as in India, steam navigation shortens service and prolongs furloughs —is "one time yam come up, twel' moon." If kept beyond their limits, they begin by waxing surly, they proceed to refuse work, and they end, African like, by taking the law into their own hands. I have known cases where they have threatened to fire a factory, and many in which they have plundered the store, launched a boat, and gone off no one knows where.

The object of the Kruman's expatriation is to make money, with which he can return home—the thing has been done in England—enact the gentleman, and marry a wife; when his purse is empty he sets out once more; not willingly, for to use his own phrase, he is "nigger for ship, king for country." After four or five voyages, he has learned English enough to become a headman, and by peculating in his turn, he lays the foundation of a large family. Until then, he has ever been received, as he returns, with noisy festivity, but his gains have been appropriated by the family council, and applied to the common stock. Now he spends his own money, chiefly in purchasing wives. The whole superstructure of

Kru society is built upon polygamy, which is much after the Mormon principle, a division of labour.* Servants do not exist, the language has no name for them, and domestic slavery is very limited; moreover, as no gentleman in Africa can demean himself by work, which he considers in the light of convict labour, the institution winds itself round every heart. He is a "small boy" when yet unmarried; he begins life with one wife, and he hopes to end it with a dozen or two, when he retires

---

* The Rev. Mr. Wilson remarks: "It is not a little singular, however, that the females, upon whom the burden of this degrading institution (polygamy) mainly rests, are quite as much interested in its continuance as the men themselves. A woman would infinitely prefer to be one of a dozen wives of a respectable man than to be the sole representative of a man who had not force of character to raise himself above the one-woman level."—Western Africa, chap. 1-4.

There is nothing singular in this: the polygamy of the Latter Day Saints derives all its force from the preference of the women. Were they to oppose it, nothing could preserve the institution.

Moreover, it appears that in the various branches of the human family, the relative development of the female to the male greatly varies. In some, the Africans for instance, the woman's inferiority is constant and salient. In others, as the Anglo-Saxon, there is a far greater amount of equality between the sexes. We see the same thing in the lower animals: whilst in the Gallinæ the male has a marked superiority over his mate; in the Falconidæ the female is superior in strength, size, and courage; and in others—the Canidæ and Solidungulæ—the powers are as equally balanced as possible.

It is, doubtless, this superior physical and mental development which has placed the women of the Indo-Germanic family in their present exalted position. Yet they willingly abdicate it. There are no more submissive polygamists than the Englishwomen at Great Salt Lake City, except, perhaps, the Americans, who—I speak only of those whose fathers were born and bred in the New World—are somewhat highly coloured copies of their English cousins.

from business, a consummation most devoutly wished for. This seldom happens before he has reached the age of fifty. There is nothing peculiar in Kru nuptials. The girl-wife's mother is first propitiated with small presents; then the dowry is settled with her father and his family, who are the real owners of the property. The senior wife is the first in rank, and respectable men always keep a separate establishment for each spouse. On the husband's death, the wives become the property of the brothers, who can transfer them if they please. When a woman is ill-treated, she runs away to her father's family, but a "big palaver" is sure to follow this elopement. The children of course love the mother better than the other parent, but they must follow their father should a split take place between the tribes.

The religion of the Kruman is a fanaticism so vague and undeveloped that no writer has, I believe, ventured to treat upon it. It has been already mentioned that they have Diyabo*—*sing*. Diyá—or "Devil Doctors," as Europeans call them, whose preparation for the ministry and position in the community is precisely that of the North-American Indian's medicine-man. Their oracle at the Grand Devil has also been alluded to. The commonalty however appear to have few, if any, exercises which can properly be called religious. During the whole of the Niger expedition, from 1857 to 1862, only one case was observed; on the night of the "Dayspring's" wreck, Grando, the second headman, stood near the bank, quite

* The syllable -bo means, I believe, a class.

upright, with his face to the West, and howled till dawn, occasionally waving the right arm. Two or three sat around him, but no one joined with him. They will not eat blood nor the heart of cattle; they swear, by dipping the forefinger in salt, pointing to earth and heaven, and then tasting the condiment. This custom reminds one of the Salt Eaters, *i.e.*, Rice Christians of the Kongo River, and the various salt-incantations of Asia.

When a man dies a fire is kindled every evening before his house to warm his Ku,* *i.e.*, his ghost or himself, and food is placed at his grave. He may appear in one or in several children. Or leading the goat or the bullock slain at his funeral, he may wend his way to Menu of the Kwi—Ghostland, which some place at Gedeye, in the remote interior—where, after confessing his misdeeds, he will take rank according to the sacrifice made and his means. But if a wizard, he must wander about the gloomy swamp and fetid marsh for ever. These ideas show a dawning of the "continuation theory;" but the West African, unlike the Egyptian, who probably invented the idea, has no conception of a corporeal resurrection.

The Rev. Mr. Bowen ("Central Africa '), asserts that a Kruman who attempted to learn reading would be

* In Bishop Payne's Grebo Vocabulary, Ku, *plur*. Kwi, is explained —devil, dream, departed spirit. Menu, or menuke, is the intermediate place through which persons are said to pass to their final destiny, and where they review all their past deeds, before going into Kwiya Orán, the City of the Manes.

killed; this is far from being the fact now, if it was then. Of all the Pagans on the coast, the Kru have been found the most difficult to convert on account of the dishonour and expulsion from the tribe which such conduct entails. Of late years there have been a few cases, and in a future page the reader will see a fine specimen of superior rascality on the part of the "divert." In the neighbourhood of the mission stations, near Cape Palmas, the more civilized Grebos do nothing on Sundays; but, as I have said before, an African will ever be most happy to practise as much idleness as you choose to preach.

Like the negro race generally, the organs of language, as well as of time and tune, are well developed in the Krumen. They find no difficulty in picking up a few words of English, though they speak it with a savage accent; of course, correctness or extent of vocabulary is beyond their powers, yet they can distinguish a brogue or a provincial accent, and they call Scotchmen "bush Englishmen"—a definition that would come home to Dr. Johnson's own heart. They have no poetry, and few legends; whilst their music is monotonous to a degree. Yet they delight in it, and often after a long and fatiguing day's march they will ask permission to "make play," and dance and sing till midnight. When hoeing the ground they must do it at the sound of music; in fact, everything is cheered with a song. The traveller should never forget to carry a tom-tom, or some similar instrument, which will shorten his journey by a fair quarter.

They are good mimics, and I have seen some laughable caricatures of various European nations. "Chaff" is with them as favourite an exercise as in civilised London, and they can say the most biting and sarcastic things imaginable. I have met fellows whose remarks, conveyed in broken English, were as humorous as those of any Irishman. They are great at pantomime, and with some twenty English words can tell a long story, as well as a Sioux of the Prairies. There are no noisier people on the coast; in our stations they are relegated to outhouses, placed well out of hearing.

The Kru language, as has been seen, possesses about 5000 vocables. The grammatical forms are simple, and by no means numerous. Most writers declare the tongue to be exceedingly difficult of acquisition. I found it quite the contrary; and the Liberian colonists, if they cannot speak it, are generally able to understand it. Mr. Smith,* in a most amusing little work, asserts that every Kru word is made to end in O; he has misconceived the sign of the vocative to be an integral part of the word. He also opines that the "Kroo language seems to be composed of vowels only," whereas in few tongues are there more explosive consonants, harsher gutturals, or a stronger nasalization that half masters the articulation. We find in it also the duplicated initial consonants, as *nn* and *mm*, which an Englishman would pronounce with a semi-elision of a prefixed indefinite vowel. Its

* Chap. 10, Trade and Travels in the Gulf of Guinea. By J. Smith. London: Simpkin, Marshall, and Co., 1851.

chief merit seems to be the facility with which a Kruman can make himself heard at a distance, when a European would require a speaking-trumpet. The Rev. Mr. Wilson, who discovers a similarity between one-fifth of the words in the Mpongwe of the Gaboon and the Kisawahili of Zanzibar and of the eastern shores of the continent, detects none between the Mpongwe and the Kru dialects.* Yet I cannot but find most distinct resemblance, not so much in vocabulary, however, as in the grammar and the spirit of the language.

"Blackman's English," opposed to "high English," or "deep English," in this part of the world is a literature whose professor has hitherto been the British sailor. I leave to the reader's imagination the style of expression which it has engrafted upon the African mind. Queer tales are told of words starting up in the presence of ladies—words which, falling amongst an English assembly, would act like a 10-inch shell. Every traveller has made merry with the ridiculous names which the Kru boys have borrowed for themselves from the English, e.g., Nix, Black Trouble, Salt water, Bottle o' beer, and Six-finger Jack.† Yet their own names are by no means unpleasant or difficult to learn, nor can I see the force of calling Nábwe, Kofá, Tiyá, and

* Western Africa, chap. 4.
† On the Gold Coast, children born with six fingers are strangled : amongst the Kru and other tribes of Lower Guinea they are not injured.

Nákú, Black Will, Two Glass, Seabreeze, and Tom Brass.*

Remains to consider the Kruman in the light of a domestic servant. In this phase he does not shine—a more clumsy-handed, pig-headed clown could not be found even in Europe. He steals anything he can lay his hands upon; he becomes idle to the last degree, and though personally clean enough, his ideas touching that virtue in respect to plate and porcelain are still embryotic. He either breaks or he mislays everything entrusted to him, and he never works except when the master stands over him; he never attends to an order, and he would see all "master's" property eaten by white ants rather than take the trouble to remove it. There are worse servants on this coast even than the Kruman, I own; for instance, the Camaroons and the Calabar men; yet even with him, your house is as uncomfortable as fancy could conceive.

About noon on the 16th August we set out once more, and steamed down the coast, which was bright with the delightful air of the fine season. We had shipped at Cape Palmas about 5000*l.* worth of Krumen, who were proceeding to the Oil Rivers; they, or rather their employers, pay for their diet and passage $10 per head. Their supper on board was a study of savagery. Their favourite food is ever rice, and they prefer it to the best bread, and pine for it at times when they cannot

* At the end of this chapter the reader will find a specimen of Kru vocabulary, kindly supplied to a friend by Bishop Payne.

obtain it. It must be far more nutritious than that of India, for they eat it dry and get through an immense amount of labour without other sustenance. A large cauldron, containing a pint per man, was brought on deck and portioned into five messes, around which, after a furious chatting and gesticulating like excited baboons, all squatted. They ball'd the rice by squeezing it with either hand, left as well as right, thrust it into their mouths, looking like chickens being crammed, and swallowed it almost whole with a powerful action of the œsophagus. They did not drink till after the meal, as is the custom of Asia; when full they satisfied their thirst at the tank. If meat appears, it is a signal for a scuffle; the strongest manage to snatch a few mouthfuls each, and the weaker get none.

Though fresh from home they are in good spirits; they love a change, and the world is all before them. Returning after two years or so, they will be in the state described as being "strung upon wires." They have boxes to protect and their property will not be safe from thieves and the ocean till it is lodged in their huts. They have pitiably suffered in health, and are allowed no medical luxuries on board; even a change of diet is unattainable, and the attendance of a doctor is a matter of personal humanity. Some of them by touching the railings have given to the passengers craw-craw, and other horrid skin-diseases, which have found their way into English homes. It is a touching sight to see some poor fellow, with the death rattle in his throat, lying unheeded upon the deck, whilst all others are craning their necks over the bulwarks, and stepping over his almost unconscious body to get the first glimpse of "we country." Should he die, the corpse must be taken on shore, or there will be what the African dreads, a "palaver." And when "Jack Kruman" reaches his hut and greets the wives of his bosom, he cannot love them till he has perfectly satisfied himself with the strictness of their conduct during his absence.

Beyond Cape Palmas, the coast line is a beach of bright white sand, from which the slave barracoons have now disappeared; in the foreground an occasional rock or ledge rises awash from the level, and the background is a deep strip of black forest, here and there broken by tall trees. We are soon fairly beyond Liberia, formerly called the Grain Coast. This ambiguous name has caused many a mistake, but the grain in question is not a cereal but a condiment—rejecting, at least that etymology, which supposes it to have been derived from cochineal, which in those days was considered not an animal but a vegetable. It is a real cardamom (*A. Grana Paradisi*), of which many varieties grow along the whole length of the western coast of intertropical Africa. The flower is of great beauty on account of the glowing pink bracts; the shrub is cane-like, and the fruit, which appears close to the ground, is a pyriform pod with crimson skin enclosing black brown seeds, surrounded by a juicy placenta. Nothing is more pleasant or reviving on a long, thirsty march, than a handful of these cardamoms; the acidity of the pulp contrasts most pleasantly with the pungency of the spice. By the Dutch they were called Guinea Grains; by the trade, Malaguetta pepper; and the demand in Europe in the sixteenth century led to the discovery of many ports on "the coast." It was then principally used for giving fire and flavour in spirituous liquors, and especially for adulterating beer. At last its importation into England was forbidden, cases of poisoning being attributed to it; and Europeans in these regions still believe that some species are injurious, and that they were mixed with the true grains. The natives use this cardamom extensively as a condiment and a medicine: it is a stomachic, a carminative, and an external irritant. The people of the Gold Coast, when suffering from headache, rub over the forehead a paste of Malaguetta pepper. The powder is applied during the hot fit of fever, as ginger is in India for rheumatism and for fugitive pains. It is spirted out of the mouth over the part affected, or a paste made with water is rubbed on like a poultice, or applied in streaks. The dead also are perfumed with this pepper and sweet scented plants. Inasmuch as when bruised and soaked in sherry, it makes excellent bitters, it will, once more, I believe, find its way into the European markets.

NOTE.—For the following specimen of the real Kráo language, I am indebted to the kindness of Bishop Payne :—

KRU AND ENGLISH.

N.B.—The vowels are written after the system of Sir W. Jones, modified as used in Lane, Richardson's Persian Dictionary, &c.: *g* is always hard, as in get; the letters *c*, *q*, *x*, and *y* are supplied by *k*, *ks*, and *i*.

Ni-o-ju	Man	Bla-bi	Sheep
Ni-o-no	Woman	Bok-er-o	Goat
Di-u-be	Child		
Mi	Father	Na-ji-o	I see
Ni	Mother	Na-uo-i	I hear
Mi-e-ju	Brother	Na-u-ru	I speak
No-ru	Sister	Mu	Go
Ni	Water	Gi	Come
Na	Fire	Di-e	Eat
Ser-a	House	Na-ni	Drink
Bun-go	Door	Na-mu	Sleep
Bu-ōm-bi	Window	Na-dub-i	Wash
Nam-bu-ri	Seat	Ma-na	Walk
Kri	Farm	Na-pin-de	Cook
Ku-ō	Rice	Mu-ne	Carry
Kin-a	Oil	Na-nu-de	Make
To	Salt	Na-ni-em	Give
Po-pa	Bowl	Na-uk-be	Take
Ja-bi	Jar	Na-ti-e	Buy
Ja-bi	Boiler	Pu-ri-em-bu	Sell
Gi-u-ro	Sun	Bi-si-um	Thank
Tsho	Moon	Gl-rum	Love
Na-pi	Star	O-ro-de	Well
Ni-ba	River	Na-po-pa	I am sick
Ku-ra	Field		
Tu	Tree	Ii	Yes
Bu-ru-a	Grass	Ie	No
Nne	Wood	So-na-to	To-day
So-ba	Stone	Po-pla-ka	To-morrow
Du-bo	Head	So-ra-ma	Yesterday
Nu-me	Bird	Kre-kre	Quickly
Ni	Fish	Da-ka	Long since
Sŏng	Fowl	Gi	Above
Bi-li	Cow	Bre	Below

CHAPTER VII.

TWENTY-FOUR HOURS AT CAPE COAST CASTLE.

18TH SEPTEMBER, 186—

" —— If you cannot swim,
Beware of Providence."
Shelley.

To the east of the Grain Coast—in maps—lies the Ivory Coast, now a misnomer. Hardly a tusk has been exported from it for the last score of years; the animals having been driven away by the "hot mouthed weapon." The present Ivory Coast is the region south of the Camaroons Mountains, extending to the Gaboon River and Cape Lopez. The old Ivory Coast had but four settlements—Fresco, Cape Lahou or Nifá, Jack-a-Jack, Grand Bassam and Assini, the two latter French: After passing these we enter the Gold Coast; it was once a celebrated region, which produced the GUINEA for England; now, all known about it by the public at home is, that it is somewhere about Africa.* How little

---

* That popular book, Haydn's Dictionary of Dates, is the best proof. The ninth edition, published in 1860 by Mr. Moxon, informs us, under the word "African Company," that "the rights vested in the *present company* are by 23 George II., 1749," whereas that company expired about forty years ago. Another well-known book—Brookes' "Gazetteer," revised by Mr. Findlay, and published 1861—omits the

it deserves this neglect, and how much may be made of it, will be shown in a following page.

There is a question of great interest touching the discovery of this coast. The Portuguese have claimed and secured the whole honour: in our encyclopedias and school-books, which are copied one from the other, no other nation is even mentioned. Their own account of it* is that Fernâo Gomes, a worthy and honest citizen of Lisbon, obtained from the Portuguese Government, in 1471, permission to trade on these coasts for five years, with this proviso: that he should pay to the Portuguese Government the annual sum of 44*l*. 9*s*. Also that he should make annual voyages of discovery from Sierra Leone along the coast to the distance of 300 miles; so that, at the expiration of the stipulated period of five years, 1500 miles should have been explored. In consequence of this agreement, El-Mina

---

date (Appendix, 926) at which the Gold Coast became an independent, government. When shall we have in England a good set of popular, and especially educational works, in which our youth will not learn that of which they must unlearn half? Not long ago I found some young friends painfully impressing their brains with the fact that the United States "contained nearly thirteen millions of souls."

* This is quoted from "Six Years of a Traveller's Life in Western Africa." By Francisco Travassos Valdez. Two vols. Hurst and Blackett, London, 1861.

The book should have been called "Voyager's Life." It is nothing but a coasting from Lisbon to Loando and its dependencies, with an occasional *relâche* at the islands on the way. The frontispiece of the first volume is copied from M. Gamitto's "O Muata Cazembe;" the frontispiece of the second is taken from the same. It is about a parallel to Mr. Macbriar's "Africa and the Africans."

was discovered, and also Cape Catherina, in 1° 50′ south latitude and 9° 2′ west longitude.

On the other hand it has been seen that Norman Knight conquered part of the Canary Islands in 1400, and that M. Bouet-Willaumez has successfully interpreted the corrupted name, Boutou, on the Kru coast, by referring it to the old Norman establishments which were founded at "all the Bassas, great and little." The Père Labat, the Sailor Villaud de Belfons, and many writers, of whom Barbot is the most known, claim for the French, exclusively, the honour of being the first explorers of this coast. According to them a company of Dieppe merchants, in the reign of Charles the Fifth, between 1364 and 1413—nearly a century before the Portuguese entered upon their grander career of discovery —sent an expedition to the Gold Coast, which founded commercial colonies at Goree and Cape Verde, at Sestro Paris, now Grand Cestros, at Petit Dieppe, near Basa or Bassa, on the mouth of the St. John's River, and at "the Bay of France," now Rio Fresco. This is repeated in the "*Mémoire sur le Commerce Maritime de Rouen, par Ernest de Fréville*," who states the date to be November, 1364, and the number of vessels to have been two of one hundred tons each. In 1382 the merchants of Dieppe and Rouen combined sent three exploring ships, of which one, the "Virgin," reached Commenda and Mina, so called from its "gold mines," from which the blacks brought large supplies of the precious metal. In 1383—others say 1386—they built a strong factory, and left a garrison of ten or twelve men, and in 1387 the settlement, which had further been enlarged, was provided with a chapel. Large imports of gold, ivory, and pepper, found their way from these places to France, and an active trade continued till the European war in 1413 caused them all, after a career of fifty years, to be abandoned. Even in Barbot's time (1700), one of the El-Mina castles was called Bastion de France, and there was an old inscription beginning with M.C.C.C.—the rest defaced. At Goree there were, it is said, similar remains. These wars continued to agitate France till 1490, nearly eighty years after the abandonment of their West African colonies. Meanwhile the Portuguese, who had learned the way, had taken the place of the explorers, and have ever since claimed the honour of discovery.

The Portuguese are naturally wroth at this attempt to pluck a leaf from their laurels. Let me quote M. Valdez: "Respecting the early settlers, ridiculous follies were propagated by Père Labat, and the seaman Villautbelle-fond (sic), but these were invented 270 years after the Portuguese historian, Gomes Ennes d'Azurara,[*] who was contemporary with the discovery of Canagá, or Senegal, and who was honoured with the confidence of the celebrated Infante D. Henrique; and therefore we

[*] Chronica de Descobrimento e Conquista de Guiné, escrita por Mandado de El Rei D. Affonso V., pelo Chronista G. E. de Azurara, precedida de una introducção e illustrada com algumas notas pelo Visconde de Santarem, 8vo., Paris, 1841. Also, Memoria sobre a prioridade dos Descobrimentos Portugueses n' a costa d'Africa Occidental, pelo Visconde Santarem, Paris, 1841.

must believe (*"Je n'en vois pas la nécessité"*) the assertion made by this writer in his 'Chronicle of the Discovery and Conquest of Guinea,' that the Portuguese were the first who discovered the entrance of the Senegal. The claim of the Norman pirates of the fourteenth century (N.B., this is hardly fair) to the discovery is supported by an allegation that Norman words may be traced in the language of the natives, and that an inscription has been discovered as follows—'M.C.C.C.'!!! Now I defy the quickest ear to discover anything resembling the Norman in the language of the Mandingoes, Jaloffes, Cassangas, Bauhans, or Feloupes; but he whose eye is so clear as satisfactorily to decipher the inscription above mentioned, may possess an ear capable of defining sounds such as those referred to. So much for national enthusiasm and fanaticism!" Such verbiage is by no means satisfactory in face of M. Bouet-Willaumez. Nor is the Rev. Mr. Wilson's remark at all more conclusive:— "This account of French discovery in Africa is not sustained by any contemporaneous writers, either French or Portuguese. The natives of Africa have no traditionary knowledge of any such visitors to their country; and what discredits the picture still more is, that Azembuja, the man sent out by the Portuguese government to build the castle at Elmina, found no traces whatever of any fort or castle at that place." As if Africans in 1856 had any tradition extending back for centuries, or as if a Portuguese or any other official of those days, when ordered to erect a fort for his sovereign in the Land of

.Gold Mines would confess priority of claim on the part of another and a rival nation !

It is to be hoped that a question of such historical importance will not be dropped. *A priori*, the claims of the French are strong, but they have been suffered to rest in obscurity. Their weak point at present is the absence of contemporary evidence. But the Bayeux tapestry, a chronicle of far older date, has been found, and perhaps some fortunate discoverer may alight upon a document which shall set the question at rest.

The history of English transactions on the Gold Coast is equally interesting. The first commercial voyage made by our countrymen was in 1551, when Captain Thomas Wyndham, who afterwards died of fever in the Benin River, after loading his ships with Malaguetta pepper at the Cestos River, reached the Golden Land and returned to England with 150 lbs. of dust. On the 10th January, 1662, the Royal Company, or Company of Royal Adventurers of England trading to Africa, was incorporated under patronage of the Duke of York, afterwards Charles II., and in the same year James Fort was built at Accra. Its object was nearly entirely the carrying on of the slave trade, and the attacks of the Dutch under the great De Ruyter compelled it, in 1667, to surrender its charter to government. The second, or Royal African Company, was incorporated on the 27th September, 1672, with powers and privileges to maintain and extend the African trade. It entered upon its functions with vigour, and soon possessed fifteen forts and factories on the coast, of which, however, Bosman* gives a poor account. Despite the Assiento contract the company became indebted, and followed in the way of its predecessor. In 1752-4 the "African Company" was established with free trade` on the Gold Coast to all His Majesty's subjects: this bound them not to interfere as before with private adventurers, or what was then called "interlopers." This was the first blow to the prosperity of the coast. The American Revolution ensued; the Abolition movement followed, and the establishment of Sierra Leone struck the final blow. In 1821 the African Company, being bankrupt, was abolished: the British forts, settlements, and possessions on the Western coast of Africa from 20° N.˙ to 20° S. lat. were made dependencies on the colony of Sierra Leone; and the bill passed through Parliament in 1821. In 1827, owing to the expenses of Sir Charles Macarthy's Ashantee war, the home government gave up the forts to the merchants as factories on various conditions, especially that Cape Coast Castle and James Fort, Accra, should remain dependencies of Sierra Leone, and that affairs should be managed by an African committee of three merchants, and a paid secretary, resident in London and appointed by government. A parliamentary grant

---

* William Bosman was chief factor for the Dutch at Elmina, in the days of the Royal African Company, and he seems not a little to have despised his neighbours. He was an active and most efficient man, and his "Description of the Coast of Guinea," is equally valuable for its observation, and amusing by its dry humour.

of 4000*l*. per annum was allowed for the repair of forts, the maintenance of schools, and presents to the various Fanti chiefs. The local establishments were a lieutenant-governor and president of the council, a council, justices of the peace, civil commandants at Annamaboo, British Accra and Dixcove, and the officers of the guard—100 men— with surgeon, schoolmasters, and interpreters. Pending these arrangements, Mr. John Jackson was made president, but as it was considered desirable to choose an officer wholly unconnected with trade, Mr. George Maclean, who had served in the African corps, and had accompanied, in 1826, Colonel Lumley as military secreary to the Gold Coast,—of him more anon,—was made lieut.-governor and president in 1830. The crown resumed possession of the Gold Coast in 1844, and the first governor was Commander Hill, R.N.

The East Indies and Western Africa both began to attract the attention of England in the days of the Virgin Queen. Her Majesty granted, in 1585, a patent to Lords Leicester and Warwick, allowing them to treat with the Barbary States for twelve years, and in 1600, two hundred persons petitioned their sovereign to establish the Governor and Company of Merchants of London trading with the East Indies. But West Africa is distant 3000, India 10,000 miles from England, and the difference enabled the company that ruled the land from the Himalaya to Cape Comorin, though younger by 15 years, to outlive for 37 years the company that ruled 40° of intertropical Africa.

The annals of the two great rivals are instructive: British Africa being near home has been greatly neglected, because mostly under home orders; it is, and long has been, a string of ruinous forts and settlements. British India, on the other hand, being beyond the range of interference from head-quarters, soon became the most splendid possession ever held by a European nation.

India, I may observe, has been conquered despite of England. Had het steamers and the electric wires of the present day been in operation a century ago, we should still have had a comptoir at Calcutta, Madras, and Bombay, with perhaps a strip of protected territory; our possessions, in fact, would have been like Bathurst, Sierra Leone, and Cape Coast Castle. But happily for England, a letter in those good old times took a year before its answer came. Every new governor or governor-general was tempted to war by some native king or chief; perhaps he was not unwilling to distinguish himself, and—rich men rarely ran the risks of climate— he might sometimes have had an eye to profitable results. Thus, hostilities were declared and duly reported to the Court of Directors. At the end of a year arrived a loud objurgation from those elderly ladies, rating at all aggressive measures, repudiating a policy of territorial aggrandizement, and much "bunkum" of the same manner. But it reached too late. A province, in which probably you could wrap up Great Britain, had been in turn fought down, well looted, and annexed with the tax-gatherer in full activity. Nothing more of course was to be said about the matter. The Court of Directors saw before them new patronage for sons and nephews, and the *Imperium in Imperio* became great *malgré lui*.

I am now firm astride upon India, an old hobby which will take the lead; in truth—may the reader pardon me! India was once the "gorgeous East;" a bit of the "Arabian Nights," which home people delighted in, and highly overvalued. This was followed by a reaction. The Indian uncle died out: the old Nabob was found to look at every sixpence. The Pagoda-tree, when struck, yielded no rupees. Presently the Public—shrewdly suspecting that their Eastern Empire, far from being worth untold sums, was actually in arrears, (despite all its gold bedsteads and jewelled saddles,) some 2,000,000*l.* per annum—waxed wroth, rose up, laid hands upon it, and, after discussing the idea of giving it up, began to treat it by administering to it homœopathic doses of scientific political economy.

Were Russia or France blessed with such a field for labour, they would soon make it pay five or six millions of pounds sterling, by some such "unconstitutional" means as these:—

> They would at once clear off two governors, who are mere head-clerks—two commanders-in-chief, mere major-generals—and two councils, viz., those of Madras and Bombay: in both these places business could be transacted quite as effectually by a secretary to the Supreme Govern-

ment and a major-general in command of sundry brigadiers.

They would abolish the civilian system and its high salaries, recruiting the ranks from military officers, who could be eligible after suitable examinations. They might retain Suddur and Supreme Courts, and organise Cassations, and even Chancery Courts, at the several Presidencies, for the benefit of wealthy natives who wish to ruin themselves by law; but these luxuries should not extend beyond a radius of fifty miles.

They would cherish the Panchayat, or native jury, merely superintending it to obviate unjust decisions.

They would not inflict upon the natives their own taxes,—income-tax, licence-tax, stamp duties, heavy import dues, and other hateful foreign appliances. They would prefer the indigenous system of a capitation or poll-tax, the house-tax, the Nazaranah or succession duties, and benefices levied from each Pergunnah, according to popular settlement, and in due proportion, as did the English of the old day when burghers were first returned to Parliament.

They would transform all their regular black army into irregulars, and never allow an East Indian to learn the scientific branches of the service—artillery and engineering.

They would systematically disarm the population, by transporting all those who fabricated, and by imprisoning all who possessed, weapons of war.

Finally, they would cleave to hereditary offices—which would create a conservative party in the country, and confirm all tenures of "hak" or vested rights.

But a constitutional people would not attempt even the first of these measures. Its idea of economy and its policy must be to cut down the pay and allowances of the ensign and the assistant-surgeon, and to spend some 30,000*l.* a year upon local governors, commanders-in-chief, and members of council.

I now return to the Gold Coast.

During the night of the 18th August we steamed past the mouth of that queer formation, called picturesquely, and not unaptly, the Bottomless Pit. Here the great bank of gradually shelving sand is split by a submarine valley, funnel-shaped, and opening seaward. At the head of this gully, close to the beach, there are twenty fathoms of soundings, with a soft bottom of bluish mud. At one mile off shore the breadth between the two sides of the ravine is less than a quarter of a mile, with 100 fathoms of depth; at three miles' distance it is about one mile by 200 fathoms. As the lead brings up pieces of coralline, and a madrepore formation is observable in most places east of Accra to the river bottom, this valley may be a depression, like the submerged Coral Islands once known to exist near Zanzibar.

The next point of interest was Grand Bassam, a clump of villages at the mouth of the Costa River, where the French, in 1843, built Fort Nemours. According to some, the experiment was a failure; others declare that a good business in gold is still done there. The same may be said of Assini, or Fort Joinville, another Gallic possession about twenty-seven miles east of the Costa River. Three miles to the west of the latter is the Gold River, which Bosman makes the western boundary of the Gold Coast. Beyond Assini lie the Four Hills, or Hummocks, of Apollonia, called by seamen Cape Apollonia; the name reminds one of the Apollo Bunder, which should be named Palawa, at Bombay—ridiculously classical. Here the English had a fort, which is now crumbling to ruins. In 1848, Captain Winniett, who succeeded Captain Hill as governor, attacked "Quawe Accah," King of Apollonia, who had killed the French Commandant of Assini, and took him prisoner, and became Sir William Winniett.

We are now off the Windward, which is here the western division of the Gold Coast.* It extends from Cape Apollonia (2° 35′ W. long.) to the mouth of the Secoom River (0° 3′ 2″ W. long.), about eight miles west of Fort James, Accra, about 170 nautical miles. The leeward, or eastern districts, begin at the Secoom River, and stretch to the mouth of the Volta, in 0° 41′ 2″ of east longitude, or 44·4 miles of direct distance. Thus, in modern times, the Gold Coast, bounded by Cape Apollonia, and the Volta River, has a sea front of 225 miles. In Bosman's

* It is regrettable that geographers encourage this most ambiguous style of momenclature. Thus the Windward Islands in the West Indies are the western; in Eastern Africa, windward means eastern.

day it had narrow limits; "the Gold Coast, being a part of Guinea, is extended about sixty miles, beginning with the Gold River, twelve miles above Axim, and ending with the village Ponni, seven or eight miles east of Accra."

The gold export, and afterwards the slave-trade, studded this coast with forts and factories; twenty-five are mentioned—about one to each eight miles; of these, three were Danish, two Brandenburghers, and the rest belonged to the English and Dutch. At present seven English and four Dutch establishments are kept up;*

---

* In the windward coast the English possessed, going from the West, Apollonia, Dixcove, British Secundee and Commendah, Cape Coast Castle, Annamboo, Fort Coromantine, Tamtamquerry, Gúmwah, Mumford, and Winnebah. The latter place was destroyed in 1812, when the frigate "Amelia," Capt. Irby, revenged the murder of the commandant Mr. Meredith, who had been tortured to death by being compelled to walk over burning grass and shrubs. The fort was blown up, and "for many years afterwards, English vessels passing Winnebah were in the habit of pouring a broadside into the town, to inspire the natives with the idea of the severe vengeance which would be exacted for the spilling of European blood" (Mr. Brodie Cruikshank's "Eighteen Years on the Gold Coast," London, 1853). To which may be added, that they fired into the wrong place, the real culprits being the people of a neighbouring village, who remained unhurt.

On the windward coast the Dutch had Axim, Brandenburg, Hollandia, Accoda, Bootry, Tacorady or Tacorary, Dutch Commendah, Chuma, Mouree, Dutch Coromantine, Apam near the Devil's Hill, and Barracoe.

On the leeward coast the British had only Fort James, Accra; the Dutch, Dutch Accra, Labaddi, Pona, Temma, and Pramprnm or Kbuprán, or Kpukprán; whilst five belonged to the Danes, viz., Christiansborg with its out-station Frederiksborg, Augustenborg near Tesha or Tassy, Fredensborg at Great Ningo, Kongenstein at

the other fourteen issues for the life-blood of Africa which these leeches sucked to some effect, have been abandoned with the traffic which called them into being. These deserted forts and ruined castles affect the voyager with melancholy as he passes these sunny shores. And even the posts, which are still maintained, appear ruinous and squalid; really, for appearance' sake, Britannia ought to look after this out-of-the-way corner of her estate, or give it up altogether. Half of the sum now wilfully wasted upon the Dover harbour, a work pronounced practicable by those engineers who maintained the Suez Canal to be impossible, would prevent our being ashamed of out-stations, than which

Adda on the Volta, and Prindsenstein at Quittah. Slavery being abolished throughout their colonies by the Danes in 1803, these places became useless. On the 17th August, 1850, the king of Denmark sold his forts on the Gold Coast to the British Government for 10,000*l*. England thus obtained exclusive possession of all the seaboard from Accra to the Volta, a rich country, of which, hitherto, no use has been made.

The real site for a settlement would be at Addah, near the mouth of the Volta, and on its right bank, where the Danish fort is fast falling to ruins. The river called by the Accras Shilau, by the Akwimbas Ainzá, by the Addas Joh or Firao, and by the Portuguese, on account of its windings, Rio Volta, is a good highway into the interior. On 28th October, 1861, Lieut. Dolben, R.N., ascended it in boats for 120 miles, until near the Kpong Rapids, where he turned back. He reported the country on the banks to be fertile and well cultivated, and the people, though a slave trade was still established amongst them, in the main, friendly. Lieut. Dolben was of opinion that the rapids could be passed by a short portage, and that the upper course of the river is of considerable length. Now that Accra has been ruined by the earthquakes of 1862, the head-quarters might be more easily transferred to Addah.

at present even Portuguese India shows nothing more wretched.

At sunrise we were off Cape Trespuntos, or Three Points, an excellent land-mark, the three headlands of which—the central is the proper Cape—lie, respectively, fifty, forty-five, and forty miles from Cape Coast Castle; the two more distant from the stream are densely wooded; the third, or nearest, is a bare "neat's tongue," backed by a growth of forest. A little to the west lies Axim Bay, where the Portuguese built Fort St. Anthony, which soon fell into the hands of the Dutch, who also became finally possessed of Fort Brandenburg, originally belonging to the Elector of that name. In 1700 it was a large depôt of gold trade; now it is a crumbling ruin, perched on an eminence, and backed by black bush and tree, which stand out from the glistening white sea-sands on both sides. East of the Cape is another Dutch ruin—Acquidah, or Accoda. The seas about Trespuntos were animated with shoals of fish pursued by gulls, and fishermen with huge straw hats were casting large seines from small canoes.

After doubling the third point, we sighted Dixcove, originally Dick's Cove. At this point begins the Ahanta, or Anta Country, once rich in gold, which may still be procured there, and ever gifted with a rich and fertile soil. It extends to near Seconda, with about forty miles of seaboard, and thirty of depth, being backed by the equally rich, but turbulent, "Wassaw"

Country, which the English have named after "Thaddeus of Warsaw." Behind that, again, lies the land of Dinkira, whose early battles with the Ashantee kings were famous in their day. Dixcove dates from 1681; it was finished in 1688, and became the strongest outpost on the coast; it has a territory totally independent of Ahanta, about five miles of sea-shore, and twenty miles inland. From the sea we could distinguish the large whitewashed building some ninety feet above the water, and about the dwarf bay were some apparently fine houses. The place contains an officer and four men, together with an assistant-surgeon—all supplied by the Gold Coast Artillery, and the little garrison ever feels suicidal. It is well backed with wood, which, however, the people are unwilling to see felled; and upon the glassy roadstead floated a single French brig. The coast now becomes a succession of settlements. Within sight of Dixcove, and separated by a black islet and reefs, called Sanco Stone, lays Boutry, upon whose ruins Fort Bartenstein, an *enceinte* apparently half way up a hill, still flies at times the Dutch flag. Five miles, going westward placed us opposite Pompendi, a native town guarded by a treacherous formidable reef, upon which the waves dashed with a long swell. About six miles from Pompendi was Takorady Point, a long, low tongue, dark at this distance, but when nearer, red: a native town appeared from the sea in the shape of a few huts; a single schooner composed the shipping, and the Dutch fort, once a place of importance, could hardly be distinguished. It was the scene of severe troubles in 1837, when, on 23rd October, the Dutch military commandant of Boutry and his assistant were treacherously slain by one Bonsoo, chief of the Ahantas. The latter followed up their success by attacking the Dutch troops at the pass of Takorady, and killing many men and four or five officers. In July, 1838, Governor Verveir revenged the outrage by capturing Bonsoo, and dispersing his men. Within the seaboard is the "Adoom country" of old geographies. Another four miles placed us off Point Secondee, where the whitewashed remains of Fort Orange occupy a bold rocky cliff, some fifty feet above sea level.

The next point of interest was Chama, also written Chumah and Essama, and by the people pronounced Ishámá. Its fort, St. Sebastian, built by the Portuguese, fell as usual into the hands of the stout Hollanders. We could plainly distinguish from our deck a large and solid European building, overlooking a native town. About a mile eastward of the fort, a sudden depression in the long wavy curtain of cliff from seventy to 300 feet high, denotes the position of the two lagoons, between which the Chumah, or St. John's River, finds its way into the sea. The Chumah people call it Prah, and prefix to it the word Bossum, meaning fetish, or sacred. Little is known of this, the largest stream on the Gold Coast, except that the bar at the mouth, being barely two feet deep, renders it useless. Col. Stahrenberg, as reported by Bowdich, ascended it for three days in a canoe, till stopped by a large cataract, near which his men would not venture; and it is reported as flowing through fertile plains, between banks clothed with magnificent timber. The outfall discoloured with bubbly green the pure blue waters off the mouth, and the bottom was the soft mud, which navigators prefer to the hard sand. They can plough a way through the former; the latter, aided by the surf, soon breaks, by bumping, the ship's back.

The Bossumpra River is the western boundary of the Fanti people,* and separates them from their powerful neighbours, the Santi or Ashantees. The former country is now, like the Ionian Islands, under British protectorate, the general nature of our tenure being a ground-rent paid to Caboceers and headmen; the former mediatorial influence, rendered necessary by the slave trade, has of course ceased. Crossing the Prah, on the part of the Ashantees, is considered equivalent to a declaration of war, as passing the Border was in the olden time, when England and Scotland amused themselves by invading each other. It is the general opinion in the colony that the Volta is an arm of the Prah; if this be the case, our maps require considerable alteration. Strange that during two centuries of residence in these regions we should not have taken the trouble to lay down so crucial

---

* The "Ethiopic Directory" (p. 390), asserts that "the Fanti country, after a dreadful war of extermination, may be now considered as incorporated with the kingdom of Ashautee," and that "in 1824 the Fantis were nearly annihilated." They are still, however, a powerful tribe, wholly independent of the Ashantees.

a point. Should the Prah and the Volta prove to be one, anastomosing at some place to the north-east of Kumasi, the capital of Ashantee, and south of the Sarem country, we have a gold country in equilateral-triangular shape whose base is a sea-line of 150 miles, and whose sides may conjecturally be laid down at 220 miles, or an area of more than 15,000 square miles, of which the greater portion is rich in hitherto partially exploited gold.

The history of Ashantee wars, which began in 1807, is that of the African coast generally. In these lands there are two great axioms of native policy. The first is never to admit strangers into the interior for trade, which it is the interest of the maritime tribes to monopolise, and they live in idleness at the expense of the "Bushmen," or people of the interior. For this point, which is first in life to them, they will fight to the last, and hence the main difficulty of opening up the "Dark Continent." The second is the ambition of the inner peoples to obtain a point *d'appui* upon the coast, where they can sell their goods at their own price. This explains the frequent wars and irruptions of Ashantee and Dahomey against the maritime people, and the want of permanency in the latter. They become demoralised by indolent living, intercourse with white men, the disuse of arms; and the deleterious climate of the lowlands, and thus they are less fitted to resist the hardier and more warlike tribes that pour down upon them. Dr. Livingstone (chap. 21) asserts "no African tribe has ever been destroyed." Nothing but the profoundest ignorance could have dictated such a declaration. I affirm, on the contrary, that from the Kru country to the Gaboon, there is not an ancient people now settled on the seaboard, including even Dahomey; that they supplanted the races who formerly possessed those civilized seats; and that many, the Mpongwe and the old Calabar people, are likely to become extinct before the close of another century. The margin of Africa, in fact, like that of other solid bodies, is continually wearing off.

The Ashantees fought hard for their primal African desideratum. Their first southerly movement, in 1807, was headed, according to Bowdich, by Sai Tootoo Quamina. Mr. Meredith ("Account of the Gold Coast") has accurately described the siege of Annamaboo, in which, though our countrymen showed the greatest possible gallantry, the Ashantees had the upper hand, and Col. Torrane's concessions encouraged them to repeat the attempt. In 1811 they again defeated the Fantis at Apam, and carried to Kumasi the bell of the Danish Fort at Addah. In 1816 the Fantis were obliged to own their supremacy, and to pay an annual tribute. The mission of Messrs. James, Bowdich, and Hutchinson, in 1817, kept the peace by means of a treaty for six years. On the 11th March, 1822, Brigadier-General Sir Charles Macarthy, who had long served upon the coast, returned to it as Governor of Sierra Leone and its dependencies, and proceeded on board H.M.S. "Iphigenia," Commodore Sir Robert Mends, to take possession of the forts on the Gold Coast. He encouraged the Fantis to resist the annual subsidy paid to the King of Ashantee, and when that monarch marched down with 15,000 warriors in January, 1824, he proceeded to meet him with about 1000 white soldiers and a mob of native auxiliaries. The Governor seems to have fallen into the mistake of despising his enemy. A fight took place at Assamacow, near the Bossumpra River, on the 21st January, and Sir Charles Macarthy was killed, together with eight officers of the 2nd West India regiment and the Cape Coast militia.* According to Major Ricketts ("Narrative of the Ashantee War"), "his heart was eaten by the principal chiefs, that they might *imbibe* his bravery; his dried flesh and bones were divided amongst the Caboceers, who always carried them about as fetishes for courage, and there is a local tradition that his head, with his spectacles on, was exposed upon a pole." The Ashantees ravaged the coast, and through the year fought with British native forces now successfully then with loss; but failing to take the castle, they were compelled by sickness and want of provisions to retire. In 1826 they again advanced upon the seaboard, but on the 7th August they were utterly routed—though they attacked on Monday, their lucky day—at the fatal field of Dodowah, so called from a village on a bushy plain, about twenty-four miles north-east of British Accra. According to Major Ricketts,

---

* As has appeared in a previous chapter; the people of the Gold Coast assign to their beloved Macarthy the fate of Cato.

"among the sad trophies of the day was supposed to be the head of Sir Charles Macarthy, which was sent to England by Lieutenant-Colonel Purdon; it was taken by the Aquapim chief. The king carried it always with him as a powerful charm, and on the morning of the battle he poured rum upon it, and invoked it to cause all the heads of the whites on the field to lie beside it. The skull was enveloped in a paper covered with Arabic characters and a silk handkerchief, over all was a tiger skin, the emblem of royalty." The skull, however, was subsequently suspected to be that of the King Tootoo Quamina, who perished in the action. The people of Cape Coast Castle still swear by Karte Ukuda, or Macarthy's Wednesday, a strong oath with high penalties for perjury.* Finally, peace was concluded with the Ashantees, and trade with the interior was reopened on the 27th April, 1831.

Since that time, though there have been many rumours of wars, the Ashantees have remained at peace with us; but, as in the case of Russia and Turkey, such a state of affairs can hardly be expected to continue.†

East of Ishama lay a line of reddish cliffs, here

---

* All the tribes upon this coast have a different oath. The Ashantees swear by Meminda Kormanti (Coromanti Saturday), when their great king Osai Tootoo was slain by the Akims. The Fanti chief of Abra, by the "rock in the sea," near Annamaboo, where he took refuge from the Ashantees in 1807. The Annamaboo chief, by Igwah, or Cape Coast Castle, which protected him when he fled from the Ashantees.

† This was written more than one year ago; 1863 proves the prediction to be correct.

patched with wood, there bare of forests, springing from a straight sea beach, in which baylets with dwarf arms and shallow chords succeeded one another. About noon we passed Commenda Point, which before 1820 was an important post to English and Hollanders; the former chose the eastern, the latter the western bank of the little River Soosn. Native huts cluster around them both, and a background of lagoon poisons the air. Viewed from the westward, Commendah, or, as the natives call it, Ekky-Tikky,—some write Akataykin—is backed by a high arm, an insulated formation known by the promising name of Gold Hill. One feels once more in "Californy."

At 1 P.M. we were abreast of the castle of St. George del Mina, popularly known as Elmina, the first European establishment upon the Gold Coast.* All the landing-places upon these shores are infamously bad, causing great loss of life, except at Elmina and Apam, both belonging to the Dutch. Here the little river Beyah (Byham?) allows light vessels to unload in safety under the castle walls, and supplies good water; the want of which, causing dysentery and various diseases, has given to Guinea what Bosman calls its "dreadful mortal name." The lower fort, called St. George, stands obliquely fronting the sea, on a black rock a little above water level; it has double walls and long batteries, with rectangular towers instead of bastions, and a tall

---

* Built by the French in 1383, rebuilt by the Portuguese in 1481, captured by the Dutch in 1637, and finally ceded to them with its dependencies in 1641.

dungeon-looking work in the rear. Above it, on a hill about 100 feet high, and commanding both fortress and tower, stands Fort St. Jago (St. James), a parallelogrammic whitewashed pile, with a single central tower, and somewhat resembling a hospital with its chapel; it is, however, strongly laid out. The large native town, with its red-brown mud walls and bistre thatching, is divided into two parts: one on the peninsula formed by the *embouchure* of the little river, and under the guns; the other extends along the beach to the westward of the stream. These defences have repeatedly resisted the whole force of Ashantee. A single schooner, the "Ionian," of Salem, lay off the port, which in the early part of the eighteenth century exported 3,000,000*l.* of gold. The settlement contains a governor, secretary, and a commandant of troops, about seventeen white officers, and sixty men, who are clad in blue dungaree. They are by no means healthy; the high walls exclude the air, "sopies" induce liver-complaint, and "personal economy" is neglected. According to Dr. Robert Clarke, late of H.M.'s Colonial Medical Service,* no less than twelve officers died in the eight years between 1851 and 1860. They are on the best of terms with their neighbours of Cape Coast Castle, but intercourse is necessarily rare. Animals being wanted—wholly

* "Remarks on the Topography and Diseases of the Gold Coast;" an excellent paper read before the Epidemiological Society, Monday, 7th May, 1860, and partly published in No. II. of the Parliamentary Reports of Her Majesty's Colonial Possessions, issued February, 1861.

unable to live on this part of the coast—they must call upon one another in hammocks; the distance along the beach, only eight miles, thus takes three hours, and the expense is about ten times that of a London Hansom. Dr. Clarke calculates the expense of locomotion by "dawk," that a journey of some ten miles on the Gold Coast costs nearly as much as to travel by third-class train from Aberdeen to London.

Beyond Elmina we passed a small bay, with its country residences and farms, where the governor and the principal merchants live, and the Sweet River and its village that divides the English protectorate from the Dutch. The country behind was a line of downs, a broken surface of little wooded hills and intervening basins, which tells distinctly its tale of gold, and which morning fogs prove to be swampy. The mysterious malaria we know is there, and men die off as if in a scurvied ship, yet it shows no sign. The German traveller Monrad, asserts that he never saw on this Costa Rica a European past fifty. In such places all officials ought to be in couples, one present, the other on leave in England; nor ought residence ever to be prolonged beyond three years. This is the system which is gradually growing up in the Oil Rivers further south, and until lands are drained and water is distilled, it would be advisable to try it here.

Presently the profile of Cape Coast Castle became

> "Distinct in the light clear air, with
> A flood of such rich dyes
> As makes earth near as heavenly as heaven."

It charmed our senses after the foul, gloomy reek of the S'a Leone coast. At a distance it was a long green-grown tongue of reddish land, broken with dwarf cliffs and scaurs, and lined below with clean sand. Upon the outline appeared three projections: a fort at the root, a second about the centre, and a castle with a mass of native huts at the tip. The first, which lies north-west of the settlement, is Phipps' Tower, alias Fort Victoria; a martello thing, abandoned, but kept in repair, and so placed in defiance of Vauban, that in the hands of an enemy it would command castle and town. The second, or central post, is Smith's Tower, now Fort William, built by Mr. President Maclean, another artless martello, pretty, but circular below, and, in defiance of all architecture, square above, mounting twelve guns, commanded by No. 1, and commanding No. 3. It has a lighthouse, 192 feet above sea level, but skippers declare that the light never fails to disappear at two A.M., and that a harbour master being, like York, "wanted," the reflectors will not reflect; whereas those at S'a Leone, under opposite conditions, have lost all their silver by over-burnishing. Also a ball used to be dropped from the castle's flagstaff at the instant of Greenwich mean solar noon; but since the death of the patron-saint of the place, Mr. Maclean, few of the governors of Cape Coast Castle have been addicted to astronomy. The principal castle is upon the tip of the tongue and the native town clusters behind it.

At two P.M. we anchored one mile off the landing-place; the water was low, no bad condition, and the day was that of the dry season. A local superstition, however, declares that the surf is always worst between the new and full moon. Presently we were surrounded by canoes, wall-sided rudderless troughs, from twenty to forty feet long, with gunwales rather bending inwards from the right angle. All had weatherboards in the bow, planks raised two or more feet out to keep out the seas,—such as the forec'sle of the British navy in the days of Henry VIII. Others are provided with a funnel of woodwork at the fore, in the shape of a huge thimble. The only danger of this craft is of their "turning turtle." The paddles are small trefoils, short and stoutly made, to lift the vessel over shallow water. In the smooth, deep rivers of the South we shall find them with long and broad lanceolate blades, the better to hold water. The crew are Fantis, once a currish race, thoroughly cowed by the more warlike Ashantees; under our peaceful rule, however, they have waxed rather insolent. They catch us dexterously from the dangerous ladder, and, as they make for the shore, all sing "Whi' man cum agen," —White men come again,—with remarks, in their vernacular, doubtless highly personal. The great art of landing without a sea is to watch when the wave breaks, backing water, if necessary; a calm interval is found, all "clap on steam," and riding over the crest of a billow, run upon the sand before the rise of the next breaker. They all then tumble out, land the passengers upon their shoulders, and haul up the canoe.

On this occasion, however, we did not escape well, there were too many in the boat to be carried off pick-a-back at one trip, and we were received upon the beach by a host of starers.

The rollers are feared at Cape Coast Castle. The landing-place is a small bay under the north-east bastion, protected by a reef jutting out from a ledge of rocks. The Harmattan season, December, January, and February, shows the smoothest seas; from May to August there is generally a terrific surf, the full violence of the Atlantic rolling in from the south and west, and for days together canoes cannot put out. An excellent landing-place and a wet dock might be made behind the main outcrop: it has often been proposed—the excuse is that there would be difficulties. The fact is, that, after the sand has been removed, the rock would require a little blasting, which would be too much for Cape Coast energy.* What can be expected, when a colonial engineer passes some twenty years at a place, and leaves, as the only memory, a temple of Cloacina, already hastening to decay? Again, at the disembarking place, about twenty yards from the castle and sea-gate, lies a lot of thirty-two pounders. They were landed here some fifteen years ago, and have been left to rust away because no one had industry enough to remove them. Throughout the castle indeed I would rather fire with blank cartridge than with ball;

* I am happy to say that many of these remarks are obsolete in 1863.

paint fills up honeycombs, but is a poor protection against gunpowder.

Ascending the few feet of ramp, we entered the long gateway of the Cruizing Cape Castle.* The foundation is called Tabara, *alias* Tahbil, *alias* Tabirri Rock, and a similar solitary outcrop to the westward is known as Tabara's Wife. The former is the supposed residence of a great fetish, who comes forth at night white and giant-like, to drive away malicious ghosts. During the yam season, sacrifices of goats, fowls, and vegetables are made to it, and they attract a multitude of "turkey-buzzards." The material is a dark gneiss, through which granite and quartz have protruded. It rises eighteen to twenty feet above sea level, yet in violent storms, the rollers, dashing clean over the rock, which echoes to their thundering roar, sweeps heavy spray over the out-lying batteries of the southern front up to the mess-room windows, forty feet high. The castle is a most irregular building, of quadrangular shape, if any, with bastions at each angle, and batteries originally intended for 100, but now mounting some sixty to seventy useless old iron guns. It is comfortable enough as quarters,

---

* The Portuguese called it Cabo Côrso, the latter a sea-term, meaning a cruizing; Bosman uses the word Cabocors, and the English ridiculously perverted it into Cape Coast Castle. (S. Lopez de Lima, Ensaios sobre a Statistica das Possessaõs Portuguezas, Libr. II. part i. p. 7.) He also corrects the following English inaccuracies: Biafra, St. Thomas, Annobona, Escardos, Chama, Axim and Cabo Lopez into Rio das Maffras, San Thomè, Annobom, Escravos, Sama, Axem and Cabo de Lopo Gonçalves.

but useless for modern warfare; it has all the vastness of Europeo-Oriental architecture in the olden time. Such erections in these days are impossible. Probably built piecemeal, it covers several acres of ground; in parts it is four stories high. The gateway leads into a large triangular space, occupying the east of the *enceinte*, used for drill, and adorned with two thirteen-inch mortars, and five fine old Danish brass guns, lately brought from Quittah. To the north of this *terre pleine* are double-storied buildings, used as barracks and for other purposes; on the south is a sea wall, twenty feet high with the Tabara bastion mounting two mortars and nine guns; which fortification unmistakeably wants casemates. The west is flanked by a long transverse line of double-storied buildings, that divide the castle into two unequal parts: they contain the council chamber, or the *palaver* hall, and the civil quarters. A double flight of steps leads to this north and south range of buildings, which are high, solid, and roomy, and are not destitute of a certain magnificence. The western gallery is paved with squares of black and white marble, like the Sayyid's Palace at Zanzibar, and His Excellency still occupies the office where President Maclean used to transact business, at the head of a small staircase separating it from the old observatory, a kind of cockloft, afterwards the dressing-room in which Mrs. Maclean was found by her servant lying dead across the door. Passing through this central building by an arched gateway, guarded by two cohorns, you enter a smaller triangular space called the spur battery; casemates in its northern side are used for stores, and in those opposite some of the troops are lodged; the centre is occupied by a guard-room, built over one of the best tanks in the place, and there is a gateway opening upon the town.

Before mess, which was at the unnatural hour of four P.M., we went forth to attend a *cause célèbre* in the Court-house. Walking along the main portion of the building, which, fronting the sea, forms the conspicuous curtain between the two bastions at the flanks, we walked into the barracks, and found the men in a state more merry than wise. This is the Yam Feast, or Black Christmas; a ceremonial intended, it is said, to impress upon the native mind the risk of using the unripe, or even the young vegetable whilst it continues soft and waxy. It may not be gathered under severe pains and penalties before the day appointed by the chief. On such festivals the Kings of Ashantee and Dahomey put to death a certain number of their subjects, the better to teach Hygiène to the rest. The harvest-home is in September, at which time all who can afford it enter the state known as "half-seas over." Armed companies, commanded by their captains, carrying their flags like regiments in New York, promenade the streets, and faction fights are disagreeably common. It has not been found possible to abolish this system of "companies," which causes great disorders on the Gold Coast. The barracks are decidedly overcrowded, and than overcrowding no fault can be more fatal in these lands. We saw, also, a reading and billiard-room, the table of which was, at any rate, superior to that of S'a Leone; a better one, however, has been proposed. The officers' quarters are in the northern line of buildings fronting the sea; in the basement of the same is the hospital, tolerably light and well ventilated. The old slave dungeons are visited by those only who enjoy such mild morbidities as slave markets and old barracoons. Dr. Clarke describes these black holes as being under the south or sea battery, and "access to them is obtained through a winding archway, which opens into crypts formed by the divisional supporting walls of the battery, being feebly lighted and ventilated through grated apertures in the sea wall, which reeks with dankness from the percolation of water."

The Court-house, or rather room, is at the eastern extremity of the tall curtain fronting the sea; it is a dirty little hole, thronged almost to suffocation with a rough crowd busy as wasps. A certain captain of marines, lately appointed postmaster and receiver-general of revenue at Cape Coast Castle, had fallen out with an "African," formerly a tax-gatherer, then a civil commandant, and now ———. The European called the African an embezzler of customs revenue. The African instituted a counter-charge against the European of neglecting his duty, and began a civil action for defamation of character; the result of which was, that the Englishman was fined 25l. Of course the place was split in two. Some declared that Japhet was rightly served for saying anent Ham things that could not be proved. Others declared that a noted truth had been twisted into a libel by men jealous, because a local appointment had been given out of the colony. Touching juries at this place, the editor of the "West African Mail," then published at Cape Coast Castle, thus confirms the assertion of his S'a Leone brother, and being, as he says himself, "an African from scalp to s*****m," he is entitled to belief and deference on the part of a British public:—

"JURIES.—We must say a word about juries in Cape Coast. We consider juries here a mistake; the *respectable* people don't like to sit. If they can avoid it, they *won't* sit. Often persons are summoned to sit as jurors who are in fact mere ragamuffins. *These* never refuse. Their verdict can be bought for a glass of beer or threepenny worth of tobacco. We think it would be well for the court to order a list of *householders* to be made out and kept in the court, and when a jury is required, the clerk of the court should be directed to summon some dozen of these householders, whose names should be written on slips of paper, and put into a hat or a box, and then the names of six (the legal number of a jury on the Gold Coast) drawn out. In a very important case that was heard a few days ago, a man was put into the jury box who was a notorious swindler and rogue. On one occasion the defendant nominated all the jurymen, and the court permitted this. It seems to us, that in all this there is much that calls for reform; but, unfortunately, what is everybody's business is nobody's business. There are now so many judges, and each judge is so wretchedly paid, that we cannot be astonished if their Honours decline to be bothered with more court work than they can help."

There is no part of the world, I may assert, where there is a worse feeling between black and white than upon the Gold Coast. The arrogance *de part et d'autre* is most comical to a stranger. There are about 100 Europeans in the land : amongst these there are many excellent fellows, but—it is an unpleasant confession to make—the others appear to me inferior to the Africans, native as well as mulatto. The possibility of such a thing had never yet reached my brain : at last, in colloquy with an old friend upon the Coast, the idea started up, and after due discussion we adopted it. I speak of *morale ;* in intellect the black race is palpably superior, and it is fast advancing in the path of civilisation. It cries for " regular lawyers," and is now beginning, even at the out-stations to file schedules of bankruptcy.

We dined at the mess of the Gold Coast Artillery. Hereabouts begins the compulsory semi-starvation which afflicts West Africa as far south as Loando. Food is scarce, and what there is affords but little nutriment. Moreover, cooks are detestable, and there is a terrible sameness of diet. As a rule, it is all fowl, till the lean poultry—about the size of an English pigeon—ends by giving one the scurvy. Beef is not to be had, and the tasteless goat's flesh must take the place of mutton.

Turkeys are sometimes brought from the neighbourhood of Quittah; and even fruit is rare. Fish, however, is plentiful, and the older residents upon the coast adhere mainly to this lenten diet. The country-made dishes are good and wholesome, but somewhat too finely pounded and too much worked to suit the English palate. But, if rations were scarce, hospitality, Steinwein, and Moselle were not; and upon these we contrived to rough it. The mess reminded the consul of the old camping days at Kurrachee, in Scinde, or the Unhappy Valley.

The G. C. A., which initials, by-the-by, the facetious grumbler interprets Great Curse of the Army, because promotion is so easily obtained in it, dates from 1851; in that year it succeeded the Royal African corps of three companies, each 100 men, stationed at S'a Leone, the Gambia, and Fernando Po. This artillery corps began with 300 men, commanded by seventeen European officers, and it was further increased by a band of fifty supernumeraries. About 120 are stationed at head-quarters; the same number at and about Accra; whilst the rest are scattered over the out-stations, and are supposed to co-operate with the Pynims—petty head men, who act as police. The main object of the levy was to act as a preventive to slavery and human sacrifice, which is effected by breaking through the influence of the chiefs; and so far have we been successful, that even the Okros, or Fetish boys, are no longer put to death. The cost, however, cannot be less than 20,000*l*.

per annum, and I suspect that Irregulars would cost much less, and be equally efficient. The men are chiefly runaway serviles, for whom a compensation of $40 is paid to the owners—another proof, if aught were needed, how difficult it is to avoid slave-dealing,—and the soldier's price is deducted by instalments from his pay. The men have a standing grievance touching salary; they receive 7$d.$, whereas the West Indian private's pay is 1$s.$ a day; moreover, they are liable to "cuttings," and their uniform is a useless expense to them. They are armed with an efficient Enfield carbine and sword-bayonet, and they wear the Zouave uniform. Though often ragged and incomplete, wanting stockings, for instance—it looks gorgeous near the blue tuft and yellow facings of the Dutch. It is, however, cumbrous, comfortless, and unhealthy, admirably adapted for Tripoli, equally ill-suited to the Tropics. Sad tales are told of their state of discipline, and few expect to see the corps live long.*

* Since this was written, an open mutiny broke out. On the 3rd October, 186—, the troops, after vainly attempting to murder certain of the officers, fled to Napoleon, an out-station distant about four miles. Two days afterwards, the place was visited by H.M.S. "Wye," and on the 7th, Major De Ruvignes, civil commandant at Accra, whose energy probably saved the Coast, sent up some 50 suspected men in H.M.S.S. "Brisk" and "Mullet." The Europeans, 15 in all, not to mention six or seven mulatto gentlemen, were in the fort, and the mutineers had entrenched themselves in their new quarters. The serjeant-major was sent to them, but they refused all terms. Being hated like poison by the natives, and aware that the chiefs and people generally would unite to destroy them, they gave up their arms on the 9th, and on the next day they were persuaded by Mr. Usher of the commissariat, to

It would scarcely be fair to judge of the *morale* of men who are almost in open mutiny; these Fantis, however, are said at times to have fought pretty well—at least not worse than their neighbours. With very few exceptions, such as the Bijugas, the Ashantees, and the Dahomans, there is no more timid race than the maritime tribes of Western Intertropical Africa; even the three above mentioned are not more remarkable for valour than the Hindu, who, "meak and mild," as we called him, could prove himself a tiger at a pinch. It is otherwise on the Eastern Coast, and I attribute the difference to the intermixture of Arab blood.

The officers of the Cape Coast army expect a company after a period of three years' service from the date of lieutenant's commission, and after six years of actual service they are entitled to a majority; moreover, a captain may retire upon 150*l.* a year. This is being liberal of promotion with a witness: the least precaution

embark for trial at S'a Leone. Capt. Luce of H.M.S. "Brisk," carried between 80 and 90 to their destination; of these one was shot at S'a Leone, and another was landed for the same purpose on the day when I left Cape Coast Castle (13th Nov. 186—). For protection against further outrage, Capt. Luce left in the castle a party of 21 marines, with Lieut. Ogle, Royal Marine Artillery. They had rations for five weeks, and were confined to barracks between 9 A.M. and 4 P.M. Great care was taken of them, and the only loss was one man, by an accidental fall from a window. No subsequent outbreak occurred. The only danger, in these cases, is the first "flare-up." Thus ended the great Gold Coast mutiny, which, though almost bloodless, should methinks be a standing warning against employing men in their own country. We know it in England and Ireland; in Africa they have still to learn this simple wisdom.

that should be taken would be to make all colonial officers of the scientific branches pass examinations before entering the home establishments. The Dutch have made six years their minimum term of service on the Gold Coast: after twelve years an officer retires on full pay. Their system is in some points superior to ours. A man will not interest himself in the progress of a place where he pitches tent for a short time; he retires before learning a sentence of the language, or becoming at all acquainted with the people, much less with the capabilities of the country. To these short periods of service I ascribe the undeveloped, or rather the wholly neglected, state of the Gold Coast, whose resources are a matter of mystery; and such will be the probable effects of frequent furloughs to the future Anglo-Indian. On the other hand, there is the climate, against which Englishmen, apparently by reason of their habits, are unfitted to contend. Whilst Americans, Germans, and Hamburghers have passed safely through years of residence in the Island of Zanzibar, it has not a single English house, the difficulty being, to speak plainly, that of finding a man who will not drink. In these days of monthly steamers and circulating libraries, breaking the monotony of existence, when the semi-starvation of which men whose vital powers are lowered by a tropical climate, die, can now be replaced by generous living; when it is known that quinine, liberty, and constant occupation rob the most dangerous climate of half its risk; the climate of the Gold Coast has lost nothing of its sting or of its victory. Bosman's remark still, I fear, applies to the English: "Their forts are very meanly garrisoned, as if it were sufficient to build forts, furnish them with cannon and necessary provisions, without men, in which the English are everywhere deficient." Besides which, he adds, that in those days our people took six years to build a fort.

No one lands at Cape Coast Castle without pilgrimaging to the "last resting-place of the poetess 'L. E. L.,'" and, of course, without inquiring into her "sad, eventful history," which has, however, nothing of

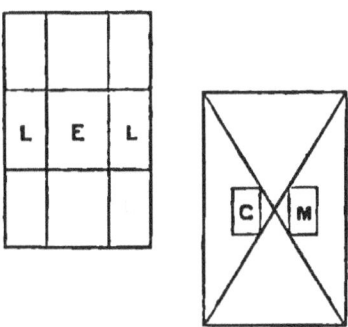

romance. For "L. E. L." is known where Miss Landon is not, and her fate has been the subject of curiosity to many that have never read the "Improvisatrice," or, "Romance and Reality." The graves of Mrs. Maclean and her deeply-injured husband are on the large triangular drill-ground of the Castle. It is a local practice to bury the dead in dwelling-houses, and the custom is not confined to Pagans; the floor of the surgery, the kitchen, and the medical store-rooms of the colonial hospital have all been used for interment. The tramping of soldiery upon the pavement had well nigh defaced all the traces of the tombs,* when the pious hand of Governor O'Connor restored them. The graves now lie parallel to each other as in p. 78: the St. Andrew's Cross denotes the nationality of the deceased.

On the wall of the north and south buildings a Latin inscription, on a neat tablet of white marble, records the death and the survivor's grief. I had always believed that upon the groundwork of a statue intended for Washington the Great, and representing a more than half-nude figure, extending its arm towards the Capitol, as if the latter had been a barber-surgeon intent upon phlebotomy, I had discovered the very worst Latin inscription in the world. My natural exultation at the success was justified by a sentence beginning with "monumentum *istud*"—ending with *faciebat*. But great is the use of travel. Cape Coast Castle supplied me with a further bathos of Latinity in the neat tablet above alluded to.

---

* The Rev. Mr. Wilson, in "Western Africa," curiously says, "that Governor Maclean and his distinguished partner lie side by side under the cold sod of this African fort." This reminds one of Sir William C. Harris's description of Eve's grave at Jeddah, being a green sod, where there is not a patch of grass. I much wonder what these gentlemen understood by sod ?

"Hic jacet sepultum
Omne quod mortale fuit
Letitiæ Elizabethæ Maclean,
Quam egregiâ *ornatum* indole," &c., &c.

There was a sister tablet a few yards off, placed, I believe, in honour of Mr. Swanzy, here a well known colonial name. It was shivered by the shock of the huge mortar fired in front of it.

The true history of Mrs. Maclean's death is known to many, but who, in writing the life of "L. E. L.," would dare to tell it? Owning that *de mortuis nil nisi verum* should be our motto, how would it be possible to publish facts whilst actors in the tragedy are still upon the stage of life? And after their death it will be forgotten. The author of a certain report on the Gold Coast, during his short and feverish residence as Commissioner, a guest of President Maclean, succeeded in casting upon his host's public efficiency a serious slur, which was afterwards satisfactorily removed by a select committee of the House of Commons. On the other hand, the author of "Eighteen Years on the Gold Coast," showed himself an injudicious friend, far worse than any foe, by asserting that, after a certain *esclandre*, the household was very successful. But enough of these private matters. Mr. Forster, M.P. for Berwick, the warmest of President Maclean's well-wishers, openly asserted that the flood of calumny poured upon him arose from the enmity of an individual in the Colonial Office, who was pettily jealous because affairs at the Gold Coast, with a miserable pittance of 4000*l.*, were managed far more effectually than at the pet S'a Leone, where economy has never been the order of the day. Hence the "President of the Council of Government," than whom a better servant of Government was never known on this coast, was charged with having encouraged slavery under the local name "pawning"—a fatal accusation in those days—and with neglecting official duty for private correspondence.

Standing over the graves we heard the story of Mrs. Maclean's death, and nothing could be less probable than the popular version. A homeward-bound vessel was preparing to sail. At 7 A.M. she left her husband's room, and proceeded to write letters before dressing in the little room opposite, once used as an observatory. A Mrs. Bailey, her servant, had been sent to the store-room to fetch some article; she returned after a few minutes, and found against the door a weight, which proved to be the corpse of her mistress. The servant distinctly asserted what has been since denied, that a phial was still in the dead woman's hand, and that the phial contained a preparation of prussic acid. But here comes the rub. The authoress's spirits had been weakened, she had ceased to play at ball, and she was suffering from a heart disease which produced fits or spasms. The local account, however, is, that she was in the habit of taking prussic acid to stimulate her energies, a use probably unknown to Scheele. At any rate, calumny found its way home, and the

President was reduced to the secondary position of Judicial Assessor at Cape Coast Castle. There he died in May, 1847, to the deep and lasting regret of the whole population, black and white.

The "balance," as Yankee Doodle says, of the twenty-four hours, was pleasantly spent at the quarters of Mr. Usher, a commissariat officer, who was serving out his two years *de rigueur* upon the coast of Western Africa. The profound quiet of a tropical night, derived a stillness deeper still from the contrast with the noisy rattle of the tiller-chains, whose perpetual jiggerty-jig made one long for a mild anæsthetic of turpentine.

Betimes in the next morning we sallied out to see the town. After 10 A.M. a European becomes a prisoner at home for the day, until his jailor, the sun, has disappeared. As there are no riding animals, and hammocks conceal the view, we used what I have heard called "Shanks his mare." We issued from the gateway at the north of the western, or spur battery, and slowly sauntered into the open. Opposite the gate is the esplanade, a cleared space for parading; from this a broad street, lined with ragged umbrella-trees, a kind of ficus, runs towards the north, dividing the town into two parts. Immediately on our left was the unfinished Protestant church, of which 600*l.* were granted by the Colonial Office and the War Department. This Africo-Gothic aspires to the honour of consecration by the Right Reverend the Bishop of Sierra Leone, and meanwhile much resembles the porter's lodge in the new style of cemetery. A large room in the upper part of the castle's northern range, or sea front, was formerly used as a chapel; it was, however, secularized into officers' quarters by the recommendation of a sanitary report published by the Commissioners 30th June, 1857. At the upper end of the main street, which rises gently, is the substantial and sober looking meeting-house of the Wesleyans, a body that is owned to have done some good in this part of Africa by abstaining from politics, and by teaching, not only Christianity, but trade. The sides of the highly irregular street are incongruous mixtures of whitewashed houses and red-brown clay huts, some double storied, and of superior dimensions, after the fashion of the olden times, but most of them palpably native; those of Europeans may show green jalousies, but the earth walls and dingy roofs of dull grey thatch, are like the Africans. The right, or east side of main street, is a straggling line of habitations that slope down into a rugged rocky hollow, and thence upwards to the side of a corresponding eminence. The shape of the native house is a hollow square; here, however, the form is undeveloped, compared with what we shall see at Abeokuta and Benin. As in all tropical countries, there are attached compounds where women do domestic work and where children gambol under the umbrella-tree. On the Gold Coast intermural sepulture has reached its climax. The pernicious practice of burying in the basement of the dwelling places, renders any improvement of the town a matter of the greatest difficulty. The custom appears to have arisen from a barbarous vain-glory; the corpse is placed in the handsome abode which it built for itself, and survivors point to the last home of a wealthy man. With the dead body, which is sprinkled with gold dust, are interred pearls, precious metals, and ornaments, Aggri, or Popo beads, and clothes of the greatest value; thus, Lombard Street being in the future, whilst the material exists everywhere, these tombs become banks of deposit, as it were, and the family, especially the eldest son, draws from them when required. The idea of burying treasures with the dead dates from the earliest days of history, and the Jews, whose rites and ceremonies show distinct traces of African fetissism, long preserved the custom. The wise king placed treasures in his father David's grave, and when Asa died, he was "laid in the bed which was filled with sweet odours and divers kinds of spices, prepared by the apothecaries' art." On the Gold Coast, even when the family vault is exhausted, they are as unwilling to part with the tomb-home, as a wild Irishman with his wretched shanty on the hill-side. The material of the walls is sun-dried brick, or more often swish, clay puddled with water; this red mixture is built in courses which are allowed to harden before others are added, and they easily dry during the hot season. They require, however, a substantial thatch and overhanging eaves, otherwise they are cut and channelled by the rain, and in damp places the foot of the walls should be protected by stone work, or by cactus, from burrowing animals. As timber is not used, it is no wonder that the habitations, after a heavy downfall, subside like the puddle palaces of Scinde.

The floors are of mud, daubed over strong lathing, the equivalent of our English "post and plaster;" the rooms are dark, damp, rarely washed, and ill-ventilated; foul linen lies upon the bed or hangs against the wall; offals, and bits of putrid fish strew the ground and encumber the corners; whilst outside, dirty green pools, and all manner of refuse taint the air. The houses are over-crowded, there are 6000 to 7000 souls in the place, and they are not sufficiently scattered. The usual number inhabiting a small two-storied tenement will be twenty; and as lodging is scarce, respectable people must live separated by a thin party-wall, if any, from some disreputable fellow, drunk all day and half the night with cheap spirits from the United States or the Brazils. Cloacinæ, public and private, are unknown; and the Galinazo and the Pariah dog are hardly numerous enough to remove the garbage about the huts. There are municipal corporations both at Cape Coast Castle and at Accra; there are also detailed police regulations for the removal of such impurities. They are, however, a dead letter, and the nuisance cannot be abated without the direct interference of the authorities, who stop their noses and say no more about it. A walk through the north-east of the town at once shows the cause of its high death rate. Those who are curious to see what an hotel may be, have only to visit Dick's or

Sam's—the *locanda* of the Apennines is a palace compared with them.

The men—I do not speak of the "native gentlemen"—are dressed after the African fashion, in a loin cloth and a larger sheet, both of cotton. The latter is removed from the shoulders on meeting or addressing a superior, and its picturesque folds assume the shape of the Roman toga. They are a tall and not ill-formed race, when they have no skin diseases, with chocolate coloured skins, noses rather high at the bridge, and a fair development of the facial angle which escapes the quasi-gorillahood of the real "nigger." The women would not shine in Mr. Barnum's beauty show; when young, however, they have the usual *beauté du diable*, and if their features are not Grecian, their limbs are. I wish "figures" might be added; unfortunately their bosoms are unsupported, and as they wear the same dress as the men, defects become painfully prominent. The Fantis are perhaps the most civilized people on this coast; unfortunately El Islam has not yet taught womankind the propriety of veiling their bosoms. Under the loose cloth all wear the "Shim"—smallest of "languti" or T-bandages, secured round the waist by a string of large gold beads when the wearer is wealthy, of glass or clay when the contrary is the case. These articles are hung in numbers about the houses, and often puzzle strangers. When due attention is paid to this article it must be beneficial to health. They have the feminine ornaments usual in semi-civilized and half-clad lands, ear-rings, necklaces, bracelets, armlets, finger and toe rings of brass, if not of gold, and metal anklets, oval shaped, and drooping over instep and heel. There are, however, in their toilettes, two very decided novelties to an English eye—whether to be recommended or not to the Hebes at home, the reader may judge. The head-dress in married women is that described by Park among the "ladies of Karta and Ludamar." The hair, which, though curly, grows eight to eleven inches long, is shaved or cleared away round the head to remove straggling pile, and to define the line of departure. The rest of the locks, well combed and greased, are drawn tightly up to a tall ridge, either wholly natural or blown out with padding. There is a back comb of gold or jewellery, if possible, and some coiffures have a terminal top-knot, whilst others end abruptly like a pillow turned upon its edge.* Women of rank would be ashamed if this monstrous *Chinoise* were not exaggerated to the utmost. In the fifteenth century, however, our ancestresses must have been as much troubled. The other *nouveauté* is a "nice thing" in "bussles." The "cankey," as it is called, is a huge pincushion, a stuffed oblong of calico, provided with two tapes, and so fastened round the waist that the two loose corners and the edge between them stand shelving upwards from the owner's back. It thus forms a continuation to the person suggesting that the caudal region has been very lately suppressed. This racing-like pad

* At S'a Leone, when people suffer from scurvy and relaxed uvula, they tie a bunch of hair, *en toupet*, tightly on the top of the head.

is supposed to act as a saddle for the baby to ride upon; unfortunately for the explanation, it is worn by little misses hardly in their teens. I therefore attribute it not purely to fashion, but to that natural and instinctive admiration of Steatopyga from which the Authoress of Crinoline does not appear to be free.

We passed one of the two graveyards lying to the windward of the castle. These enclosures are, as usual, foul places of wet sepulture, dank with fetid vegetation, and poisoning the air of the houses and huts around them. The other, I am told, is equally badly situated, and also surrounded by a dense population. Besides these cemeteries, which are appropriated to Christians, graves for Pagans are dug about the beach, and the slaves, when not thrown into the sea, are buried "promiscuously" along the lanes or pathways of the *faubourgs*. Dr. Clarke recommended "that the Christian burial-ground should be closed up, and that cemeteries should be opened to the leeward of the town, where there is abundance of land lying waste suitable for the purpose, and where a piece of ground might also be set apart wherein to bury the dead of the Pagan and slave population."

Leaving this burial-ground stained and dreary, we passed out of the town into the bush, where gamboge trees, with flowers like hollyhocks, were conspicuous, and we breasted the rough ascent leading to Fort Victoria. The soil was a reddish-brown argile, thinly clothed with quartz nodules, mica flakes, and feldspar; in places thin rivulets had furrowed the surface, and bands of quartzose rock crossing the course, would have conveyed an intelligible hint to a Californian or Australian prospector. Ascending the eminence, which is about a mile from the castle, we found an extensive prospect, bounded southwards by the sea, and northwards, or inland, the horizon was a wavy mass of little hills, paps, and hummocks, all bushy, and prolonged in crescent-shape towards the Atlantic. A few were rounded at the summits, others had table-tops; none, however, showed signs of cultivation, being shaggy and with trees between; and the only road in sight was the narrow ribbon winding through the valleys, and taking the direction of Kumasi. It is now easy to follow in the path of Bowdich, Dupuis, and Hutchinson. The King of Ashantee, however, can hardly be visited without a dash of at least 100*l.*, for which he will probably return 40*l.* in gold dust, and, as has been said, hammock travelling, especially over mountains and on long journeys, is very expensive. Besides which, an unknown visitor is compelled to await at the frontier permission to visit the capital, and etiquette will not allow this to arrive for some days,—when in Kumasi, various pretexts will prevent you seeing the king till a second delay ceremonious has taken place. And, lastly, it is said that his Majesty has invariably refused a transit northward to all travellers, fearing lest they should make some arrangements for trade with the "people on horses," probably Moors or Africo-Arabs, who, the tradition is, are impatiently expecting the arrival of white men. It was the same at Dahomey, and the reader will readily remember the difficulty with which Mr. Duncan* penetrated into the interior from Abomey. A large lake, and other geographical curiosities, are reported to exist between Ashantee and the "Kong Mountains." The country is described as consisting of rich grassy plains and savannahs, contrasting with the thick bush-forest of Ashantee, and the people are said to furrow the land with ploughs. Perhaps, in these days, by proper management and by liberal presents, the interdict might partially be removed, and the explorer permitted to advance under an escort of the king's guards.

On our left, or northward of the castle, Fort Macarthy occupies the crest of a detached little hill. Below us, and about one mile north-west of the city, lies a lagoon, like those which deform the environs of James Fort and Christiansborg, a "silver liquor" to the bird's-eye view, but nearer a pond prevalent with foulness and fever, and full of crabs more than suspected of anthropophagy. This intensely salt "marigot," which in the dry season is about one mile in length by half that breadth, is sepa-

* Mr. Duncan was sent as Vice-Consul to Abomey in the days of Gezo, father of the present sovereign. He was an adventurous traveller, but by no means an educated man or a man of the world, and the Dahoman used to say of the Englishman that he wished the King of England would "send him a man with a head." Gezo was, although we consider him a barbarian, a very remarkable man, dignified, and gifted with uncommon penetration: as my informant, who was on friendly

rated from the Atlantic by a narrow strip of sand. During the rainy season, when freshened and swollen by the drainage of the hills, and the streams that flow from the spongy and reedy morass at its landward extremity, it partially discharges itself into the ocean. Warping will be difficult, and drainage impossible here; the sole's level is below the sea. Kurrachee has its "Clifton," and similarly this lagoon has been provided with a "Mount Edgcumbe," a pigmy scaur overhanging the impure lake. Another bad formation calling loudly for reform is impartially placed at the east end of the town and intersecting part of the suburbs—a deep fiumara cribbled with water-holes and gold-diggers' pits, strewed with animal and vegetable refuse, and dammed by a sand-bar across the mouth. Whilst these things continue in *loco*, Cape Coast Castle must expect to retain as evidence maladies which, like dracunculus and dysentery, are sporadic at deadly Bathurst and S'a Leone. It can hardly wonder that scrofula, ulcers, kra-kra,* herpes, *noli-me-tangere*, leprosy, and foul defœ-

---

terms with him, said, he could tell a visitor's calibre in half an hour. His son, Badahong, the present ruler, gave promise of superior civilisation, but he has followed in the ways of his ancestors. How little the general public at home know of this class of people may be gathered from this fact: An enthusiastic lady—I will spare her name—wrote, strongly urging me to take her with me to the City of the Amazons. She intended, by a magic lantern, and by pronouncing some words in the vernacular (the list desired was duly specified), to terrify the king into abolishing human sacrifices—to become a Christian and a Roman Catholic! It is incredible, but it is true.

* A bad kind of scabies, commonly written Craw Craw. It is not

dations, are rather the rule than the exception. For the unusual frequency of ophthalmia, deafness, land-scurvy, and elephantiasis, the people have mainly to thank their own indolence. Medical men find the atmosphere surcharged, they say, with that specific poison which breeds "Yellow John" at S'a Leone and the Gambia. I should be astonished if it were otherwise. Yet even here Nature, as is her wont, has planted a remedy where she has placed the poison. "Connor Hill," or "One-tree Hill," on the north-east of the town, is said to be a sanitarium; there, and there only, Europeans should be stationed. There is a dwarf platform on the summit which is capable of accommodating all the Europeans in the station, and if the castle is ever to be defended, this is the position for a strong battery of Armstrongs. Were I governor of Cape Coast Castle, my hut should be built there during the first month.

Returning homewards, we passed, on another eminence to the west of the town, a house and school belonging to the Wesleyan establishment; both appeared neat and clean. Standing upon the balcony was his Reverence Prince John, *alias* Usu Ansah, who, with his cousin Kwántibisá, son of the King of Ashantee, were given as hostages to Mr. Maclean in 1830. The youths were forwarded to England for education. When they returned to Africa in the Niger expedition, they settled

confined to mankind; goats, and other animals, often die of it a few days after arrival at Fernando Po; it is most easily communicated, and on board ship it has run through the whole crew.

at Cape Coast Castle, where Prince John remained as "interpreter, class-teacher, and local preacher." He appeared in the shape of a very black man with a white necktie, *more Africano;* as Mr. Paul says of the Maori,* he looked "snobbish, so to speak, when clad in European costume." I could not but admire the vastness and the barbarous splendour of the houses, built by residents in the days before steamers, when men expended hundreds, whereas they now grudge a "flimsy." They reminded me of Richard Lander's description of Mr. Hutchinson's style of living at Annamaboo,—"His silken banners, his turreted castle, and his devoted vassals recalling, the manners and way of life of an old English baron." One stone pile, "Gothic Hall," built by Mr. Hutton, would be considered a handsome residence even near London. The two stags on the columns flanking the gate, and wearing crowns around their necks, are in the style of a certain tall house near Rotten Row, in the palmy days of those honoured animals.

Under the western walls of the castle women were panning the sand of the shore for gold; as in Ashantee, this washing is the peculiar office of the weaker sex. They shovelled up with their hands the finer "stuff"— the metal sinks through the coarse material—and filled, with three parts of it to one of sea water, a calabash, a wooden bowl, or a metal pan. The implement was then whirled, as in California, Australia, and all gold-washing

---

* New Zealand, as it was and as it is. By R. B. Paul, M.A., late Archdeacon of Nelson. London: Stanford, 1861.

countries, to and fro, with and against the sun. The lighter contents were thrown out by dexterously canting up the vessel, and after repeated washings, the precious metal appeared in flakes and dots, with an occasional grain shining out of the black emery that remained at the bottom. At Cape Coast Castle the scarlet beans of the *Abrus precatorius*, used from Senegal to Calcutta by goldsmiths—Ca da Mosto observed them in 1454,—are the customary weight. Bosman calls them Dambas.* In Ashantee they still employ for the purpose little figures of labourers and mechanics, the "Fetishes" of the old Dutch writers. At the end of five minutes one of the women produced a small pinch of gold, which she sold to us for sixpence.

After that I lost all patience with Cape Coast Castle. Will our grandsons believe that in these days a colony which cannot afford £150 per annum for a stipendiary magistrate, that men who live in a state of poverty, nay, of semi-starvation, are so deficient in energy as to be content with sitting down hopelessly whilst gold is among their sands, on their roads, in their fields, in their very walls? That this Ophir—that this California, where every river is a Tmolus and a Pactolus, every hillock is a gold hill—does not contain a cradle, a puddling-

* He makes 1 damba = 2 stivers,
         24 ,, = 1 angel,
  16 or 20 angels = 1 ounce.

There is also mention made of black and white beans heavier than the above, and called Tacoes.

machine, a quartz-crusher, a pound of mercury? That half the washings are wasted because quicksilver is unknown, and that pure gold, selling in England for 3*l*. 17*s*. to 4*l*., is here purchasable for 3*l*. 12*s*.? That whilst convict labour is attainable, not a company has been formed, not a surveyor has been sent for? I exclaim with Dominic Sampson, "Pro-di-gious!"

The population of the Gold Coast is rudely estimated at 400,000 souls, scattered over a surface of 8000 square miles; its scantiness and its slow increase are attributable to the destructive slavery of the last, and the bloody wars during the first decennia of the present century, with other minor causes, uncleanliness, drunkenness, neglect of hygienic precautions, and the mismanagement of children. Their occupations are agriculture, mechanics, and fishing, and the wealthier classes are acute traders. The principal manufactures are cloth weaving, mat and basket making, and working in metals; their goldsmith craft, however, is not to be compared with the rudest East Indian work. Native rings and watch-chains are bought by Europeans as curiosities; their only value, however, is in the weight of metal. They can pan salt, mould bricks, and many have learned the arts of masonry, carpentering, and cabinet work. In these trades they are far superior to the Krumen and other wilder races, but they yield to the S'a Leone men, because the latter have more European tuition. The fishermen use hand-seines and deep-sea lines, and as canoe-men they are valued at Lagos and other places on the southern coast.

There is sufficient civilisation to produce a very marked distinction of classes. Bosman divides the people into five orders, viz.:—

1. Kings or captains, synonymous words: under our protectorate, however, this class naturally languishes. Krensil, for instance, is the reigning chief of Cape Coast Castle, but the people describe him as a poor devil.

2. The Headmen, or civil fathers, called Caboceros, or Caboceers, from the Portuguese Caboceiros, with the Pynims, or sub-chiefs, policemen, who promulgate edicts and who act as criers. The former are the hereditary official representatives of towns, who keep order, appease tumults, direct the operations of their subordinates, and lead in the superstitious rites which each season brings round with it. They issue summonses by peons, who carry message-canes—long staves, with gold or silver heads, and corresponding with the chob of Hindostan—or by way of token they bear their master's gold-handled sword. These men have large households, consisting of three classes—blood relations, dependants and slaves, or pawns—*ouvriers libres*.

3. Those enriched by inheritance or trade: though slaves, they are treated by the better class as a rich Pariah by a Brahman, who risks pollution for profit. Bosman thus quaintly derides the authors who call this class noblemen: "It will not a little redound to my honour, that I have for several years successively been

waited on by these noblemen in the capacity of a footman, without having the least respect to his nobility."

4. Peasants and mechanics.

5. Slaves, either sold by their relatives or taken in war, or come so by poverty. As Sir Benjamin Pine,* then Governor of the Gold Coast, justly defined it, the whole social fabric, "woof and warp," is slavery. The mutual relation of master and servant, especially in case of the home-born, is much the same as in the days of Abraham; the slave may accumulate wealth, and theoretically what is his is his master's. Popular custom draws a broad line, and desertion in case of cruel usage is a never-failing remedy. The bush slaves, called Donkos, are brought mostly from the country north of Ashantee; they are brave and hardy, and their services in the "Krobo campaign" of 1858, and the troubles in Abrah (1859), proved them to be superior to the Fantis, their proprietors. Some wealthy men have great numbers of these chattels, and cases have been known in which claims wholly without foundation have been set up by individuals to whole families. As has been said, the okra is no longer slain; and the custom of Panyarring,† seizing one man for the fault of another—once common along the whole western coast—is systematically discouraged.

The Fanti of Cape Coast Castle, or, as purists write

---

* It is no small satisfaction to the Gold Coast that the brother of this excellent officer now holds the same position.

† The word is said to be Portuguese, but I have been unable to trace it.

the word, Fante, are a cognate race to the Ashantee.* The tradition of their separation is as follows. When at war with the Akim country, a great famine occurred in the land. The Fanti lived on fáñ, herbs or cabbage, hence they were called, from *didi*, to eat, Fanti. The others were eaters of sañ, barn stores, Indian corn, yam, &c., hence Sandidi, Santi, Ashanti. The connection between the races now separated by such fierce feuds is proved by community of language—the Oji, or, as others write it Otyi. The Fanti dialect, however, is, less soft and agreeable than the Ashantee. It has all the characteristic features of the Ga of Accra tongue, the Ewe of Dahomey and the Yoruban families, and it belongs to the Hamitic class, which extends, with many varieties, from south of the Sahara to the Cape of Good Hope. The other countries in which the Oji is spoken are Akim, Akwapim, and Akwam, called by the English Akwambu. As usual in these African languages which delight in individualising general ideas, their proverbs form an extensive and curious literature.†

The habits of the people have been greatly modified by the century and a-half which elapsed since Bosman

* I have not thought it advisable to change such words as Ashantee, Accra, and others, which have been naturalised amongst us by long residence, utterly incorrect as they are. Bosman and the other travellers write, with comparative accuracy, Asianti. The proper form is Asante, in which we first converted the difficult palatal aspiration into Ashante, and then added another error, Ashántée, accenting —like absentee—the ultimate instead of the penultimate vowel.

† "Grammatical Outline of the Oji Language." By Rev. H. N. Riis of the Basle Mission. Basle: C. Ditloff, 1854. Pp 111-136.

described the "Fantynean negroes," who "so horridly plagued the English," though to meet *perfide Albion* was like "going to the devil to be confessed." Many of the old Hollander's descriptions, however, are still to be recognised. The mass of the people are pestilent pagans, and, considering their intercourse with us, few of them speak English. The sexes eat separately, and both are equally fond of tobacco. All who can afford the luxury are polygamists, and the first wife rules the roast; but all are equally the absolute property of the husband. The men are jealous of one another, and fatal quarrels often arise. The boys are circumcised before puberty.* This rite, however, is confined to certain families, and is performed with peculiar ceremonies. At Accra, for instance, a rock rising from the sea is the proper spot. The sister's son inherits to the prejudice of direct descendants, telling with a fatal significance that it is a wise child indeed that knows its own father. There are various ceremonies for girls arriving at a marriageable age, and for women about to become mothers for the first time. During gestation there is a complete separation of the sexes, not only here, but almost everywhere up the West African coast. When a woman dies in childbed, the body is cast out into the bush. The funeral customs resemble the wakes of the Jews and the Irish; there are hired præficæ, and the men shave the head in token of mourning. For some time the shoulder

---

* For curious information upon this subject, see Dr. Clarke's "Sierra Leone," p. 49.

bone of a sheep, slaughtered to make the funeral feast, is placed upon the new grave. If a man die insolvent, his body is kept above ground till his debts are paid, and this often happens in a country where the legal interest is fifty per cent. per annum, or per diem. Travellers on the Gold Coast have often remarked corpses placed on platforms, and covered with a cloth, till reclaimed by the debtor-heirs. No one would bury a chance corpse, because, though such Samaritan inherits the property of the deceased, he also becomes liable for all the liabilities. Nothing would be easier than to do away with so barbarous a practice—"East Lynne" informs us that England is not wholly free from it—by a promise of indemnity on the part of Government to the debtor. Witchcraft is exceedingly common, especially the form called "putting into Fetish," which is rendered penal by Government. To these spells they attribute death and all manner of diseases, including the much dreaded "broke back," for which that part of the body must be treated by aphrodisiacs. The charge of sorcery must be purged by ordeals, of which there are many; amongst them the corsned, or consecrated cake, of our Anglo-Saxon progenitors. An infusion of the mellay tree, or a decoction of the Edum bark, are swallowed by the accused, who if they escape are pronounced guiltless.

The religious ideas of the Fanti are, as usual in Africa, vague and instinctive. Each person has his Samán—literally a skeleton or goblin—a private Fetish, an idol, rag, fowl, feathers, bunch of grass, bit of glass, and so forth: to this he pays the greatest reverence, because it is nearest to him. The Bosoms are imaginary beings, probably of ghostly origin, called "spirits" by the missionaries. Abonsám is a malevolent being, that lives in the upper regions; Sasabonsám is the friend of witch and wizard, hates priests and missionaries, and inhabits huge silk-cotton trees in the gloomiest forests; he is a monstrous being of human shape, of red colour, and with long hair.* Nyankupon,† or Nyame, is the supreme deity, but the word also means the visible firmament or sky, showing that there has been no attempt to separate the ideal from the material. This being, who dwells in Nyankuponfi, or Nyankuponkru,‡ is too far from earth to trouble himself with human affairs, which are committed to the Bosoms; this, however, is the belief of the educated, who doubtless have derived something from European systems,—the vulgar confound him with sky, rain, and thunder. Kra, which the vocabularies translate "Lord," is the Anglicised okro, or ocroe, meaning a

* The reader will not fail to remark the similarity of Sasabonsam to the East Indian Rákshasa, the malevolent ghost of a Brahman, brown in colour, and inhabiting the Pipal tree.

† Mr. Beecham ("Ashantee and the Gold Coast," pp. 171-2) explains this word to mean greatest friend, a poetical and phonetical misapprehension. Mr. Riis derives it from Poñ (pong), a common termination in Oji words, and signifying high, great; and from Nyáñ, to rise, raise; the whole meaning the very great, or the most high.

‡ The vocabulary explains these words to mean Heaven, the house, or habitation, of God, and of the departed spirits of good men; opposed to Abonsámkru, hell, where the devil Abousám rules over the wicked. I suspect these to be purely European imported ideas.

favourite male slave, destined to be sacrificed with his dead master, and "sunsum," "spirit," means a shadow, the man's umbra. The Fantis have regular days of rest— Tuesday for fishermen, Friday for bushmen, peasants, and so on.

The first missionaries to the Gold Coast were the Portuguese; about a century ago they were followed by the Moravians, but of these ancient establishments there is now not a trace. The first English missionary in these diggings was the Rev. Thomas Thompson (1751). After cultivating the field for four years he returned to England, taking home with him several natives for education at Oxford. Of these, Philip Quako occupied for fifty years the chaplaincy of Cape Coast Castle, and died in the savour of Fetishhood. In the autumn of 1834, the committee of the Wesleyan Missionary Society sent the Rev. Joseph Dunwell, a man spoken of as highly as Brainerd and Martyn, to the Gold Coast. He died there in 1835, and was followed by Mr. Thos. Freeman in 1838; but this is entering upon modern times, when the men who "make history" still survive. The Wesleyans have extended themselves on the sea coast of the Gold Region, and they monopolise the field as do the Church Missionaries at Sierra Leone and Abeokuta; the American Episcopals at Liberia and Cape Palmas, and the Baptists at Fernando Po and the Camaroons. Besides Wesleyans there are Basle Missionaries about Accra and Akim, and Bremen men to the east and north of the River Volta. Mr. East ("Western Africa,"

p. 289), speaking of his own sect, says, "The beneficial effects of this mission are very conspicuous." It requires a perspicacious and microscopic eye to discern them.

On the evening of the 19th August, after taking kindly leave of our good hosts, we soon passed over, under a full head of steam, the seventy miles between Cape Coast Castle and Accra. I could think of nothing but gold, and perhaps the reader may not be unwilling to receive a few details concerning the precious metal, in a continent which, when opened up, will supply us with half-a-dozen Californias.

CHAPTER VIII.

GOLD IN AFRICA.

"Slave of the dark and dirty mine :
What vanity has brought thee here?"
Leyden.

"Gold! gold! gold! gold!
Bright and yellow, hard and cold;
Molten, graven, hammer'd, and roll'd;
Heavy to get and light to hold."
Hood.

BARON HUMBOLDT first announced the theory, that gold is constant in meridional ranges of the paleozoic and metamorphic formation. In this he was followed by Sir R. Murchison, and he was *not* followed by Professor Sedgwick. The latter "has no faith whatever in the above hypothesis, though it led to a happy anticipation," which followed erroneous premises. He continues, "what we seem to know is, that gold is chiefly found among paleozoic rocks of a quartzose type," and, moreover, that, "some of the great physical agencies of the earth are meridional, and these agencies *may probably*—and in a way we do not comprehend— have influenced the deposit of metals on certain lines of bearing." He thinks, however, it would be a "hypothetical misdirection" to say that a quartzose paleozoic rock cannot be auriferous, because its strata is not north and south," and that "experience must settle this point." The supporters of the meridional theory may quote as instances East African Ghauts, the Oural Mountains, the Sierra Nevada of California—which includes the diggings in British Columbia—the Australian Cordillera, the New Zealand ranges, and the Western Ghauts of India. On the other hand, there are two notable exceptions—the Central Indian region, in which Sir R. Martin and others, as long as thirty years ago, were convinced that the natives washed for gold; and, still more remarkable, the highly productive African chain, which, for want of a better name, we still call the Kong Mountains.*

The fact is, that gold is a superficial formation, and has been almost universally distributed over the surface of earth's declivities. This want of depth, Sir R. Murchison is fond of illustrating by the hand with the fingers turned downwards; these represent the golden veins, whilst the palm denotes the main deposit. It is

---

* A similar imperfect generalisation is the old theory, that gold pertains not to islands. Malachi wore a collar of Irish gold, probably from Wicklow. It has been found in Cornwall and other parts of England, and in Scotland; and there are few Californians who do not believe that Queen Charlotte's Island will form rich diggings.

Another remark has lately been made, which pretends to no more than to discover a curious coincidence. The Oural chain lies 90° west of the Australian diggings, and the Californian Sierra Nevada 90° west of the Oural. But, on the other hand, the fourth quadrantal division falls into the Atlantic between Western Africa and the Brazils; and Eastern Africa, a highly prolific metallic region, is 20° west of the Oural, and 120° east of California.

the contrary with other metals. Gold mines, therefore, are now rare—except in newly explored or exploited lands of primitive formation, where it is common, nay almost universal; the article, whose utility was early recognised, soon disappeared from the older workings. The Californian digger, provided with pick, pan, and shovel, made $10 per diem in 1852; in 1862 he still makes $2·50 and in 1872 he probably will make $0. The anciently auriferous countries, especially Arabia, have been stripped of their treasures, perhaps before the dawn of what is called true history; * and if they linger in Sofala, it is by reason of the people's ignorance; † they never traced the metal to its matrix.

* I allude to the Hammæum littus of Pliny, which appears to coincide with the modern Hazramant. Perhaps, however, the gold of Arabia is not wholly exhausted: it is difficult to believe that the rude appliances of savages and barbarians can extract anything but the coarsest particles from the dirt.

Some years ago, an English traveller, who had seen gold dust brought to Cairo from the coast of Western Arabia, north of Yambu, applied to Dr. Walne, then Her Majesty's consul, for facilities of exploring the place. The sage reply of that official was, that gold appeared to be becoming too common. Other officials, equally sage, have since made the same remark. I refer them to the end of this chapter for my reply.

† In Eastern, as in parts of Western Africa, the natives have a curious superstition, or, rather, a distorted idea of a physical fact. They always return to the earth whatever nuggets are found, under the idea that they are the seed or mother of gold, and that if removed the washing would be unprofitable. They refuse to dig deeper than the chin, for fear of the earth "caving in;" and quartz-crushing and the use of quicksilver being unknown, they will not wash unless the gold appears to the naked eye. As late as Mohammed Ali Pasha's day an Egyptian expedition was sent up through Fayzoghlu in search of the precious metal, brought down by the eastern tributaries of the Nile: it

Setting aside the vexed question of the identity of Ophir and Sofala, and the fact that in early times gold was brought down from the eastern regions of the upper Nilitic basin, Western Africa was the first field that supplied the precious metal to Europe. The French claim to have imported it from El Mina as early as A.D. 1382. In 1442, Gonçales Baldeza returned from his second voyage to the regions about Bojador, bringing with him the first gold. Presently a company was formed for the purpose of carrying on the gold trade between Portugal and Africa; its leading men were the navigators Lanzarote and Gilianez, and the great Prince Henry did not disdain to become a member. In 1471, João de Santarem and Pedro Escobar reached a place on the Gold Coast to which, from the abundance of gold found there, they gave the name of Oro de la Mina, the present El Mina. After this a flood of gold poured into the lap of Europe, and at last, cupidity having mastered terror of the Papal Bull, which assigned to Portugal the exclusive right to the Eastern hemisphere, English, French, and Dutch adventurers hastened to share the spoils.

The Portuguese, probably foreseeing competition in the Atlantic waters, but sure of their power in the

failed, because the ignorant Turks expected to pick up ounces where they found only grains. There are many traditions still extant in Egypt, of mysterious travellers floating down the Nile in craft of antique build, accompanied by women of blackest colour, but with Grecian or Abyssinian features, and adorned with rings, collars, and bracelets of pure gold, in shape resembling those found in the tombs of ancient Egypt.

Indian seas, determined, about the middle of the 16th century, to seek gold, of which those who preceded them had heard, in Eastern Africa. The Rev. Father João dos Santos, of the order of San Domingo, has left us, in his "History of Eastern Ethiopia," a detailed account of the first disastrous expedition. According to him, Dom Sebastian was scarcely seated on the throne of Portugal* before he sent to Sofala an expedition under command of Francis Baretto, who, "penetrating into 'Macoronga'† and 'Maniça,' discovered mines of gold in these kingdoms, of which, by his prudence and valour he made himself master." Baretto, having successfully passed through, despite a harassing warfare, the territories of the Quiteva or sovereign of Sofala, who fled from his capital, Zimboo, and having contracted with the Moorish or Arab sultan‡ of Maniça a treaty of amity, which included

---

* Don Sebastian, grandson of Don João III., was born July 20th, 1554, and at three years of age ascended the throne of Portugal. His subsequent romantic history is well known.

† Mr. Cooley ("Geography of N'yassi," p. 16) has confounded the "Mucaranga" with the "Monomoezi." Captain Burton ("Lake Regions of Central Equatorial Africa," pp. 228-9) found the Wakaranga, a people wholly distinct from the Wanyamwezi: the former being a small tribe living near the Tanganyike Lake, south of the Wajiji. Mr. Cooley still, I believe, keeps his own opinion, and persists in writing these tribal names with an initial, M or Mu, which, being an abbreviation of Mtu, a man, signifies only the individual.

‡ In the "Periplus" attributed to Arrian (A. D. 64-210), chap. 16, we are told that Rhapta, probably Kilwa (Quiloa), and the adjacent regions were held by colonists from Muza, *i.e.*, Bandar Musa, near Aden. Gold is not mentioned amongst the exports, which are confined to ivory, rhinoceros' horns, and tortoiseshell.

the article that the King of Chicanga should admit the strangers to trade throughout his territories for gold dust and other merchandise, reached at length the goal of his ambition. His proceedings are told as follows: *

"The Portuguese were enchanted at having in so short a time concluded a treaty of such advantage to their sovereign, and so beneficial to the realm; they, moreover, flattered themselves with the hope of acquiring store of gold, with which to return enriched to their country; but when they saw what toil was requisite for extracting this precious metal from the bowels of the earth, and the danger incurred by those who worked in the mines, they were speedily undeceived, and no longer regarded their fortunes as instantaneously made. At the same time they were induced to reflect that the labour and risk of digging the gold from the abysses whence it is drawn, are such as to stamp that value on it which it bears from its consequent rarity.

"These people have divers methods of extracting the gold, and separating it from the earth with which it is blended; but the most common is to open the ground, and proceed towards the spot where, from certain indications, ore is supposed to abound. For this purpose they excavate vaults, sustained at intervals by pillars, and notwithstanding they make use of every possible precaution, it often happens that the vaults give way, and bury the subterranean sappers beneath their ruins

---

* Dos Santos, "History of the Ethiopians," Book II, chap. 1-3.

When they reach the vein in which the gold is found, mixed with the earth, they take the ore as it is, and put it into vessels full of water, and by dint of stirring about the water the earth is dissolved, and the gold remains at bottom.*

"They likewise take advantage of heavy rains, which, occasioning torrents, carry before them whatever loose earth they meet in their way, and thus lay open the spots where gold is embedded in the ravines. This the Caffres collect, and wash with care to purify from the grosser parts of its earthy admixture.

"Those people, also, however unpolished they may seem, yet possess a secret peculiar to themselves for discovering the gold concealed in certain stones, which they likewise have the ingenuity of extracting, constantly observing the same practice of washing it well to separate all earthy particles from the metal, and thus rendering it equally lustrous with that obtained from the earth. This gold is, however, much cheaper than the other, either owing to its being more common, or to its being obtained with more facility and at less expense than that exfodiated from the bowels of the earth.

"It is a matter of fact, that this country is rich in gold and silver mines, but these metals are not so easily obtained as is imagined; for the Caffres are prohibited, under penalty of death and the confiscation of their

---

* The reader will remark that at all times, and in all places, gold has been washed or procured in the same way—a fair instance of the instinctive faculty in mankind.

property, from discovering the site of the mines, either to their neighbours, or to those who pass through their country. When a mine is discovered, the persons finding it make wild outcries, to collect witnesses round them, and cover the spot, above which they place some object to denote the site; and far from being susceptible to be prevailed upon by strangers to point out these spots, they avoid encountering them as much as possible, for fear they should even be suspected of such a deed.

"The motive of the sovereign for enacting these prohibitory laws, and for exacting a declaration to be made to the Court of all mines discovered, is that he may take possession of them,* and by preventing the Portuguese from becoming masters of one portion, give no room for succeeding warfare on their part to seize on the remainder."

---

* The same was the practice of the Indian Rajahs. Whenever a ryot discovered either treasure or gold in situ, he was most cruelly treated, to compel him to confess and to give up what he had secreted. As, of course, he had secreted a part of his *trouvaille*, it was a hard struggle between his cupidity and the ruler's bastinado. About 1840, some peasants near Baroda, in Guzerat, found lumps of gold, which they carried before His Highness the Gaikwar, and received in return a terrible flogging. The Hindu, with that secretiveness which has ever been his shield against the tyranny of rulers and conquerors, resolved for the future to keep his good fortune to himself. The quantity of gold which from time to time has appeared amongst these people, made the shrewder sort of European suspect. But the inertness, or, rather, the terror of new things, that possessed the then rulers of the land, "threw cold water" upon all attempts to trace the diggings, which, accordingly, were worked by the people till the present year. This is the simple history of "gold mining in the Deccan."

The melancholy fate of this expedition deserves mentioning After passing through Zimboe,* where the Quiteva received him with open arms, Baretto returned to Sofala. Being now on good terms with the sovereign of that place, and Chicanga, he resolved to open a road into the kingdom of Mongas, the dominions of the Monomotapa, who opposed him with a large army.

* De Barros, describing the ruins of Zimboe, mentions an inscription over the gateway of a fort built with well-cut stones and no lime, whose surface was twenty-five palms long and a little less in height. Around this building, which, like the Kaabah, might have been a pagan Arab temple, are bastions—also of uncemented lime—and the remains of a tower, seventy feet high. The inscription was probably in the Himyaritic character, as "Moors well versed in Arabic" could not decipher it. This was repeated to Mr. Lyons M'Leod ("Travels in Eastern Africa," Vol. I., chap. 10) at Mozambique. Dr. Livingstone ("Travels in South Africa," chap. 29) discovered Zumbo in lat. 15° 37' 22" S., long. 30° 32' E., about 8° W.N.W. of Kilimani. At the confluence of the Loangwe and Zambezi, he found the remains of a church, a cross, and a bell, but no date and no inscription. The people of Sená also state that there are remains of large edifices in the interior; unfortunately they place them at a distance of 500 leagues, which would lead them nearly to the equator north, and to the Cape of Good Hope south.

† Dr. Livingstone ("Travels in South Africa," chap. 30) explains the word Monomotapa successfully, I think, to mean the "Lord (mone, muene, mona, mana, or morena, are all dialectic varieties, synonymous with the Kisarahili muinyi, which means master, sir, kyrios, &c.), and Motapa," the proper name of the chief. The ancient Portuguese assigned to the Monomotapa the extensive regions between the Zambezi and the Limpopo rivers, 7° from north to south. The African traveller, however, is not so successful in explaining the corrupted term, Monomoizes, Monemuiges, and Monomuizes—for which, see Journal of Royal Geographical Society (Vol. XXIX., pp. 166 et seq.)

Dr. Beke ("On the Mountains forming the Eastern side of the Basin of the Nile," p. 14) defends, against Mr. Cooley and Captain Burton, M. Malte Brun's "Mono-emugi, ou selons un orthographie plus

Baretto signally defeated the "Caffres," and reached Chicona, where he found no gold mines. An artful native, however, buried two or three lumps of silver, which when discovered brought large presents to the cheat and dreams of Potosi to the cheated.* Baretto, in nowise disheartened by discovering the fraud, left two hundred men in a fort at Chicona, whilst he and the remainder of his forces retired upon Senã, on the Zambezi. The Caffres then blockaded the fort, and having reduced the gallant defenders to a famine, compelled them to make a sortie, in which every man was slain.

The ruins of Maniça, north-west of Sofala, and west of and inland from the East African ghauts, are described as being situated in a valley enclosed by an amphitheatre of hills, having a circuit of about two miles. According to Mr. Macleod, the district is called Ma-

---

authentique *Mou-mimigi.*" The defence is operated by enclosing after the latter, in italics, another version in parenthesis, and with an interrogation, thus [Nimougi ?] ; and the French geographer's orthography "being fortunately based on the theoretic root," is pronounced "more authentic than any hitherto proposed in its stead." How often will it be necessary to repeat, that Mono-emugi and Mou-nimigi are merely corruptions of M'nyamwezi, a man or individual of the Land Unyamwezi ?

* A French adventurer tried a similar trick upon the Imam Sayyid Said, father of the present Prince of Zanzibar. He melted a few dollars and ran the fluid upon bits of stone, which were duly shown to His Highness. But the old Imam, whose cupidity was equalled only by his cunning, took them to his friend, Colonel Hamerton, Her Majesty's consul, who, finding the matrix to be coralline, had no difficulty in detecting the fraud.

touca (the Matuka of Dr. Livingstone's map), and the gold washing tribes Botongos.* The spots containing the metal are known by the bare and barren surface. The natives dig in any small crevice made by the rains of the preceding winter, and there find gold dust. These pot-holes are rarely deeper than two or three feet, at five or six they strike the ground-rock. In the still portions of the rivers, when they are low, the natives dive for nuggets that have been washed down from the hills. Sometimes joining together in hundreds, they deflect the stream, and find extensive deposits. Mr. M'Leod heard of mines 400 to 500 miles from Sofala, where the gold is found in solid lumps, or as veins in the rocks and stones.

The result of Dr. Livingstone's travels is, that whilst he found no gold in the African interior, frequent washings were met with in the Mashinga mountains† and on the Zambezi river; no silver, however, was met with, nor could the people distinguish it from tin, which, however, does not establish its non-existence; he heard from a Mashinga man, for the first time, a native name for gold, "Dalama."‡ The limits of the auriferous

* Dr. Livingstone places the Batonga people west of Zumbo, and 4° to 5° N.W. of Matuka, or Maniça.

† These elevations are on the western frontier of the great Marave people.

‡ In Kisawahili they have but one word for gold, Zahábú, which is palpably derived from the Arabic ذهب. None of the people living in the interior, or even the tribes beyond the coast line of Zanzibar, are acquainted with the precious metal: they would prefer to it brass or copper. The appreciation of gold on the part of the so called "Kafir"

region are thus laid down: "If we place one leg of the compasses at Tete, and extend the other 3° 30', bringing it round from the north-east of Tete by west, and then to the south-east, we nearly touch or include all the known gold-producing country." This beginning from the north-east would include the Marave country,* the now "unknown" kingdom of Abutua, † placed, however, south of the Zambezi, and coming round by the southwest, Mashona, or Bazizulu, Maniça, and Sofala. Gold from about Maniça, is as large as wheat grains, whilst that found in the rivers is in minute scales. The process of washing the latter is laborious. "A quantity of sand is put into a wooden bowl with water, a half rotatory motion is given to the dish, which causes the coarser particles of sand to collect on one side of the bottom. These are carefully removed with the hand, and the process of rotation is renewed until the whole

races points to an extensive intercourse with Arabia, if not to a considerable admixture of Arab and Asiatic blood.

* Dr. Livingstone gives six well-known washing-places, east and north-east of Tete, viz.: Mashinga, Shindúndo, Missála, Kapéta, Máno, and Jáwa.

† Mr. Cooley ("Geography of N'yassi") questions whether there be such a kingdom as Abutua, or Butwa. He derives it from Batúa plur. of Motúa (in Kisawahili wátu plur. of M'tu), signifying men. The Amazulu, when they attacked Delagoa Bay, were called by the same name; but the Portuguese throwing back the accent changed that word to Vútua, of which Captain Owen made Fetwah. So, in 1822, the tribe that fell upon the Bachwúná (Bechuana) were, we are told, called Batúa, but the missionaries recognised the meaning of the word. Though it is "now unknown," Dr. Livingstone has inserted it into his map.

of the sand is taken away, and the gold alone remains.* Mercury is as usual unknown. Formerly 130 lbs. of gold were submitted to the authorities at Tete for taxation, but when the slave trade began, the Portuguese killed the goose with the golden eggs, and the annual amount obtained is now only eight to ten pounds.

It is evident that gold is by no means half worked in Eastern Africa. As in California, it appears to be found in clay shale, which for large profits requires "hydraulicking." The South African traveller heard that at the range Mashinga, the women pounded the soft rock in wooden mortars, previous to washing; it is probably rotten quartz, and the yield would be trebled by quicksilver and crushers.

It is highly probable that the gold formations in those East African ghauts, which Dr. Beke is compelling to become the "Lunar Mountains," are by no means limited to the vicinity of the Zambezi. In gold prospecting, as every geologist knows, the likeliest places often afford little yield and sometimes none. The author of "The Lake Regions of Central Africa," describes a cordillera which he struck, about 100 miles from the Eastern coast, as primitive, quartzose, and shaly; unfortunately time and health hindered him from exploring it. The same writer, in "First Footsteps in East Africa" (p. 395), indicates such formation in the small ghauts, and on the western side of that range he

* This is absolutely the present practice on the Gold Coast, and perfectly agrees with Mungo Park's descriptions.

is reported to have found gold. What steps he took do not appear; he was probably disheartened by the reflection that all his efforts would be opposed with might and main in official circles. Possibly he feared the fate of Mr. Hargreaves, of Australia, who obtained a reward of 10,000*l.*, when 1 per cent. of export would have made him master of eight millions. Local jealousies at Aden also certainly would have defeated his plans, if permitted to be carried out; and the Court of Directors had already regarded with a holy horror his proposal to build a little fort, by way of base upon the seaboard near Berberah. Leaving, however, these considerations, we are justified by analogy of formation and bearing in believing that at some future time gold may be one of the exports from Eastern Intertropical Africa.*

Returning to Western Africa, we find in Leo Africanus, who is supposed to have died about 1526, that the King of Ghana had in his palace "an entire lump of gold"—a monster nugget it would now be called—not cast nor wrought by instruments, but perfectly formed by the Divine Providence only, of thirty pounds weight,

---

* I cannot, however, understand the final flourish of Dr. Beke's paper above alluded to. He declares that the discovery of gold in his "Mountains of the Moon" will occasion a complete and rapid revolution, and ends thus : "We shall then, too, doubtless see in Eastern Africa, as in California and in Australia, the formation of another new race of mankind." We have seen nothing of the kind in Western Africa, where for four centuries the richest diggings have been known. In fact, they have rather tended to drive away Europeans. Why then expect this marvel from Eastern Africa?

which had been bored through and fitted for a seat to the royal throne.* The author most diffused upon the subject of gold, is Bosman, who treats, however, solely of the Gold Coast.

The first region which he mentions is Dinkira, under which were included the conquered provinces of Wásá (our Wassaw, or Warsaw), Encasse and Juffer, each bordering upon one another, and the last upon Commany, (Commenda). There the gold is fine, but much alloyed with "fetishes," oddly shaped figures used for ornaments, and composed sometimes of pure mountain gold, but more often mixed with one-third, or even half, of silver and copper, and filled inside with half weight of the heavy black earth used for moulding them. The second was Acanny, the people of which brought the produce of their own diggings and of their neighbours of Ashantee and Akim: it was so pure and fine, that the negroes called all the best gold "Acanny Sika," or Acanny gold. The third was Akim,† which "furnishes as large quantities of gold as any land that I know, and that also the most valuable and pure of any that is carried away from this coast; it is easily distinguished by its deep colour." The fourth and fifth are Ashantee and Ananse, a small province between the former empire and Dinkira. The sixth and last is Awine, our Aowin,‡ which formerly used

---

* Similarly, the king of "Buncatoo" had a solid gold stool, which caused his destruction at the hands of his neighbours of Ashantee.

† It still supplies gold, and will be alluded to in a future page.

‡ The old traveller, however, is wrong, when he says, "I take it

to export large quantities of fine and pure gold, and they "being the civilest and the fairest dealers of all the negroes," the Dutch "traded with them with a great deal of pleasure." They were, however, finally subdued by the Dinkiras.

According to Bosman (Letter vi.) "the illustrious metal" was found in three sites. The first and best was "in or between particular hills :" the negroès sank pits there and separated the soil adhering to it. The second "is in, at, and about some rivers and waterfalls, whose violence washeth down great quantities of earth, which carry the gold with it. The third is on the sea shore, near the mouths of rivulets, and the favourite time for washing is after violent night rains.* The negro women are furnished with large and small troughs or trays, which they first fill full of earth and sand, which they wash with repeated fresh water till they have cleansed it from all its earth; and if there be any gold its pon-

---

(Awine) to be the first on the Gold Coast, and to be far above Axim." Aowin is the région to the west of the Assini river, whereas Axim is to the east of the Ancobra river; thus the two are separated by the territory of Apollonia. He apologises, however, in the same page for any possible errors. "I cannot inform you better, because the negroes cannot give any certain account of them (the various diggings), nor do any of our people go so far; wherefore I must beg of you, my good friend, to be contented." Despite which, however, he may yet be right, and his critic wrong.

* So, "in Coquimbo of Chili," says Sir Richard Hawkins, "it raineth seldom, but every shower of rain is a shower of gold unto them, for with the violence of the water falling from the mountains, it bringeth from them the gold."

derosity forces it to the bottom of the trough, which, if they find it, is thrown into the small tray, and so they go on washing it again, which operation generally holds them till noon; some of them not getting above the value of sixpence; some of them pieces of six or seven shillings, though not frequently; and often they entirely lose their labour."

The gold thus dug is of two kinds, dust gold and mountain gold. The former is "fine as flour," and the more esteemed because there is no loss in melting. The latter, corresponding with our modern "nugget," varies in weight from a farthing to 200 guineas; it touches better than gold dust, but it is a loss from the stones adhering to the stone.

The natives, in Bosman's day—and to the present time—were "very subtle artists in the sophisticating of gold." The first sort was the Fetish before alluded to.[*] They also cast pieces so artificially, that whilst outside there was pure gold thick as a knife, the interior was copper, and perhaps iron—then a new trick—and the most dangerous, because difficult to detect. The common "false mountain gold" was a mixture of the precious metal with silver and copper, extremely high coloured, and unless each piece was touched, the fraud passed undetected. Another kind was an artificially cast and

---

[*] We are also informed that the same Fetishes were cut by the negroes into small bits, worth one, two, or three farthings, and the people could tell their value at sight. These Kakeraa, as they were called, formed the small change of the country, as our 3d. and 4d. bits do now.

tinged powder of coral mixed with copper filings : it became tarnished, however, in a month or two.

The official tests of gold were as follows :—If offered at night or in the evening large pieces were cut through with a knife, and the smaller nuggets were beaten with a stone, and then tried as above. Gold dust was cast into a copper brazier, winnowed with the fingers, and blown upon with the breath, which caused the false gold to fly away. These are not highly artificial tests. Bosman, however, strongly recommends them to raw, inexpert people (especially seafaring men), whom he bids to remember the common proverb, that "there is no gold without dross." These greenhorns, it seems, tested the metal by pouring aquafortis upon it, when ebullition or the appearance of green proved it to be false or mixed. "A miserable test, indeed!" exclaims old trunk-hose, justly remarking that an eighth or tenth part of alloy would produce those appearances, and that such useless niceness, entailing the trouble of drying, and causing the negroes to suffer, is prejudicial to trade.

With respect to the annual export from the Gold Coast, Bosman reckons it in peaceful times, when trade

They were current all over the coast, and seemed to pass backwards and forwards without any diminution. The reason for this was, that they sold in Europe for only 40s. the ounce : the natives mixing them with better gold tried to palm them upon the purchasers, but the clerks were ordered to pick them out. A similar custom down the coast, was to cut dollars into halves and quarters, which thus easily became florins and shillings.

is prosperous, to be "23 tun." The 7000 marks are disposed of as below.* Mr. M'Queen estimates this exportation at £3,406,275. The English trade has now fallen to £360,000 to £400,000 per annum.†

The conclusion of Bosman's sixth letter may be quoted as highly applicable to the present day. "I would refer to any intelligent metallist, whether a vast deal of ore must not of necessity be lost here, from which a great deal of gold might be separated, from want of skill in the metallic art; and not only so, but I firmly believe that large quantities of pure gold are left behind, for the negroes only ignorantly dig at random, without the least knowledge of the veins of the mines. And I doubt not but if this country belonged to the Europeans, they would soon find it to produce much richer treasures than the negroes obtain from it;

---

* The Dutch West India Company yearly exported, Marks 1500
The English African Company . . . ,, 1200
The Zealand interlopers as much as the Dutch, viz. ,, 1500
The English interlopers about 1000, usually, which they have doubled . . . . . . ,, 1000
The Brandenburghers and Danes together, in times of peace . . . . ,, 1000
The Portuguese and French, together . . . ,, 800
                                    Which makes 7000

For several years before Bosman's time, the Dutch export had been reduced by one-half (750 marks). Mr. Wilson, however ("Western Africa," chap. IV.), is evidently in error, when he makes Bosman to estimate the "amount of gold exported from the Gold Coast at 800 marks per annum."

† Dr. Clarke ("Remarks," &c.), gives 100,000 ounces. This was the

out it is not probable that we shall ever possess that liberty here, wherefore we must be content with being so far masters of it as we are at present, which, if well and prudently managed, would turn to a very great account."

In several countries, as Dinkira, Tueful, Wásá,* and especially Akim, the hill region lying due north of Accra, the people are still active in digging gold. The pits, varying from two to three feet in diameter, and from twelve to fifty feet deep, are often so near the roads that loss of life has been the result. "Shoring-up" being little known, the miners are not unfrequently buried alive. The stuff is drawn up by ropes in clay pots, or calabashes, and thus a workman at the bottom widens the pit to a pyriform shape: tunnelling, however, is unknown. The excavated earth is carried down to be washed. Besides sinking these holes, they pan in the beds of rivers, and in places collect quartz, which is roughly pounded. The yield is very uncertain,

---

calculation of Mr. Swanzy before a parliamentary committee in 1816. Of course it is impossible to arrive at any clear estimate. Allowing the African Steam Ship Company a maximum of 4000 ounces per month, we obtain from that source 48,000 ounces. But considerable quantities are exported in merchant ships, more especially for the American market. Whilst, therefore, some reduce the total to 60,000 ounces, others raise it to half a million of money.

* Wásá (Wassaw, Warsaw, Wossa, Wasau, &c., &c.) has been worked both by Dutch and English; they chose, however, sickly situations, brought out useless implements, and died. The province is divided into eastern and western, and is said to be governed by female chiefs—Amazons?

and the chief of the district is entitled to one-third of the proceeds. During the busy season, when water is abundant, the scene must resemble that described by Dr. Livingstone near the gold-diggings of Tete; as in California and Australia, prices rise high, and gunpowder, rum, and cotton goods soon carry off 'the golddust. During the repeated earthquakes of July, 1862, which laid waste Accra, the strata of the Akim hills were so much shaken and broken up, that, according to report, all the people flocked to the diggings and dispensed with the shafts generally sunk. There are several parts of the Gold Coast where the precious metal is Fetish, and where the people will not dig themselves, though perhaps they would not object to strangers risking their lives. One of the most remarkable is the Devil's Hill, called by Bosman, Monte de Diablo, near Winnibah, in the Aguna (Agouna) country. In his day, a Mr. Baggs, English agent, was commissioned by the African Company to prospect it. He died at Cape Coast Castle before undertaking a work which, in those days, would have been highly dangerous. Some authorities fix the Seecom river as the easternmost boundary where gold is found. This is so far incorrect that I have panned it from the sands under James Fort. Besides which it is notorious that on the banks of the upper Volta, about the latitude of the Krobo (Croboe) country, there are extensive deposits, regarded by the people as sacred.

The Slave Coast is a low alluvial tract, and appears to

be wholly destitute of gold.* According to the Rev. Mr. Bowen, however, a small quantity has been found in the quartz of Yoruba, north of Abeokuta; but, as in the Brazils, it is probably too much dispersed to be worth working. And the Niger, which flows, as will presently be seen, from the true auriferous centre, has at times been found to roll down stream-gold.†

The soil of Fanti and the seaboard is, as has been seen, but slightly auriferous.

As we advance northwards from the Gold Coast the yield becomes richer. In Ashantee the red and loamy soil, scattered with gravel and grey granite, is everywhere impregnated with gold, which the slaves extract by washing and digging. It is said that in the market-place of Kumasi there are 1600 ounces' worth of gold—a treasure reserved for State purposes. The bracelets of rock-gold, which the caboceers wear on state occasions, are four pounds in weight, and often so heavy that they must rest their arms upon the heads of their slave boys.

In Gaman, the region to the north-west of the capital, the ore is found in large nuggets, sometimes weighing four pounds. The pits are sunk nine feet in the red granite and grey granite, and

---

* Some years ago the late Consul Campbell, of Lagos, forwarded to Her Majesty's Foreign Office bits of broken pottery, in which he detected gold. When submitted to the School of Mines, the glittering particles proved to be mica.

† Silver is also said to be found near the Niger, but of this I have no reliable notices.

the gold is highly coloured. From 8000 to 10,000 slaves work for two months every year in the bed of the Barra river. There, however, as on the Gold Coast, the work is very imperfect, and in some places where the metal is sacred to the Fetish, it is not worked at all. Judging from analogy, we might expect to find the precious metal in the declivities inland and northwards from Cape Palmas, and in that sister formation of the East African ghauts, the "Sierra del Crystal." The late Captain Lawlin, an American trader, settled on an island at the mouth of the Fernan Vaz, carried to his own country, about the year 1843-44, a quantity of granular gold, which had been brought to him by some country people. He brought back all the necessary tools and implements to the Gaboon River, but the natives became alarmed, and he failed to find the spot. Finally, according to the tradition of native travellers, the unexplored region called Rúmá,* and conjecturally placed south of the inhospitable Waday, is a land of goldsmiths, the ore being found in mountainous and well-watered districts. It is becoming evident that Africa will some day equal half-a-dozen Californias.

Mungo Park supplies the amplest notices of gold in the regions visited by him north of the Kong Mountains. The principal places are the head of the Senegal

* This may be the "Runga," of our maps, with whose position Rúmá corresponds. My informant wrote down the name from the mouth of a Waday man at Lagos.

river, and its various influents; Dindiko, where the shafts are most deep, and notched, like a ladder; Shronda, which gives two grains from every pound of alluvial matter;* Bambuk and Bambarra. In Kongkadu, the "mountain land," where the hills are of coarse ruddy granite, composed of red feldspar, white quartz, and black shale, containing orbicular concretions, granular gold is found in the quartz, which is broken with hammers; the grains, however, are flat. The diggings at present best known are those of Manding. The gold, we are told, is found not in mines or veins, but scattered in sand and clay. They vary from a pin's head to the size of a pea, and are remarkably pure. This is called Sana Manko, or gold-powder, in contradistinction to Sana birro, or gold stones, nuggets occasionally weighing five drachms. In December, after the harvest-home, when the gold-bearing Fiumaras from the hills have shrunk, the Mansa or Shaykh appoints a day to begin Sana Ku—gold-washing. Each woman arms herself with a hoe, two or three calabashes, and a few quills. On the morning before departure a bullock is slaughtered for a feast, and prayers and charms are not forgotten. The error made by these people is digging and washing for years in the same spot, which proves comparatively unfruitful unless the torrent shifts its course.

* This would be $\frac{1}{3500}$ (avoirdupois), whereas the cascalhão, or alluvium, of Brazil is $\frac{1}{15000}$ and remarkably rich and pyritical ores in Europe give $\frac{1}{500000}$. Yet M. D'Aubrie estimates the gold in the bed of Father Rhine at six or seven millions of pounds sterling.

They never follow the lead to the hills, but content themselves with exploring the heads of the water-courses, which the rapid stream denudes of sand and clay, leaving a strew of small pebbles that wear the skin off the finger-tips. The richest yield is from pits sunk in the height of the dry season, near some hill in which gold has been found. As the workers dig through the several strata of sand and clay, they send up a few calabashes by way of experiment for the women, whose peculiar duty it is to wash the stuff, and thus they continue till they strike the floor-rock. The most hopeful formation is held to be a bed of reddish sand, with small dark specks, described as "black matter, resembling gunpowder," and called by the people Sana Mira, or gold-rust: it is possibly emery. In Mr. Murray's edition of 1816, there are illustrations of the various positions, and a long description (Vol. I. p. 450, and Vol. II. p. 75) of the style of panning. I will not trouble the reader with it, as it in no way differs from that now practised on the Gold Coast and Kaffir lands. There is art in this apparently simple process. Some women find gold when others cannot discover a particle; and as quicksilver is not used, at least one-third must be wasted, or rather, I may say, it is preserved for a better day.

The gold dust is stored in quills, stopped with cotton, and the washers are fond of wearing a number of these trophies in their hair. The average of an industrious individual's annual collection may be two slaves. The price of these varies from nine to twelve minkali,* each of 12*s.* 6*d.*, or its equivalent in goods, viz., eighteen gun-flints, forty-eight leaves of tobacco, twenty charges of gunpowder, a cutlass, and a musket. Part of the gold is converted into massive and cumbrous ornaments, necklaces, and ear-rings, and when a lady of consequence is in full dress, she bears from £50 to £80. A proportion is put by to defray expenses of travelling to and from the coast, and the greater part is then invested in goods, or exchanged with the Moors for salt and merchandise.

The gold is weighed in small balances, which the people always carry about with them, and they make, like the Hindus, but little difference between gold dust and wrought gold. The purchaser always uses his own "tilikissi," beans, probably, of the Abrus, which are sometimes soaked in Shea butter, to increase their weight, or are imitated with ground-down pebbles. In smelting gold, the smith uses an alkaline salt, obtained from a ley of burnt corn stalks. He is capable, as even the wildest African tribes are, of drawing fine wire. When rings—the favourite form in which the precious metal is carried coastward—are to be made, the gold is run without any flux in a crucible of sun-dried red clay, which is covered over with charcoal or braize. The smith pours the fluid into a furrow traced in the ground, by way of mould. When it has cooled, he reheats it,

* May not this word be an old corruption of the well-known Arabic weight, miskál?

and hammers it into a little square ingot or bar of the size required. After a third exposure to fire, he twists with his pincers the bar into a screw shape, lengthens out the ends, and turns them up to form the circle.

It must now be abundantly evident to the reader that the great centre of West African gold, the source which supplies Manding to the North, and Ashantee to the South, is the equitorial range called the Kong. What the miueral wealth must be there, it is impossible to estimate, when nearly three millions and a half of pounds sterling have annually been drawn from a small parallelogram between its southern slopes and the ocean, whilst the other three quarters of the land—without alluding to the equally rich declivities of the northern versant—have remained as yet unexplored. Even in northern Liberia colonists have occasionally come upon a pocket of $50, and the natives bring gold in from the banks of streams.

Mr. Wilson* remarks upon this subject, "It is best for whites and blacks that these mines should be worked just as they are. The world is not suffering for the want of gold, and the comparative small quantities that are brought to the sea-coast keep the people in continual intercourse with civilised men, and ultimately, no doubt, will be the means of introducing civilisation and Christianity among them."

I differ from the reverend author, *toto cœlo*. For such vain hope as that of improving Africans by Euro-

* "Western Africa," Chap. X.

pean intercourse, and for all considerations of an " ultimately "vaguer than the sweet singer of Israel's "soon," it is regrettable that active measures for exploration and exploitation are not substituted. And if the world—including the reverend gentleman—is not suffering for the want of gold, there are those, myself for instance, and many a better man, who would be happy at times to see and to feel a little more of that " vile yellow clay."

CHAPTER IX.

A PLEASANT DAY IN THE LAND OF ANTS.*

20TH SEPT., 186—.

VERY early in the morning of Friday we arose, and walked the quarter-deck, wihsing to see as much as possible of the coast of gold. The land about Winnibah, "the Forest Country," as it is called, extending as far west as Cape Apollonia, is a curtain of undulating rocky hills, none apparently above 200 or 300 feet in height, with deep grassy valleys, swampy, and discharging little rills. The vegetation, which clothes almost every foot of soil, is of that dense oily kind most fit to sustain life under alternations of excessive humidity and of extreme drought. We could easily distinguish from the quarter-deck acacias and mimosas, wild dates, adansonias, and guinea palms. Most conspicuous in the morning grey was the Devil's Hill, a tall cone between Apam and Winnibah, a celebrated mining locality, dignified by many a local legend. Then came the woody hill, on whose seaward flank is the

---

* I cannot swear that Accra means the Land of Ants, nor that Mnyamwezi signifies the Land of the Moon, still there is a certain significance about them both which justify me in using them,—at least, when not writing a report to the Royal Geographical Society.

ancient Dutch port of Barraco. Lastly, Cook's Loaf, much in the shape of a *petit pain,* introduced us to the shallow bay of Accra, where we cast anchor at nine A.M. The scenery was a yellow shore, dotted with green, and backed with pale blue hills. For landing on this coast, there are no worse months than July, August, and September. Fortunately for us it was a dull day, and the wind had not power to raise the dreaded surf. Eyes were cast anxiously towards the edge of the beach at times, as thin white froth appeared above the smooth but undulating sea, with its livid leaden tints, but a glance was sufficient to satisfy us that in landing we risked nothing but wet jackets.

Seen from the offing, Accra is imposing, in its own way. A jotting of azure blue hill, the threshold of the Aquapim highlands, distant from sixteen to twenty miles, rising 1500 to 2000 feet above the sea, and forming an amphitheatre for the plain below, appears upon the far horizon. The old capital of the leeward districts stands upon a red beach, which pronounces itself, not condescending to a slope, and its base is lined with black rocks and ledges that chafe by opposing the invading tides. The centre of attraction is James Fort, a picturesque old building, which must have been regarded with awe in the days of falconets and culverins. The "negro quarters," which spread out to the north-east and north-west of the fort, do not show from this offing, which confines our view to the large square and parallelogramic houses that take open distance along the sea frontage. There are two which attract every eye: westward—the castle-like pile called the Commodore, and nearer to the fort, the Big House. Here and there a wind-wrung cocoa, forming a natural vane, whilst bent away tremblingly from the bullying south-west wind, broke the somewhat bald and monotonous scatter of habitations. On the eastward, or to the right of James Fort, lies the Dutch Crevecœur—why it should so be called I have not yet discovered, as an order to capture it ought not to break a man's heart—sedulously white-washed, and more protentous in appearance than its English neighbour; and further still, after a long narrow strip of yellow sward, surmounted by a stratum of equally bright green verdure, appears upon a jutting rock the once magnificent castle of Christianborg. It rises boldly from a black rock, at whose feet the tides ceaselessly surge, and beyond it is a ledge upon which the waves incessantly break in the calmest weather.

Landing in a canoe, with high weatherboards—the surf here is a litle worse than at Cape Coast Castle—we made for a dark reef to the westward of the fort, and we passed behind it through a little channel which might easily be improved; there is, however, a better place nearer the fort. The sea-horses reared and shook their foamy manes outside the rocks, inside we had nothing more than a high tide at Dover or Weymouth. We were seated in chairs in the fore part of the canoe—the usual place in these landings—and as she touched the sands, our "pull-a-boys" springing into the water, carried us all out high and dry. A dollar is well laid out on such occasions; a moment's delay may often see the stern of the canoe half swamped by a breaker. Ascending the unclean bank by a stiff rampart or *tranchée* of red clay, banded with strata of what is about to be sandstone, we entered upon the Parade-Ground, or Esplanade, an open space between James Fort and the whitewashed stone-box called the hotel. The "Grande Place" did not look well: a rough square, with a few gutters for drains, strewed with bits of brick and bottles, and backed by negro quarters and shabby huts facing the sea.. Like Stamboul, the capital of the Leeward Districts of the Gold Coast, loses all its picturesqueness by closer inspection, and the place has the quiet, hopeless, cast-down look of a veteran bankrupt.

Mr. Addoe, the African proprietor of the British Hotel, was civil and obliging: the interior of his establishment was in Anglo-Indian style, combining menagerie with old curiosity-shop, and not without a touch of Booksellers' Row, as I believe Putea-Sancta Street is now called. In the unswept yard was sunk a large tank of solid masonry, with mildewed walls, and a surface overgrown with a broad-leaved duck-weed, which is supposed to keep water sweet. Dysentery, according to Dr. Clarke, is "by far the most fatal disease on the Gold Coast, both to the European and native," and the people consider it highly contagious.* I ceased to

---

* It is dangerous in the tropics to despise popular opinions touching the contagiousness of a disease, which is notably not so in colder

wonder at this being the case; after tasting the water, and a month or two subsequently spent in the country climates, such as phthisis in Italy, and "morbus gallicum"—without actual contact—in Persia. Central African travellers have also remarked that in those old homes and birth-places of small-pox, it falls upon a village or a caravan like a plague, and the Portuguese of Goa will not pass to leeward of a house where a confluent case is known to be.

It may be presumptuous in a non-medical man to offer an opinion upon such a point. I cannot, however, but concur in all the advice which Dr. Clarke offers upon the treatment of the West African scourge, dysentery. He informs us, p. 37: "That whereas European medical officers almost always prescribe soups, slops, and farinaceous substances; the natives diet the patient with dry and nutritive aliments, in fact, animal food. And this," says Dr. Clarke, "is the secret of the great success attained by the people of the country." In my experience, I always found the same thing. The vital powers of the sufferer being greatly lowered, he requires as much support as possible: good meat, beef tea, but no slops, essence of meat, fresh fruit, and mild stimulants, port or champagne. These will not create acidity, the invariable effect upon a deranged stomach of vegetable food; moreover the latter does not support the patient sufficiently. In all dysenteric cases, however, the first point for consideration is the existence or non-existence of hepatic complications. If these be absent, and the disorder be entirely local, opium may be used; it is a fatal treatment when an organic derangement of the liver has given rise to the disease. Above all things, relapse is to be guarded against.

In dysenteric cases the natives have another adjunct to their multifarious simples and tisanes. The patient is directed to rise at daybreak, and to sit wholly undressed in the cool and pleasant morning breeze until 6 A.M. He is then washed in a cold unstrained infusion of macerated plantain-roots, lime-tree leaves, cassava plant, and roots of the water-lily; the skin is anointed with Shea butter; "pampa," a gruel of Indian corn, is given to drink; and the process is generally followed by a sound and refreshing sleep. This cold "air-bath" is a form of cleanliness which has yet to be adopted in England; it will doubtless follow in the wake of the Turkish bath. Its merits have long since been discovered in India, where, after the sensation of living in a poultice—the effect of European clothing—the exposure of the skin is greatly enjoyed.

convinced me that the fatality of the climate might be greatly diminished by a distilling machine. Mr. Addoe does a little business in stock. Accra is better provided than most part of the coast with supplies: small but good turkeys are brought from the breeding-places at the mouth of the Volta,—Jellakofi, usually called "Jelly-coffee," and Quittah, with its now deserted fort. They are bought here for 6s., and a little down the coast are worth at least $2: at Fernando Po one of them has cost a pound sterling. Pigs and poultry are bred at head-quarters. The interior supplies excellent farm land, and a man might soon make a small fortune by breeding sheep and goats, and by selling milk and vegetables to mail-steamers and cruisers. But "sun he be too hot, mas'er!" There are also curios at the British Hotel—monkey-skins for dames' muffs—there are inland some pretty specimens, jetty black, with pure white beard and whiskers; they are worth $1 per dozen. A fierce dog-faced baboon or two, with a strong propensity for a bite at your tendon-Achilles,[*] amuses himself in captivity with perambulating a rail; and dozens of Guinea parrots—little valued because they cannot speak, though they want the voicelessness for which the Greeks envied the wives of the Cicadas—twist and turn upon their perches on the

---

[*] It is this tendency in the monkey that induced the learned and Rev. Dr. Adam Clarke, in his "Commentary on the Bible," to propose that the ape should take the place of the old serpent in the Book of Genesis,—that most curious of cosmologies.

ground-floor piazza; whilst an eagle is chained to a post in the yard corner.

Not much prepossessed by the appearance of the establishment, where precocious urchins, hardly in their teens, were chewing sápo,* and laying the cloth for breakfast, the consul and I prepared for a walk round the town. We were accompanied by poor Hollingworth, of H.M.'s ship "Prometheus," one of the best and kindliest fellows that ever wore a blue jacket. Six months afterwards he fell a victim to the deadly climate of Lagos. Before setting out we had a palaver with a "cook-boy," as Anglo-Indian ladies persist in calling him, who was willing to engage himself for "Nanny Po." The cook-boy, however, owning to a proclivity for "sucking the monkey," and demanding as wages £5 per mensem, we did not subject him to expatriation. In most parts of India a stranger, if wise, would have hesitated to expose himself to the sun at 10 A.M. On this coast, however, even Europeans enjoy immunity from sun-stroke:† the natives, as the black-skin everywhere seems to do, enjoy themselves in the living "lowe."

* A bunch of fibres of the plantain and other trees, which, like the lff of Egypt, is used as a sponge; a mouthful is chewed to clean the inner part of the teeth, and is then applied outside like a tooth brush. Some of these fibres are bitter astringents, and doubtless beneficial.

† Dr. Clarke attributes this immunity to the relaxation of the system, by which profuse perspiration follows the least exertion, thereby equalising the circulation and preventing local congestions. This is true: it is dangerous to sit, though not to walk, in the sun. But I would also suggest that the humidity of the atmosphere, forming at all seasons a veil for the sun's rays, greatly mitigates the absolute heat.

Our first walk was to the British Salt Lake, as the Accra Lagoon, lying west of the town, is called. These formations are of two kinds, which I may term longitudinal and latitudinal. The former is disposed at an angle, more or less rectangular, to the coast; it is usually in a sink between two waves or tongues of high land, the lower bed of some watercourse, which flows only during the rains, and which, being below sea-level, is fed by percolations through the raised sand strip which acts as its embankment. The latitudinal is generally the formation of a permanent river, which spreads out over the depressions on either side of its bendings: the Volta river offers the perfection of this feature. Nothing can be worse than British Salt Lake, which runs far into the interior; it is historic ground, the fatal field of Dodowah lying near its head. Though fetid with decomposed mud, and haunted by sand-flies and mosquitoes, it is the favourite walk and ride with the Europeans of Accra. Between it and the sea are a number of pits, where the natives—fair and not fair—bathe in a touching approach to the pure Adamical costume. Turning inwards past "the Commodore"—as the large and well-built pile belonging to the Bannerman family—its tank contains the purest water in the place—is called, we walked towards the north, and had a fine view of the Aquapim and other hills, of which two cones, named Mount Bannerman to the west-north-west, and to the north-east, Kwabenyang, called on our charts Mount Zahrtman, are the most conspicuous,

The nearer country was adorned with the Palmyra, the French Ronnier, and it is everywhere a tree of good omen. The roads were bordered with datura—fortunately the people ignore its poisonous narcotism—and with thick hedges of prickly pear, whose only fault is a proclivity to extend itself unduly: the fruit is eaten by children, but the whites have not yet learned to appreciate the Maltese favourite.* The people whom we met on the road were mostly she-"pawns," sauntering towards the plantations; they did not, however, neglect to address us with the normal Heni odse — where thou comest from? To which we were taught to reply Ble-e-e-o— meaning softly—*tout doucement*—it is peaceful here. At some distance from the town, stood Garden House, once a shooting-box, whence sportsmen issued to slay leopards and moose-deer — probably the Koodoo. It was a fine old building, but, like the rest, dark, deserted, and sadly ruinous, whilst the grounds around it were a mere waste of bush. We strolled into the cemetery, whose hingeless, rusted gate offered no obstruction, and found it on a par with the habitations of the living. Returning by the north-east of the town, we passed by the Big House, another stately pile, that belongs to the Hansen family; it is even more broken down than " the

---

* On the Mediterranean shores it is considered cooling and wholesome, especially in summer. Englishmen at first dislike its insipidity, but they soon accustom themselves to it. The only difficulty about it is removing the thorny peel, which cannot be done without much practice.

Commodore." Mr. Addoe has married one of the daughters of the house, which, as usual, has a burial-ground on the lowest or ground-floor. Query, how is it that these houses are never haunted? What can become of the ghosts? It is said to have cost £12,000, in a place where money is worth double what it is in England, and the original proprietor died before he had carried out his plans of purchasing and clearing the frontage. A little beyond it was the French factory, and the Wesleyan Mission-house, bought from old Mr. Bannerman. In the town the women had their legs stocking'd and striped, like a clown's face, with some whitish, clayey substance; they were "making custom." The men as we passed bared themselves to the waist, which is equivalent to a cavalry-man dropping his right arm. All appeared civil and respectful: they are said to enjoy English rule, and to wish that we were sole possessors of the land—a great contrast to the East Indian. The pot-bellied children never appeared without a lump of native bread in their hands, a circumstance which accounts for the inordinate mortality of these juveniles—about one in three arriving at the years conventionally termed "of discretion." The alleys—streets they could not be called—were dirty and slovenly; sweeping seemed to be unknown; and the lank, sharp-snouted, long-legged pigs that haunted the heaps, were engaged in anything but rooting up truffles. This nuisance can hardly be abated: at times private orders are issued to cut short the days of Paddy's friend, as Pariah dogs are slaughtered in India; but the people attributing it to a porcine pestilence, send their pets into the country for change of air. The houses were of the hollow square form, more preserved than those of Cape Coast Castle, but less so than the Yoruba habitations. In most courtyards a female slave was bending, with pendent bosom and perspiring skin, over a stone roller, which, working along a concave slab, reduced the maize and obdurate holcus to a fine flour. Nothing can be more gloomy than these mud huts; their never whitewashed walls and seedy brown thatches are sad to behold. A few yards placed us once more upon the parade-ground.

Re-entering the hotel, we refreshed ourselves with brandy-pawnee, the pawnee being Patent Quinined Water, which has a high local reputation. After a disconsolate glance at the interior, and a gloomy anticipation of breakfast, a bright thought suggested itself. We walked over to the fort, passed inside despite the lowering glances of a shoeless Zouave, whose chestnut-coloured stockings, not unmatched with toes protruding through the tips, gave his legs the appearance that the English-woman in Paris seems to love—of two large chocolate sticks, and introduced ourselves to the Civil-Commandant, Major De Ruvignes, who, whilst finishing off business for the forenoon, welcomed us most kindly. He had brought to Africa a goodly stock of East Indian campaigning experiences, and we found ourselves in for pleasant day, when we had no right to expect any such thing.

I must break the thread of my tangled discourse to moralise "some," as Jonathan, or rather the two Jonathans, have it. In extensive travel there is catholicity of experience, especially in the cuisine. Few races, except the Esquimaux, the Hottentots, and the Australians, possess not a dish or two that might profitably be naturalised at home; whilst we in England have too many, which might, equally advantageously, be changed for others. Nor is the subject one of light import. *L'homme d'esprit seul sait manger.* Only fools and young ladies care nothing for the *carte.* Who but the idiot would affront his polarity (as Mr. Emerson, if I rightly understand him, terms man's individuality) by adhibiting to powers exhausted in a tropical climate, a refreshment of boiled mutton (*proh pudor!*) and caper sauce,* or a stuff invented, when meat was dear, to choke off appetite, and for which the speech of Europe hath no name—"pudding?" "Religion," says the sage Soyer, "feeds the soul, Education the mind, Food the body." *La destinée des nations dépend de la manière dont elles se nourrissent* is the wisdom of another wise man. This age of high progress is beginning to suspect a fact of which it never doubted in its days of barbarism— namely, that the babe at the breast imbibes certain peculiarities according to its nutrition.

---

* Well do I remember, in days of youth, our "elegant" and chivalrous French chef at Tours, in fair Touraine, who at once retired from the service because he was ordered to boil a gigot—"*Comment, madame, un—gigot!—cuit à l'eau, Jamais! Neverre!*"

These reflections, philosophical as good gastronomy is the truest philosophy, emanate from the memories of that day's breakfast. The people of Accra are notoriously good cooks; but, as amongst unpolished races, the men, who in civilisation attain heights of excellence to which the humbler sex may not aspire, are here notably inferior to their partners. The best of *cuisinières* are, of course, those of birth and breeding, and in their places Madame can direct the actions of her slave girls without compromising herself, as would be the case in an English kitchen, where we find Mrs. A——, with arms akimbo, ruling the roast, and brooking no rival luminary in her firmament. I can name and describe the qualities of the dishes to which we paid more particular attention, but their composition is complicated and tasteful enough to puzzle the brains of the lady who writes the cookery book. "Kankie" is native bread: the flour, at first not unlike the "yaller male" of the Land of Potatoes, must be manipulated till it becomes snowy white: after various complicated operations—soaking the grain, pounding, husking, triturating, and keeping till the right moment, it is boiled or roasted and packed in plantain leaves. It is as superior to the sour, brown, sodden mass tasting of butter-milk—like palm-wine and mildew, used by Europeans on this coast and called bread, as a Parisian roll to the London quartern loaf. "Fufu" is composed of yam, plantain, or casava; it is peeled, boiled, pounded, and made into balls, which act the part of European potatoes, only it is far more savoury than the vile tuber, which has potatofied at least one nation, and at which no man of taste ever looks, except in some such deep disguise as a *maître d'hôtel*. There were also cakes, seasoned with the fresh oil of the palm kernel, but they had a fault,—over richness. *En revanche*, the fish and stews were admirable; the former is the staple supply of the coast, and old residents live upon it.* "Kinnau" is fish opened, cleaned, stuffed with mashed green pepper, and fried in palm oil. The oil used for these purposes must be freshly made, thoroughly purified by repeated boilings, till free from water and fibre; the sign of readiness is a slight transparent yellow tint, supplanting the usual chrome colour. ."Palaver sauce" is a mess of vegetables, the hibiscus, egg-plant, tomato, and pepper, boiled together, with or without fowl or fish. "Palm-oil chop" is the curry of the Western coast, but it lacks the delicate flavour which turmeric gives, and suggests coarseness of taste. After some time Europeans begin to like it, and there are many who take home the materials to Europe. Besides palm-oil, it is composed of meat or fowl, boiled yam,† pepper,

---

* The fish is mostly a kind of herring, of which large quantities are cured and sent to the interior, even as far as Ashantee. Turtle is turned in the Hamattan season, beginning with December: after March they breed, and are unfit for food.

† The West African yam is of two kinds—white and yellow: the former is sweet, the latter bitter, and consequently preferred by the natives and by old hands amongst the whites. It never has the internal light purple tinge, nor the drug-like flavour which renders this vegetable anything but a favourite in India. The best yams in this part of the world are grown by the Bubes of Fernando Po.

and other minor ingredients. I always prefer it with rice; pepper, however, is the general fashion. The best and only sensible drink with this "chop," is palm wine, but the article is seldom to be procured sweet, and it mixes very badly for the digestion with all other fermented liquors. Next to it claret, but by no means Burgundy, which would recall a flavour, perhaps already too strong. And I advise the young beginner to conclude his "palm-oil chop," especially when eaten at a native house, with a "*petit verre.*" The last dish which shall be mentioned—it affects the palate of reminiscence with a pleasant humidity—is "kickie," a most intricate affair of finely minced and strongly flavoured fish or fowl; it is served up in Accra-made pots of black porous clay, into which the pepper sinks so thoroughly that after a few months it heats its contents. It has the one great advantage, like the West Indian "pepper-pot," of always coming up to table fresh from the fire.

After the *déjeûner dînatoire*, not without *aliquo mero*, we walked round poor old James Fort, which dates from the days of Charles the Martyr. It is an irregular square, flanked by bastions, and provided with two stories; the eastern side contains, or rather contained, a large saloon used for business purposes, and on the ground floor are the dungeons in which prisoners were immured. The sides of the fort proper are about 145 feet long; outside the gateway, however, there are the courts, surrounded by loopholed walls, and separated by a tumble-down building called a court-house. It is built upon the outer extremity of Accra Point, on a rocky foundation, about 36 feet above sea level. A low ledge of reef projects far into the sea, and at an expense of 5000*l.*—20,000*l.* being annually wasted upon a local corps — a breakwater of rough stone might easily be made there. It has been repeatedly recommended, and it was even expected to be undertaken: but who cares for Accra on the Gold Coast? This place, once the great ambition of Europe, has now fallen—fallen—fallen—even from the memory of the Gazetteer. In Brookes and Findlay (MDCCCLI.) we read, for all information—

* "ACRA, or ACCARA,"—neither spelling admissible—"a territory of Guinea on the Gold Coast, where some European States have forts, and each fort its village. N. lat. 5° 25′, W. long. 0° 10′."

A fine-looking massive building it must have seemed to the eyes of its own generation. It was the furthermost of their works upon this Coast, which will never look upon its like again. When I first saw it, however, the gateway was bending humbly forwards, the walls were lézardés, by rain dripping through the mortarless interstices, the ramparts were in holes, the rooms ruinous, the old iron guns, of some dozen various calibres, were scaly as the armadillo, and the whole place wore the tristest aspect of desolation. Some 1000*l.* per annum would have kept all these places—Cape Coast Castle, Accra Dixcove, and Christiansborg—in proper order; no great addition to an expenditure of £24,000 or £30,000 per annum. Now all is ruin. Books tell us that the coast, from El-Mina to Benin is still rising, and that rocks and ledges, before below, are now flush with the water. The earthquake of 1858 tended to hasten the growth.*

No one visits Accra without inspecting its neighbour, Christiansborg. Our coach and six presently appeared at the door; a quaint contrivance,—a four-in-hand of negroes to the fore, holding little cross-bars, and two pushing in the rear. The late Lieutenant Forbes, of Dahomian celebrity, used to wax extremely wroth at this degradation of men to cattle. I regret to own that it felt very refreshing after the banalities of hammocks, palanquins, and sedans. Horses, which die at Cape Coast Castle after a few months, here live for years : their owners, however, are careful not to take them into the bush. The reason generally given there is, that they catch complaints which are fatal. I cannot, however, but think that it is the tzetze, or some kindred fly, which destroys them. Wherever the bush and the tall grass are cleared away, these noxious animals, whose poison seems to be derived from the rank vegetation surrounding them, disappear. They are no longer upon the actual seaboard, which, perhaps, has been too much denuded of trees,—Nature's screen-work against the malaria of

* About April, 1862, seventeen distinct shocks, extending through six weeks, added increment to it, and on the 10th of June, 1862, when the rolling of the ground split every stone house in Accra, I distinctly saw that the level of the rock ledge had been upraised from the sea. The same day, however, was fatal to the three forts ; and the clerk of the works, sent from England to report upon the state of those belonging to us, declared that it was useless to attempt repairs.

the inner marshes. Within five miles north of Accra, I was severely stung by a large brown gadfly, of which specimens were secured. They were unfortunately lost; but though without books of reference and preserved specimens it is impossible for me to identify the animal, my impression is that it is the true tzetze, which Dr. Livingstone has limited to the southern branch of the Zambezi. The author of the "West Regions of Central Africa," brought home with him a fine large glossina, which was pronounced at the British Museum to be the true G. morsitans. Mules and asses might succeed even where horses fail. The only trouble in keeping these animals is the difficulty of finding proper attendants. Nothing can be more inhuman or neglectful than the West African stable-boy; he mounts his charge when unobserved, and rides him like a beggar, wears the cloths by night, and unless the master is present robs the grain and kankie with which his charge is fed. Besides which the fellows seem constitutionally unable to keep a horse clean, and to ride an animal out of condition and one quarter groomed is to drink *Romané glacé* out of a tin pannikin—both lose all their pleasure.

Our novel go-cart dashed through the streets at full speed. We passed through the Salt Bazaar, a kind of market, where women were sitting, before them were stores of fish and vegetables, ground-nuts, and palm-oil, and large flat baskets filled with the infinity of small cheap articles chiefly required in barbarous life. This led us to another square. On its seaward side stands the Dutch fort Crève-cœur, which M. Bouet-Willaumez described as an "abandoned ruin." It is a large pile of building, at the edge of the cliff, with a tall turret and a large courtyard. Being freshly whitewashed it wore an aspect somewhat superior to our ruin, but during the earthquakes it fared much worse, which was bad indeed. A Dutch negro soldier or two sat at the door, but never ventured upon the least sign of salute, eyeing us with all the repose which marks the caste of Canaan bin Ham. We also found a Wesleyan chapel, standing solitary at the landward side of a square, not unlike the parade-ground. Its style of architecture was that of the olden meeting-house, generally copied from that useful but not ornamental tenement, a barn. It disdained steeple, and being a week-day the doors were of course shut. Under its shade a small party of young negresses were enjoying their favourite relaxation of a dance. Nothing is more grotesque than their style of saltation. A couple stands up *vis-à-vis*, and raising the foot alternately both stamp upon the ground as bears are taught to do. This presently becomes a leap in the air, during which the hands are thrown out, palms forwards, and are met by the partner opposite. If there is any failure the couple breaks off with loud shouts of laughter, and another set stands up in their stead. On great occasions at Accra there are, I believe, dances which are as ceremonious as the East Indian Nautch; we had not, however, time to see them.

Presently we emerged from the town upon a level high

road of no despicable construction. Originally the work of the merchants at Accra, it is now kept in order by the civil commandant. The hard red clay, often the *débris* of ant masonry, dispenses with the necessity of metalling, though not with that of repairing at the end of the rainy season. The avenue of umbrellas and tamarinds which, bending to the N. E., acted as natural waves, gave it almost a south-European look. The country around, although in the heart of the dry season, afforded me an unexpected pleasure. Not a trace of bush, jungle, or mangrove swamp around: in the yellow daylight the rolling surface, here gently swelling, there sinking with a graceful curve, was clothed with golden grass; and here and there a tall tree, a "motte" of underwood, a solitary cactus, or a clump of evergreen woo'd the traveller to its green shade. Herds of cattle browsing in the distance gave it a pastoral appearance, and beyond the prairie formation of the lowlands rose forest,—not primeval, as Dr. Daniell calls it, but rather land that has lain fallow for some scores of years. The people call this Ko, as opposed to Ná, the grassy savannah. The consul had never seen so many ant-pyramids since leaving the Somali country: they studded the land; tall broken cones of red ferruginous earth, the favourite building material of the white termes bellicosus, the bug-a-bug of S'a Leone, which gives to the region a mistaken name.* There is game to be found in the land—" horse-deer," 13 to 14 hands high, ante-

---

* Accra is derived, through the Portuguese, from Inkran, or

lopes, the noble African partridge, and the "bush-turkey," which I believe to be a floriken: the animals, however, take to cover at once, and cannot be dislodged without curs. There is a kind of wild cattle, called on the Gaboon river, Nyára: it seems to exist everywhere in the maritime region—I found the same animal on the Gold Coast. Mr. Thompson ("Palm Land, or West Africa," p. 168) mentions it in the grass plains near Sherbro, and Mr. Valdez calls it Empacasso in Portuguese Africa,—Empacasseiros are the huntsmen who make a profession to kill it. Leopards are only too numerous. Hippopotami and crocodiles are plentiful in the Volta river. Spur-fowl exist in the bushes. I prefer, small as they are, the delicious curlews that pace the sands. Wild geese appear at certain seasons; the meat is fat, rich, and juicy. Elephants must exist in the interior, as the people are plentifully supplied with scrivellos and tusks of moderate dimensions. The only drawback to a gallop over this fine open country is the number and size of the crab holes, which rival the biscacheros of the South American pampas. During the rains, when verdure invests these charming slopes, and a thicker herbage clothes the woodland, the view must be a repose to the eye.* The horizon in the north showed a distant line of fading blue hill, the

---

"drivers," not white ants. Others say it was so called on account of the ant-like swarming of its numerous population.

* Compared with S'a Leone the rains in Accra are light, averaging a little above 60 inches. They are sufficient, however, to flood the

threshold of Ajumanti, Akim, and Ajuapim. In the latter, Akropong, the king's residence, and Abude, are now stations of the Basle mission: the distance is laid down at 20 to 30 miles from Accra, the height is 2000 to 2500 feet above sea level, and the climate is described to be delightful. The Ajumanti range is a day's hammock march from James Town, and being drier, is preferred by many to Akropong or Abude: the air is delicious, the water pure, and abundant stone and timber everywhere, whilst mechanics and supplies, at slightly advanced prices, are readily procurable from Accra. On the seaward slopes there is still a Danish ruin, bearing the inscription—

Frederiksgave
VI.
1832.

and intended as a sanitarium for the officers of Christiansborg. The fine estate around it, called the Queen's Plantations, has been granted to Major De Ruvignes, the civil commandant, on consideration of his paying annually a pine-apple quit-rent. Anything—from coffee to cotton—would grow here, and will grow well, whilst the air is pure and cool, and the mosquito plague of Accra is unknown. At the foot of the range is Abokobi, another station of German missionaries, and in the hills various farms and plantations belonging to the merchants of Accra. Coffee has been grown there, but all has now run wild. Mr. Freeman has been much more successful

lowlands, and as the soil is clayey, to stop travelling. The best season for excursions into the interior is the Harmattan.

near the Secoom river: at this time he has, I suppose, 10,000 plants. The German missionaries in Ajuapim also attempted it, but want of gardening skill made their efforts vain. Cotton was tried, and succeeded admirably. Mr. Swanzy, an eminent merchant, laid out large sums, and produced an excellent staple; since his day, however, the trees have been entirely neglected. The Accra copal is of poor quality, and fetches in the market far lower prices than that of Angola, Benguela, Kongo, or S'a Leone. Guinea grains are procured spontaneously everywhere in the hills, but this once celebrated spice, like the Balm of Meccah, has now become a weed. The mountain land of Akim lies about a week's easy travel to the north, with a little westing from Accra; it is divided into two districts, the eastern, of which Ojadan is the capital, and the western, whose capital is Chebi. The people, who know, though they cannot avail themselves of, their country's resources, are desirous of seeing it colonised by Europeans. Two very rich diggings have lately been discovered in Akim. There is no doubt that by paying a certain per-centage to the king and his Pynims, Europeans would be allowed to work them. It is described as a beautiful region, abounding in fruits and flowers: its botany would doubtless instruct Europe, but where are the botanist, the geologist, and the student of natural history on the Gold Coast? The great industry throughout Akim is gold. According to travellers the local fetish is called Kataguri; it appears in the shape of a large brass pan, which dropped down from heaven; in token of its high descent it is secured with all mystery in a fetish house, and is surrounded by drawn swords and axes overlaid with gold.*

After a two miles' drive through a country which it was a pleasure to look at, we reached the outposts of Christiansborg. The first sign was a cemetery, where the missionaries lie apart from "*dee hayden*," with whom they have associated during life. Ensue some quasi-European houses in which the "consort,"—such is the ambiguous term which the native "housekeeper" enjoys in these lands,—is located by the absent "householder." A martello tower, once considered a strong defence, stands sentinel on this approach to the main work. Around it, and to the northwards, clusters a native town, rising phœnix-like from it ruins. It was bombarded to correct a mutinous tendency, in 1854, by H. M. S. Scourge, followed by a squadron of six English vessels, and a large native force, which had collected, was easily dispersed. Unfortunately the lines of streets have been carelessly laid down, and, as has been explained, it is more difficult to remove a Gold Coast town than a West Africo-English

---

* At Accra the commandant showed me some of these swords, which had been sent in token of submission by one of the chiefs of Krobo, a highland about 60 miles north-east of James Town. They were short, broad, and heavy falchions, apparently of rusty hoop iron, in shape somewhat like the dreaded Turkish scimitar of the olden time—now known only in pictures—but adorned with open work near the end, like fsh-slicers or Highland dirks, the handles and pommels being thinly plated with worked gold sewn together, and hammered close to the wood.

settlement. The holes from which the earthen material of the houses was excavated are allowed to remain, and, filled by every rainy season they must be small hotbeds of malaria. The native town showed us a peculiar sight. "Can the Ethiopian change his skin?" is a question which has been asked some time ago, in distinct expectation of a negative reply. My day at Accra enables me modestly, but decidedly, to reply that he *can*. Outside a hut sat a strange-looking being, a spotted man, such as we read of in books that treat of ethnology and of skin-diseases. The ground-colour of his superficies was an unwholesome pink white, and the rest was a series of deep black splotches. He was well-known to all in the place; a few years before he had been a negro; he gradually changed to a white man, and when we saw him he was again recovering his *rete mucosum*. I saw another anthropological curiosity at Accra. The Albino in Africa has been noticed by every traveller, the semi-Albino has not. My specimen was a man with features and cranium distinctly belonging to the "poor black brother." His complexion, however, was *café au lait*, his hair a dull dead yellow, short and kinky as that of all his tribe, and his eye-pupils were of a light and lively brown. I afterwards saw many of the same temperament at Benin, and one—the chief Sandy—at Batanga: my little "Travellers' Library," however, does not allude to this *lusus naturæ*.

Near the entrance of the old Danish castle there are some large whitewashed quarters, occupied by the Basle

Mission's Gesellschaft, and a number of white-haired children broke the monotonous prospect of little waddling niggers and long-legged trotting pigs. This Mission holds the hill-country, and by combining commerce with Christianisation, has succeeded in establishing half a dozen stations. The members arrive in Africa like timid sheep, very humble; they wax bolder in time, as the fox in that fable where he met the lion, and they end by being as offensive to the community as were the frogs to King Log. An abominable charge was brought by their superior against a highly respectable English merchant at Accra: an action for libel of course ensued, the cause came into court, and the defendant altogether failed to substantiate his calumny. Yet the jury—partly negroes and partly whites, lower in the scale of creation than black men—brought in the peculiar verdict that the accusation was a libel, but that it had been made without malicious intent. These Germans carry matters with a high hand. An English brother happening to come under their displeasure, they took from him his wife and children—by a process of divorce which they had no right to pronounce—and actually married her to one of their own number. I will not mention names unless the truth of this assertion be disputed by the culprits, in which case I will.

Christiansborg Castle, like its brethren Crève-cœur and James Fort, is founded upon a rock, and bears upon its walls the date of erection, A.D. 1694. This strong point, flanked on both sides by sandy bays, stands some thirty-five feet above sea-level; it is fronted by scattered ledges and outliers, upon which at most seasons, a heavy surf breaks, consequently the landing is fit only for canoes. Built by degrees, it has grown into a large but irregular building, a square of 190 feet on each side, with a variety of party-walls, ramparts, bastions, and outworks, all of solid stone masonry, which must have cost a "pretty penny." The first room is a fine *salon*, called the council-chamber, enlivened with bright blue bands of paint; under it, however, are noisome dungeons. Besides this there is a chapel, now closed, a hospital, sundry store-rooms, and officers' quarters. It is garrisoned by a detachment from Accra, and so scanty are supplies, that the Europeans never miss mail-day, and generally dine away from home; no skipper can pass the place without being mulcted in a bit of fresh beef, or, that failing, salt pork. The air is damp and unwholesome; articles hung against the walls generally mildew, and the human animal fares even worse. The fort was built originally by the Portuguese, but after repeatedly changing masters, it was confirmed to the Danish crown in the year inscribed upon its walls. In 1850, the King of Denmark, as has been said, sold all his northern provinces for the sum of 10,000*l*., to the English. I should have preferred paying these moneys for the archives; they were, however, removed with the establishment. The Danish trace is still met with in the interior, although the names of the towns do not end in —by. You meet, however in out-

A DAY IN THE LAND OF ANTS. 159

of-the-way villages, with Miss Hesse, Miss Engmann, and other unmistakeable signs of the Danes.

The view from the ramparts is extensive and picturesque. Under the north-eastern walls of the Fort is a clump of cocoa-nut trees, where the "wa 'ful waddie" is erected when required. A little beyond it is a lagoon, or rather a hole of stagnant water, fit only for crocodiles, and well accounting for the unsanity of the place. Looking eastward, about two and a-half miles along the sandy tract which runs uninterrupted as far as Sandy Bluff, the western point of the Volta's embouchure, we see a clump of trees on rising ground, denoting the site of a well-known village, Labaddi, by the natives called Lá, and the seat of the Great Fetish Lá-Kpá. The people are fierce and fanatic, and show a disposition to be troublesome. The commandant had pointed out to me, within the *enceinte* of St. James Fort, the grave of a Labaddi fetishman, who had been lately hung for a barbarous murder. The operation, owing to the struggles of the patient, had been long and severe, and the corpse had been buried and kept under surveillance in James Fort, lest the people should believe in a local Resurrection. The fellow had declared under the death-tree that he would return and haunt the man who caused his destruction, and there are those who believe that he has returned—once at least. Three miles beyond Labaddi is a country whose prettiness is difficult to describe; in a charming stretch of park land, tapestried with grass, and relieved by clumps and scattered trees, lies Tesha, or Tassy, properly Tesi, once guarded by Augustenborg, a Danish fort. But no more shall European eyes view these charming scenes from that *point de vue;* the inexorable earthquake came, shook Christiansborg down to the rock, and breaking the head of an assistant-surgeon, compelled the garrison to camp out upon the plain.

Bidding adieu to this "Castle o' Balwearie," we walked to the north and entered a large building, not unworthy of comparison with the Commodore and the Big House. The owner was not at home, so we ascended the stairs, and sitting in the saloon, made ourselves comfortable with cocoa-nut water, "laced" with cognac. The house, which had all the qualifications for a Governor's palace, belonged to a Mr. Richter, a Danish merchant, one of the wealthiest. His portrait still hangs upon the wall, a kitcat, showing a mild and gentlemanly unmoustachioed face, supported by a swathe of muslin, around which was a high horse-collar, that formed part of a blue cloth coat, and brass buttons; as the intelligent reader will have anticipated, a bunch of seals hung from the fob. And yet this quiet old gentleman must have been a terrible Turk—skeletons have been found in his under-ground dungeons, and his name is like that of "Draque" in the New World.

After this we walked still further north for about half a mile, to the old Fredericksborg. On the road we passed a most forbidding-looking German missionary, who was driving before him a herd of little negroes, habited in striped calico. Not a hand was raised to the hat: in a country "croom" not a soul would have passed us without a kindly greeting. It is one of the worst points in these Christianisers that they are ever endeavouring to raise man against man; their theory is "love one another," their practice is jealousy and hate. After a quarter of an hour we came upon the outskirts of the place, where our men began to tread cautiously. Serpents in exceptional numbers come forth to bask in the burning sun, and some are so full of fight, that, instead of running away, they will, it is said, rise and fly at an intruder. The land also is covered with a tall growth of spear-grass, which at once works its way through serge, and hooks its barbed points into the flesh; *crede experto*, and never travel in the inner Gold Coast without antigropelos (is that rightly spelt?) or top-boots. Frederiksborg contained only two stone houses, but they were handsome and well built of cut slabs. They are now uninhabitable; the material has been filched by the garrison at Christiansborg, and a wall half-pulled down in these regions is soon level with the ground. It was not safe to enter the *débris*; we therefore contented ourselves with an outside view. The Gold Coast has already more remnants of antiquity than the American Republic, where the Nauvoo Temple is the only ruin between the Atlantic and the Pacific Oceans.

We then remounted our coach and six, and proceeded at a spanking pace, which spoke well for the wind and bottom of our cattle, towards James Town. The beauty of the view, the contrast of ruin and perennial growth, the terrible sereneness of Nature, unchanged, inexorable, so utterly beyond the emmets, black and white, that burrow and nest upon earth's surface, filled my mind with a sudden and profound sadness. Like the builders of these deserted homesteads, I have sought this coast, determined to show what can be effected by energy not undirected by intellect. And now, under that glowing sun, and with that ever-smiling prospect before me, a voice seems to say that all my efforts shall be vain, perhaps even vainer than theirs. I felt relieved when we had plunged into the alleys of James Town.

A succulent dinner prepared us for the ever-increasing *disette* of the A. S. S. We are now lapsing into tropical diet,—beef that looks like dead horse, fowls barely the size of pigeons, and turkeys whose breast-bones pierce through their skins. The gallant captain of the " Blackland " began to bang his pop-guns before the ground-nut soup was off the table—the only object of which proceeding was to double-shot a 24-pounder, in case he might be disposed, contrary to contract, to give us the slip. Nothing so unpleasant, however, occurred. We dined in peace; and I bade adieu to my excellent host with a regret, lightened only by his promise to accompany me, at the first opportunity, to Kumasi, capital of Ashantee. A rush through the breakers, and a frantic paddling;—in half an hour more we were on board.

The tribes of the eastern Gold Coast, Accras, Krobos, Krepis, Agotims, Awunahs, and Addahs, differ greatly from the Akan, or western races, in *morale* and *physique*. There the people are larger and finer men than on the windward coast; I have never seen such tall, muscular, and powerful negroes as at Addah. The women are equally well-grown, and withal remarkably hairy. Their complexion is rather a dark red than black. Placed between the two great despotisms of Ashantee and Dahomey, they are free even to anarchy, and though fierce as *coqs de combat* they are disunited, or rather hostile. According to Bowdich, the people of Accra, like those of Mombas, rose up against the Portuguese,—they had settled here in 1492, and were guilty of great cruelties,—executed the governor and the garrison on the spot where they still take the earth to rub on a new-born child, in memory of the event. They show considerable improvability. The children on the Gold Coast are named after the days on which they are born. Kwashi, or Sunday, our well-known Quashie; Kajjo (Cudjoe), Kwábino, Kwáko (Quacco), Kwaw, Kofi, and Kwamina, or Saturday. The same is the case in Ashantee, where the king's last name is the birthday, which necessarily returns once a week, and the first is the title Sai or Osai, borne also by the principal nobles. Here the first-born son is Tete, the corresponding daughter Dede; the second pair are Te*te* masculine, and Koko feminine; the third, Mesa and Mansa; fourth, Anan and Tsotso; fifth, Anum and Manum; sixth, Nsia and Sasa; seventh, Ason, masculine and feminine; eighth, Botfe; ninth, Akron; tenth, Badu. The three latter are common to both sexes. With few exceptions, they are taken from Oji numerals, as amongst the Romans, Quintus, Decimus, &c. European officials get a native prenomen from the day on which they land; the real *nomen* is some nickname, which the witty knaves choose with peculiar felicity. Thus an esteemed friend of mine rejoices in the style and title of Kajjo (Cudjoe) Frafra—"Monday Flatface." They respect Europeans beyond their fellows; there is no personal risk in travelling through the wildest parts of the country, and the people would willingly see our power extended. In the smallest crooms, or country villages, a house is cleared for the traveller, and in the larger settlements there is always a guests' room set apart for strangers. Where the chief resides he will prepare an excellent breakfast of pepper-soup, kankie, and native stews, and the table will be loaded with champagne and claret, gin and cognac. If they find any fault with our policy, it is the lax hand with which the reins of government are held; they respect the Dutch, because these treat them with greater severity. Under President Maclean the Krobo troubles would have been settled in six weeks, now they have lasted four years.* These shortcomings

* Krobo is a protected territory, a mass of highlands about 10 miles west of the Volta, and 45 from its mouth. There are two main divisions of the mountain, eastward or near the river, including Kpong (Pong) and Mámyá, is under the chief Odonko Azu. Westward is Yilau, the capital of the chief Ologu Patu. The troubles began in 1858, with a turmoil between the rivals, arising, it is said, from a dance at a festival, in which a neighbouring village interfered, and they

on our part are doubtless owing to the frequency of "gubernational changes," necessitated by the nature of the climate.*

It is not a little curious that on this coast several heathen tribes practise circumcision,† whilst their neigh-

are not settled. Odonko Azu and his principal chiefs were taken prisoners, and kept for nine months in captivity. They escaped from Christiansborg by the unjustifiable carelessness of the officer who had charge of them, and who escaped all injury concerning a transaction which would have cost him in India his commission.

* The following is a list of the governors and the acting governors up to the present time :—
 1. Commander Worsley Hill, R.N., made in 1844. Lived to return to England.
 2. Dr. Lilly (acting), 1845. Superseded.
 3. Commander afterwards Sir William Winniett, 1846. Returned home.
 4. J. C. Fitzpatrick, Esq., Jan. 1849. Superseded.
 5. Sir William Winniett, Jan. 1850. Died at his post. He was one of the best of governors, and steadily pursued his favourite scheme of making the colony self-supporting, till it was cut short by death.
 6. J. Bannerman, Esq. (acting), Oct. 1851. Superseded.
 7. Major G. J. Hill, Dec. 1851. Returned to England.
 8. J. C. Fitzpatrick, Esq. (acting), June 1853. Superseded.
 9. B. G. Cruikshank, Esq. (acting), Aug. 1853. Ditto.
 10. Major G. J. Hill, Feb. 1854. Returned home.
 11. Henry Connor, Esq. (acting), Dec. 1854. Ditto.
 12. Sir Benjamin C. C. Pine, March 1857. Ditto.
 13. Col. Bird (acting), 14th April, 1858. Superseded.
 14. E. B. Andrews, Esq., 20th April, 1860. Returned to England.
 15. W. A. Ross, Esq. (acting), 14th April, 1662. Superseded.
 16. Mr. Pine, 20th Sept., 1862. Still there.

Thus it will be seen there have been 16 governors, commanders-in-chief, and vice-admirals in 18 years; and the almost total disorganisation of the colony, or rather the garrison—for colony it is not—can hardly be wondered at.

† The rite is called Keteafo, or shortening. It is practised by both

bours do not. A similar circumstance of sporadicity in the rite is noticed by a late traveller in the Lake Regions of Central Africa. Morality, despite the precaution, appears to be at a low ebb. The *morbus gallicum* and its varieties are almost universal in some places, *delirium tremens* is by no means rare, poisoning is common, and abortion is generally resorted to, when a woman nursing, contrary to the custom of the coast and the dictates of Nature, is threatened with once more becoming a mother. There is no difficulty in procuring a temporary native wife, locally called a "consort," by the week or "by the run," as it is termed. The principal diseases are dysentery, fever, and dracunculus.* Owing

Gá and Adanme tribes, and is in the keep of a certain family, though not directly connected with religion. The boys—not the girls, as some authors represent—are circumcised about 13 years of age. The missionaries believe this to point out a Hebrew or a Moslem origin; I think not. They should bear in mind that the Jews derived the rite from Egypt, that is to say Africa, where it had been used for ages immemorial, and that in the very depths of the Dark Continent, where Jew or Arab never penetrated, it is practised under a variety of modifications.

* The *Vena Medinensis* was called from this coast the "Guinea worm." The natives deny that it is produced by drinking impure water, and they are right. It is doubtless the product of some animal which deposits its ova in the skin. The Gold Coast people say that it prefers those with sweet flesh, avoiding acid and acrid skins. The great proof of its external origin is that the legs and feet are the parts most affected, cases occur most frequently during the rains, when the lower extremities are liable to be wetted, and those who sleep on the ground or on mats are more liable to the disease than those who use cots. The people, according to Dr. Clarke, believe in a male and a female Guinea-worm; the former is the thickness of a crow's quill, the latter of a stout linen thread. The only part of the body not liable to dracunculus

to the relaxing nature of the climate, unexciting life, unnutritious and unchanged dietary, unwholesome water, and absence of cold weather, a man once "down" remains so for a long time.

A rude native smith-craft is the favourite industry at Accra, where zodiacal rings may be found upon every one's finger. The gold is first melted and reduced to proper size; it is polished by a mixture of nitrate of potash, soda, and water, boiled together in a large limpet shell (Achatina). The mould is cut out in the soft part of the dead cuttle-fish, and the ring, when made, is polished with borax and lime-juice, forming a weak acid. They also make studs, watch-chains, and other ornaments, which, to say the truth, are utterly destitute of artistic beauty. The sonmesi, or blacksmith's shop, as in parts of Europe, is a weird place, where thieves are detected, wounds healed, and so on. The land is full of tales and legends of gold-dust and doubloons buried under trees, and the people are credulous upon this point as the Hindus.

The Accra English is superior to "Black-man's *mouf*" generally. In addressing them it is not necessary to use, for comprehension, the horrid jargon of the S'a Leone man or the Kruboy. There are, however,

---

is the hairy scalp. Some persons have been known to have 30 Guineaworms at the same time. The average time of cure is laid down at three months, but if the worm be broken, it will last six. Lameness is sometimes caused by it, the Tendo Achilles and other sinews becoming permanently fixed and contracted by the inflammation.

many English expressions which no Englishman would at first understand. "Put him in log," means fasten his leg to a log; a "house master" is the proprietor of the house; to "put in fetish," is equivalent to our old excommunication; to "make customs," is to mourn for and wake the dead; and, to quote no more specimens of this quaint and queer old trading English, a "tail-girl" is a young woman whose only dress is a T-bandage, with a long extremity pendant behind. It is, say Europeans, as usual wrongly, a sign of fetish.* All such names of places as Accra or Jamestown, Dutch Accra, Christiansborg, Labaddi, Tassy, and others have their native duplicates in Gá, Kinká, Osu, Lá, and Tesi, and the names are mostly significant; the latter would mean, for instance, "stone land."

The languages, or rather dialects, spoken upon this leeward coast are, like the Fanti, of Hamitic origin, and cognate with the tongues of Ashantee, Dahomey, and Yoruba. As all the family, they have no peculiar character, and they were probably never written till Moslems and Europeans appeared. Of late years speeches, histories and legends, proverbs and tales, of which there are thousands, have been published by mis-

* Girls amongst the Accras and eastern tribes are not properly allowed to wear any cloth but a narrow strip. When marriageable, they are taken home, kept from work, highly fed, well dressed, and profusely ornamented. After many ceremonies, they are exhibited in the town by the advertisements of finery, dancing, and playing; thus it is pretty much the same in barbarous Medidsiasikpong (Africa) as in civilised England.

sionaries and others. So extensive is this literature, that the people have a name for a single branch, *e.g.*, Anansesem, or spider-stories.* This insect *(ananu)* plays a principal part in animal fables; it has a bad influence upon children sleeping in the same room, it speaks through the nose like a malignant ghost, and its hobbling gait, and other fancied peculiarities, are correctly imitated by the gestures of the relater.† On moonlight nights, when men, like other animals, feel gay and frisky, they sit in circles, and listen to these wild tales, which are recounted with an appropriateness of gesture, a power of imitation, and an amount of fun worthy of Mathews and Robson. The people are fond of singing, and compose extempore, whilst playing, dancing, or working,—the African can do nothing without a chant,—short songs, often highly satirical, and much relished by the listeners. The children in

* See a "Grammatical Sketch of the Akra or Ga Language," by the Rev. J. Zimmerman. Stuttgart : J. F. Steinkopf, 1858. It is a useful publication, but ineffably tedious, as such German "sketches" ever are, and not without a fair share of linguistic arrogance—another Teutonic peculiarity. The spelling is abominable, in parts unintelligible ; but what can be expected from Stuttgart English ?

† There is a large Arachnis upon this coast, which may become of commercial importance. It is black with a broad golden band down the back, and the web is not circular, but in long lines thrown from tree to tree, as if it did not prey upon flies. The thread is a deep yellow, stronger than silk, moreover a single insect easily produces more than the largest cocoon. There is no reason why this spider should not be naturalised in Europe, and though my specimens of spider-silk have hitherto been lost, I still hope to send home sufficient for a veil or a lace shawl.

the Krobo mission schools are said to have extemporised little hymns sung to very sweet native tunes. This shows linguistic powers which few European children possess. Perhaps, however,—I am not prepared to support the thesis,—precocity of intellect, as a rule, results in inferiority in later life.

There are two main languages upon the leeward coast, Gá proper, and its mother tongue, the Adánme; the general language, however, is called the Gá family, and is spoken by about 100,000 or 120,000 out of 400,000 souls.

The Gá Akpa, or Gá Proper, is the speech of the sea-towns, from the Sakumofio or Secoom, west of Accra, to the town of Tesi, about five miles east of Christiausborg. It is spoken by about 40,000 or 50,000 people, and is bounded on the east by the Adánme, on the west by the Ojí of the Akan tribes.

The Adánme, or Adá-gbe, "voice," or "language of the 'Adá people," extends from Tesi on the west, eastwards, to the Volta; northwards, its area includes the Krobo country and towns at the foot of the Aquapim mountains: to the north-east, on the Volta's left bank, it is spoken by three towns of the Agotim people. It is used by 50,000 or 60,000 souls; but, though more extensively spread, it is by no means so important a tongue as the Gá, which is the speech of tribes enjoying both moral and political supremacy. The missionaries found their assertion that the language of 'Adá is the mother dialect of the Gá, upon these reasons: it is harder and shorter, purer, and unmixed with Ojí—*ergo*, it is more primitive. The difference is described to be as great as that between the Saxon, or High Deutsch, and the German of Switzerland or Suabia.

The missionaries thus briefly state the theology of the Gá tribes. God, called "Nyonmo" and other names, is the highest being, the only one, Creator of heaven and earth. The Fetishes (Wodsi) are spiritual and personal beings, either sub-deities who govern, or demons who disturb, the world. There are such Fetishes —*e.g.* earth, air, and sea—common to all men; others, as rivers and trees, peculiar to distinct tribes, towns, families, or individuals. A person may possess a Fetish, or $\delta\alpha\iota\mu\omega\nu$, and is called Wontse, which is translated by Fetish man or priest. Or he may be possessed by some one, which possession is called Wonmomo, or Fetish-fury.* Besides these there are innumerable things sacred to, belonging to, or made effectual by a Fetish.† Such things are cords (wonkpai) tied about

---

* Cases of this affection are frequently seen even in the streets of Accra. If hysterics denoted possession in modern, as epilepsy did in olden times, what a high development of demonism Europe would present!

† This is poorly explained. The West Africans, like their brethren in the East, have evil ghosts and haunting evestra, which work themselves into the position of demons. Their various rites are intended to avert the harm which may be done to them by these Pepos or Mulungus, and perhaps to shift it upon their enemies. When the critical moment has arrived, the ghost is adjured by the Fetish-man to come forth from the possessed, and an article is named—a leopard's claw, peculiar beads, or a rag from the sick man's body nailed to what Europeans call the

the body or the house, teeth, skins, rings, chains, and other similar articles, which gave rise to the absurd belief that the African makes everything, even a rag or a bit of glass, his god; and the missionaries assert that "a comparison with religious things"—I presume that is Stuttgart English for "relics"—"and superstitions in the heart of Christendom, would have fully explained the matter, without casting the Africans together, no more with men, but with brutes." *

I am ready to concede that the people of the Gold Coast have emerged from the utter atheism which characterises the so-called Kafirs and other tribes of Eastern Africa. But as yet their ideas are too vague, and connected with material objects, to rank them with deistical peoples. They have neither a personal and local Deity like the heathens, nor the atomic gods of Epicurus. "Nyonmo" is their word for the Almighty, but the same means the sky, the rain, and even thunder and lightning; thus they say God drizzles or God knocks, *i.e.*, it thunders. The missionaries explain this by the people considering God to be the "spirit or soul of heaven, or heaven the face or outward appearance of

---

"Devil's Tree,"—in which, if worn about the person, the haunter will reside. It is technically called Kehi or Keti, a "chair" or "stool."— See "Zanzibar and two Months in East Africa," Blackwood's Magazine, February, 1858, pp. 220, 221.

* The preceding note will illustrate the difference between the two absurdities, the African Fetish-chain and the European relic. It must ever be borne in mind that the former is haunted by an evil influence, whereas the latter carries with it a blessing.

God." This, however, sounds much like applying German metaphysics to the absurdities of heathen fable. When men associate in language and idea the material with the immaterial, the former is the real thing worshipped. Thus we also find "Sikpon," earth, considered a personage, and adored as well as "Nyonmo," sky, perhaps with more reason, as the former exists, whereas the latter does not. There is the usual African tradition to account for the superiority of Japhet over Ham. God, say the people, made two men, one white, the other black. To these he presented for choice a calabash full of writing materials, and another full of gold—it is needless to say how the selection was made, and what the results were. For this reason the people of the Gold Coast always consider the precious metal their peculiar property, and resent all attempts on the part of foreigners to work it without some royalty. And they mightily despise the mulatto—the "white blackman," they say, is silver and copper, not gold.

In the land of the Akan and Gá races there is a curious dawning of a belief, not in metempsychosis, but in transmigration, not of soul, but of life. The 'Kla or 'Kra* of a person is the principle which animated a

---

* The word is better known as Okla or Okra, which some authors write Occro or Ocro, and translate Fetish or Sanctified boy. It is a slave chosen by his master to be his companion in this life, and to be sacrificed over his grave, that he may accompany him, not in the world to come, but in that state in which man exists—if I may use the word —after death. Most Africans are real Swedenborgians as regards "continuation." I cannot but reflect with horror upon our future

relative or other person before dead. When parents have lost several children, they sometimes cast the body of the child that died last into the bush, any congenital deformity or defect in the next infant, which they believe to be the same child whose corpse is thrown away, is attributed to injuries received from wild beasts or other influences in the jungle. Hence, children born with supernumerary fingers or toes, have been strangled or burned alive. When one or two infants have been lost by death, they mark the next born by making one indelible cut on each cheek. If that fails, they make one vertical and three transverse incisions, and so on. The pregnant woman always visits the Fetish-priest, and asks the 'Kla of her child that is to be; the priest summons it, listens to its voice, and answers her question. A man's 'Kla is considered partly himself and partly not; it is a being like the demon of Socrates, who gives him good advice, and receives thanks and thank-offerings as a Fetish. Moreover, every person has two 'Kla, male and female, the former of a bad, the

---

prospects, if we are to be for ever liable to a summons from Mr. Hume, if we are doomed to communicate with friends by rapping, and if we are, like Shakspeare and Milton—in their ghostliness—to rap out the feeblest nonsense imaginable. *Revenants* in Africa are at any rate dreaded. In Europe the "spirit" becomes a thoroughly contemptible being, whose knuckles must supply the want of tongue, and who has apparently a mania for prophecy despite perpetual self-stultification.

After all, superstition, like happiness—of which perhaps it is a branch—is equally divided amongst men, and the civilised, generally, have not a tittle of right to deride the most ignorant or the most barbarous of their brethren.

latter of a good disposition. This recals to mind the Jewish and Muslem Kiram el Katibin, the two mysterious beings who, sitting upon man's right and left shoulder, whisper their virtuous or vicious suggestions into his ears. For El Islam, despite the sublimity of its truths and the higher law of unselfishness, which is its real spirit, has retained—as all of human must—some old leaven of superstition, directly derived from man's earliest dawn of belief in things unseen—Fetishism.

The Yara, or funeral customs of the Gold Coast are not less barbarous than those of their neighbours. They consist of washing, dressing, and providing necessaries for the corpse, which is then interred by the burial women, or "Klageweider" (Keeners). Weeping and lamentation, singing and dancing, all accompanied with copious rum drinking, are kept up sometimes for weeks together, and at certain stated periods are repeated. Formerly 'Klas and wives were slaughtered on the graves of people of importance — a custom almost universal amongst barbarians from the days of Homer downwards. So the ruffian Achilles, addressing the ghost of Patroclus, promises him that—

Δώδεκα μεν Τρώων μεγαθύμων υἶας ἐσθλούς
Τους ἅμα σοι πάντας πῦρ ἐσθίε.

It is now as difficult and dangerous a ceremony as a Sati in Hindostan; yet it is secretly practised whenever found possible.

The principal festival in the year is the Yams Custom, which Europeans call native, or black Christmas. It is celebrated at the end of August or the beginning of September, and at the same time their New Year's Day occurs. The first eating of that vegetable is connected with many ceremonies; the Fetish must begin, then the king, and so on.* This is called Yereyelo. Follows Homowo, literally the "outcrying" or "mocking of hunger;" a harvest-home, celebrated on the coast with gun-firing, singing, dancing, music, eating, drinking, and merrymaking, in the interior with the human sacrifices now familiar to Europe.

I proceed now to discuss the three great obstacles to improvement on this coast,—the presence of the Dutch, the peculiar style of taxation, and the use of a military instead of a police corps.

The forts and stations of the British and Dutch governments closely intersect one another from Apollonia to Accra, and this causes endless troubles. Our Netherlandish neighbours have not much improved since the days of Jonathan Swift; they are still—in Africa at least—the most selfish and obstinate of colonists. If the English place a duty of 2 to 2·50 per cent. upon the invoice price of landed imports, the Dutch establish a free port. Overtures have, it is said, been made to give up our windward for their leeward territories; though heavily in our debt, they have turned a deaf

---

* The custom has been explained as a hygienic measure; and Fetish law generally is resorted to when some measure beneficial to the commonwealth is to be strictly carried out; such as the prohibition of eating pork, cutting down trees, or collecting gold.

ear to all our proposals, and have even prepared to re-occupy their deserted posts. Whilst the English make 7000*l.* per annum, and expend nearly 30,000*l.* a year—a little more than the Maynooth grant—upon their possessions in this quarter of the world, the Dutch, defended by the moral influence of our squadron and troops, require only two officers, commanding 200 negroes in "blue baft," and including their civil department, maintain themselves for 6000*l.* to 8000*l.* per annum. Free trade would evidently not dislodge them.

At Accra, where the British Jamestown and the Dutch Kinka are dovetailed into one another, only an imaginary line separating St. George and Tricolor, the workings of the two systems become apparent. After Dutch Accra had been captured by us, the Netherlands were allowed as a favour to rebuild their factory, but not to appoint a commandant. When old Mr. Hanson, originally Hansen, a Danish mulatto, who at one time had charge of both factories, died, our rivals began to exercise jurisdiction, and we "let it slide." At present they claim almost all Jamestown, except a few houses near the fort, because Kajjo, the king of Dutch Accra, is king over the kinglets of Gá, Osu, Krobo, Akim, and Aquapim. They keep a commandant, a sergeant, and four to six men. English ships are charged 3*l.*, and foreign bottoms 3*l.* 18*s.* 4*d.* for wharfage at British Accra. The Dutch take 12*l.*, but there is neither wharfage due nor import-tax; ships therefore naturally prefer the Dutch roads.* Our merchants are charged even for imported machinery, here more wanted than in America: it is a suicidal policy.† Of course they are unable to compete with their Dutch rivals, whose free ports are frequented by Akims, Ashantees, and the inland tribes generally, who would rather travel a month than waste a dollar. They have even rejected all proposals to co-operate in the imposition of duties, and they are contented to remain a thorn in our side, and to collect occasionally a heavy fine, as $12,000, which was lately imposed on the occasion of a manslaughter.

Were the Dutch to be removed, even at the price of 100,000*l.* our deficit of 23,000*l.* would soon change to a surplus of 50,000*l.* The duties on rum, spirits, arms, and ammunition might gradually be raised to 50 per cent.: a measure a hundredfold more beneficial to the natives than even to ourselves, and gold exploiting might commence in real earnest.

And now for taxation. In April, 1852, a council of British officials and native chiefs was assembled at Cape Coast Castle, to "take into consideration the advantages

---

* The Dutch roads, however, are not so safe as the English. South of Fort James, according to the Directory, there are eight or nine fathoms water with very soft clay, which requires a light anchor, as a heavy one could not be drawn up from the ground.

† There are men who object to using labour-saving contrivances in Africa, because these would foster the indolence of the people; the idea appears to me exceedingly absurd. Methinks it is better that men who will not work much, should work a little rather than not work at all. But possibly this is not an "elevated view" of the case.

which the country derives from the protection afforded to it by Her Majesty's Government, by submitting, from time to time, to pay such taxes as may be determined on by the majority of chiefs assembled in council with His Excellency the Governor." Hence the poll-tax on families, of which the "house-master," or the pater-familias, was made responsible for each member—after the fashion of Mahommed Ali in Egypt. It began with the Good Intentions which are said to pave the way to a Certain Place. "The revenue derived from the tax, after paying the stipends of the chiefs, and other expenses attending its collection, shall be devoted to the public good, in the education of the people, in the general improvement and extension of the judicial system, in affording greater facilities of internal communication, in increased medical aid, and in such other measures of improvement and utility as the state of the social progress may render necessary." A poll-tax collector at Christiansborg informed Mr. Consul Hutchinson ("Impressions of Western Africa"), that he had received in 1855 about 337 ounces of gold, at the rate of a shilling a head, and that in the Akim districts the people would pay more if they received for it value in protection or information.

As our fine words buttered no parsnips, the natives began to murmur. In the earlier Italian railways there was little to gain because of the impossibility of finding an honest *employé*. So on the Gold Coast, the poll-tax was collected, but instead of going to judges, schoolmasters, and roads, it restored bankrupts to wealth and position.

Letters upon the poll-tax and taxation in general appeared in the local papers, headed with the safe but not novel reflection on the part of a writer, who signs himself, " Yours obediently, an African," "a nation is only the aggregate reflex of 'the man's a man,' the minutial agglomeration of a nation." It—"Lord Grey's pet tax"— is described to be an "oppressive, invidious and ill-managed impost, signifying thraldom and oppression, causing children to be sold or pawned." As regards the promises of the local Government, they are stated to be "false and deceptive as moonshine." The consequence, however, of the "dwarfish demon convention" was that the native towns of Christiansborg, Labaddi and Tesi were demolished by bombardment in 1854 ; that in 1855 Accra was threatened with the same fate, because she also would not pay; that in 1856 a commissioner, sent to inquire into the state of affairs, reported that although Kajjo (Cudjoe), King of Kinka, and his subject chiefs, were all loyally disposed towards our Government, they would not pay poll-tax, and that in 1857 a mob plundered the French factory at James Town.

However presumptuous may be the supposition, one is almost disposed to think that our Wilsons and Laings, so admirable in the algebra, have not mastered the elemental arithmetic, of tax-gathering. Mr. Wilson left his home, after enunciating in many a postprandial oration the farcical sentiment, that "what is good for England is good for the world." Mad as a hatter, he gave India an income-tax and a flood of paper money.

No subaltern in a native corps would have made such a blunder. Peace to his manes, for

> "To his natal shore,
> Enriched with knowledge, he returned no more,"

dying just in time to escape seeing the failure he had made.

The true art of taxation, allow me to say, is honestly to speak out what you want, and less to regard the theoretical excellence of the tax than the practice which the people have had in paying it. For taxation shows the genius of a nation quite as much as its ballads: what men have imposed upon themselves, they will prefer to the political economy of the stranger, however cunning. There are those who like indirect taxation, which to others seems the dealing of a vampire that sucks your blood whilst you sleep. In my humble opinion, the main, if not the only, injury which American Secession has done to the world, is that it has prevented the trial on a gigantic scale—in a highly civilised and commercial people—of direct, and the total abolition of all other, imposts. In the meantime the items must be sedulously studied and subjected to the local popular system. The Hindu, I have said before, will contribute half his income in the familiar forms of poll-tax, succession dues, "benevolences," and local imposts raised in the Pergunnahs. The African will pay fifty or perhaps cent. per cent. upon imports of arms and ammunition, salt and tobacco, whilst rum is his incense and his eucharist, without which the necessaries of worship cannot be supplied to him.

To conclude with police considerations. I will not insult the reader's understanding by treating upon the inapplicability of soldiers to police purposes under an English Government. Two companies of any West Indian regiment would be amply sufficient for the general military wants of a colony like this; besides which, the police corps might be armed, drilled, and trained to working the guns of the several forts. The present expense of the Gold Coast Artillery, including all charges, cannot be less than 20,000*l.* per annum. For this we have seventeen European officers and 300 men, who are worse than useless for protection duties. Being regularly enlisted soldiers, it is difficult to punish them, and the jealousy of rival departments has enabled them to show a bold front to the Colonial Secretary, who on this coast stands next in rank to the Governor. The officers who fail in securing civil appointments naturally prefer a sick certificate for England or Tenerife to living a wretched, starveling life at Cape Coast Castle or Accra; and though the warrant under which they obtain promotion requires them to serve three years on the Gold Coast, it is generally considered enough to have served for that period in the Gold Coast Corps.

The following distribution of, and estimate for, a police corps of 355 officers and men was drawn up by a friend whose judgment and experience justify my introducing it to the public.

The distribution would be as follows:—

Stations.	Head Constbls.	Constables.	Sub-constables.	Policemen.
1 Dixcove	1	1	3	30
2 Cape Coast Castle	1	2	6	90
3 Annamaboo	1	1	3	20
4 Winnebah	0	4	6	25
5 Accra, &c.	1	3	6	90
6 Addah	1	4	6	35
Total	5	15	30	290-300

A grand total of 355.*

At five of these stations—Cape Coast Castle does not require one—there would be commandants acting as magistrates and collectors of customs. Addah has been included, because it now equals Whydah in slave exportations. There are shiploads hid in the town, even within cannon-shot of our cruisers. It is a pity that this fine port is not taken up by some English company; it is the only point from which a future can be expected.

The annual estimate for the commandants and the police force would be as follows:—

	£	s.	d.
1 Chief Civil Commissioner, including table allowance	600	0	0
Ditto, ordinary travelling allowance	150	0	0
5 Commandants (each 350*l.* per annum)	1750	0	0
Ditto, ordinary travelling allowance (each 75*l.*)	375	0	0
5 Head Constables (each 30*l.* per annum)	150	0	0
15 Constables (each 18*l.*)	270	0	0
30 Sub-Constables (each 13*l.* 10*s.*)	405	0	0
300 Policemen (each 9*l.*)	2700	0	0
Clothing, at rate of three suits each man	1000	0	0
House rent	100	0	0
Total	£7500	0	0

* In these sickly climates there must always be supernumeraries: I allow, therefore, five extra officers and ten men.

For complete efficiency this police corps should be placed entirely under the civil power, which has ample jurisdiction to punish those offences—plundering the natives and living upon threats of accusation—which are now committed with all impunity on the outstations. The five commandants should transmit monthly estimates for the pay of their establishments to the Chief Civil Commissioner; the latter, after checking and signing them, would forward them to the Colonial Secretary, who, in his turn, would submit them to the Governor. This functionary should not, of course, be commander of the corps, as he is Commander-in-chief of the Coast, but he should be charged with drawing up a code of regulations for the force.

I am certain that by such happy changes order would soon grow out of confusion and misrule upon the Gold Coast.

* * * * * *

At Accra we left our Spaniard, who, suffering severely from sea-sickness, appeared nothing loth to quit us. He was a gentleman fond of his bed and also of his Madeiran wicker-work arm-chair. He read a little; but, when excited, which was rare, he would declaim loudly against the practice of "lecture" as worthless, touching the main enjoyments of human life—eating, drinking, visiting friends, and attending the theatre. According to him the *summum bonum* of human life was to lie upon his back smoking cigarettes and looking at the moon or at all the stars. He once, but only once, gathered energy to sermon me upon the subject of over-curiosity. I had remarked that the thermometer stood unusually high. "To me," quoth Don ———, "it is hot when I am hot; it is cold when my body feels cold. What do I want to know more?" Perhaps that Don was not so far wrong.

As the "Blackland" steamed along the coast we could see a long succession of open grassy savannahs backed by dark curtains of bush and forest, and many a tongue of land, forming by its gentle rise little valleys which would become swamps during the rains. About three to four miles beyond Tesi, on the eastern end of a little ledge, stands a small black boulder—Greenwich Rock: it transported us in thought far enough north of the Gold Coast. During the night we passed Cape St. Paul's, the western boundary of that ill-omened region the Bight of Benin. And whilst sleep sealed our eyes, the indefatigable ship—how superior is her continual diligence to the best of travelling even by railroad—was bearing us past the infamous regions of Little Popo, Great Popo, and Whydah.

CHAPTER X.

A DAY AT LAGOS,

WHERE
"In July you must die,
August go you must;
In September remember,
October it's all over."
Old Rhyme describing Rainy Season.

FORMERLY the great centres of the export slave trade from Africa were these three :—

1st. The Semiticised and often Moslem negroes, extending from the Gambia and Senegal, as far inland as Takrur or Sokotu. They were principally Mandengas, Jolofs, and that pseudo-punic tribe of Africa whom men have derived from the lost Cyrenaican Psylli or Psulloi, and called by a variety of names Peul, Púlá, Puloh, Fulá, Phúlá, Pulbe or Fulbe, Felatah and Felláni.* All these people drove the heathen negroes of the Sudam to the coast, although they did not sell or enslave their brother religionists.

* M. Koelle ("Polyglotta Africana") calls the language Pulo, and the people Pula, which is properly an adjective, "yellow," or "brown." Fulbe is the plural of Pulo; Fulání is the plural of the Hausa name Fuládsi, and Fulatah is Bornuese. The original home of this people is said to have been near Futa Toro, and in the eighteenth century they moved to Hausa, and built Sokotu.

2nd. The despotisms of Ashantee and Dahomey, Yoruba and Benin, large pagan states, which maintained standing armies well armed and disciplined, and used chiefly for the purpose of forays and slave commanders; all, except Dahomey, have fallen from their former power, and Dahomey will, by self-exhaustion, if not by a foreign blow, follow their example.

3rd, and last. The whole coast about the mouth of the Kongo River, one of the great African four, the others being the Nile, the Niger, and the Zambezi, and without any exception the most neglected. Known to the natives as the Zaire, its name is to be traced, I believe, in Claudius Claudianus,. himself an African, born at Alexandria, and who wrote about A.D. 400.

"*Gir*, ditissimus amnis
Æthiopium simili mentitus gurgite Nilum."
De Laudib. Stilich. lib. i. v. 252.

For dit- some read not- —" notissimus,"—but not so correctly; at any rate, it is far from being the superlative of " notus " now. The name again occurs in a Latin form.

" Domitorque ferarum
Guirræus, qui vasta colit sub rupibus antra,
Qui ramos ebeni, qui dentes vellit eburnos."
Idyl. iv. v. 20.

And be it further remarked that the Zaire still gives the best ebony—a tree which does not extend beyond 4° north latitude: thus rendering the common theory which identifies it with the Νίγειρ or Νίγιρ, untenable—that river notoriously wanting ebony. Pliny (Nat. Hist.

lib. v. 10) makes the Nile, after an underground march of twenty days, spring again from the source called Nigris, and form the limit between Africa and Ethiopia. He adds: "cui quoque etiamnum Giris, ut ante, nominatus per aliquot millia, et in totum Homero Ægyptus aliisque Triton." A modern writer identifies Giris or Gir, with Wed Mzi or Djidi of the Sahara, but nothing can be more unsatisfactory than his remarks.* The negroes on this part of the coast are savage and degraded, and, as in northern Guinea, are settled in small independent communities of 1000 to 5000 bodies. The first treaty between England and Portugal restricted our squadron to the north of the equator, and enabled the export trade, assisted by an admirable waterway, to recruit itself from the very heart of the continent.

These three great centres are now reduced to two, which, separated by a long interval, are incapable of mutual support. The first is the Bight of Benin, still

* I allude to the Rev. Mr. Tristram's "Great Sahara," appendix I., p. 262. Barbarously as eastern languages are treated, the exceeding cruelty of this gentleman's practice beats belief. Who could believe that Beni Yssou could mean Beni Isa, sons of Jesus ? When the Arab "looked sadly disconcerted" at his hearer's want of sympathy, and his assurance that *Inglez mafish hinné arrhua*—"that the English never would come here"—the expression of countenance must have been that of utter despair. What would even an English guide understand by "English there is none eer (for here) I go away ?" And so throughout the book, the names of animals: *e.g.*, Nemeur, for Nimr, a leopard; and el Guett' bá, for Katá, a sand-grouse ; and hundreds of other horrors are perpetually offending ears and eyes. Had not the reverend gentleman a spare hour for submitting his cacography to any one who has read Arabic for a few months !

appropriately termed the Slave Coast, and extending from the Cape of St. Paul's to the Nun outlet of the Niger, a coastal length of 350 miles. The root of the evil lies between Little Popo and Whydah, which are separated by not more than thirty miles. Public attention has been drawn to it, and it is now in a fair way of being extirpated. During the last year steps have been taken in the right direction, the bombardment of Porto Novo, and the annexation of Lagos with its old dependency, Badagry. The next year, I hope, will see the submission or the capture of Whydah and the two Popos.* The Kongo river still awaits modern exploration, and the difficulties thrown in the way are so great, that without assistance from Government it would be vain to attempt it.

The slave coast offers peculiar facilities for shipping cargoes. Low, marshy and malarious, it could hardly be held by foreign garrisons. The dreadful surf which beats upon the shore defends the barracoons from land

---

* At Great Popo there is an inlet which leads up the lagoon to Whydah direct. If it be proved—the point, however, is not yet settled—that there is a beach between the Victoria Lagoon of Lagos and the water that passes Whydah, this entrance, distant only ten hours from the great slave market, will be the best line of attack.

Whydah is perfectly protected from the sea by a strip of land half a mile broad, and it lies north of the lagoon, which is here four feet deep. It is within shot. The people show as Fetish a cannon-ball, fired by a British cruiser seventeen to eighteen years ago, and embedded in earth. Shipping must lie outside the sand-bank when the surf is very heavy. The town is described as poor and squalid, and the people suffer from intermittent fever.

attack, and can be safely braved in canoes only. The bush and jungle conceal the movements of those on land, and the succession of lagoons forming natural canals along the seaboard, enables the trader in human flesh and blood to ship his cargo where and when least expected. The French and English, Spaniards, Portuguese, and Brazilians established themselves there in old times, and by rich presents persuaded the "tyrant" of Dahomey to supply them with the fruits of his annual raids. In 1842, Captain Broadhead saw "thirteen vessels lying in the roads of Whydah at one time." Of late years the vigilance of the cruisers has tended materially to check the traffic, and nothing can now be done openly. Still shipments take place. But lately a large vessel, the "African," carrying 500 to 700 negroes, ran the gauntlet of the coast-guard, passing the African steam-ship "Armenian." Her captain politely raised his hat to his agent, M. Soarez, who, the late Lt. Hollingworth told me, was so delighted with the

* Her Majesty's Commissary Judge, Havana, writing in February, 1861 (Class A. "Correspondence with the British Commissioners"), estimates that the safety of one adventure amply repays the loss of ten empty, or five full ships. These are the figures :—

Cost of vessel and provisions	$25,000
Cost of 500 negroes at $50	25,000
Ten per cent. mortality	2,500
Wages and presents to master and crew	30,000
Expenses of landing 450 slaves, at $120 each	54,000
Total	$136,500

present prospect of 100,000*l*.,* the normal profit of a full cargo, that he offered to "stand champagne" to all on board.

The English and Dutch had formerly fortified factories, which still await our return to Whydah. Some years ago the French restored their establishment, and used it as a palm-oil store. They have missionaries there,* and according to our Frenchmen, the King of

Brought forward	$136,500
Add one year's interest, ten per cent.	$13,650
Total expenditure	$150,150
Sale of 450 slaves, at $1200 a head	$540,000
Profit on the adventure	$389,850

The loss of an empty slaver is estimated at $27,500 only, the cost of the ship, provisions, and interest thereon; the wages, &c., being contingent on success. If the negroes are on board, it would amount only to $55,000. These figures perfectly account for the continuance and persistency of the traffic.

* "Annales d'Afrique," Nos. XI. and XII., of November and December, 1861.—Lettre de M. François Borghero, supérieur de la Mission de Dahomey, à M. Planque, supérieur du Séminaire des Missions Africaines, à Lyon. "Whydah, 28th April, 1861.—We learn that the reverend fathers were well received by what they call the Jevoghan (Yavogar) of Whydah, and celebrated their first mass on the 21st inst., in the long-abandoned Portuguese Fort, before a hundred men." An old steeple with two bells, and ornamented statuettes in the sanctuary, showed that Fetishism had not quite won the day. The people of Whydah were estimated at 20,000, of whom 300 have been baptised; but they live in utter ignorance, ' Quomodo audient sine predicante?' The snake-worship is well described, and it will be remarked that whilst the men of Whydah worship, those of France curse 'l'abominable animal.' May not the poor serpent, when he speaks, exclaim with Friday—

'Je n'ai mérité
Ni cet excès d'hommage ni cette indignité.'

Dahomey had sent two of his "sons " * for education to Marseilles.

About midday on Saturday, the 21st of September, we were off Porto Novo, sixty miles distant from Lagos, and separated from the sea by the lagoon and sandbank. This town and the little province around are called " Ajáshi: " properly speaking " Newport" is the name of a factory, barracoon, and village built upon the shore by the celebrated, or rather the notorious successor of Da Souza, who died in 1849, the Brazilian, Domingo José Martinez, who used to receive at times from the King of Dahomey a present of 600 negroes, a bakshish worth a " plum." The town itself was founded on the south-east frontier of Dahomey, by Huenbomu, a younger brother of Takudumu, the first recognised Dahomian King, and the

---

At Great Popo, we are told, the boa, like the Irish pig, is allowed to eat small children. Poison is said to be profusely used. Of the "roi Badou"—*i.e.*, Badohong, the present king—a great truth is told, "Quand nous lui demanderons de permettre à ses sujets d'embrasser le Christianisme, nous aurons autour lui les féticheurs, *devant lesquels le roi lui-même doit se courber.*" The King of Dahomey has no more power to prevent human sacrifice than the Prince of Wales has to forbid morning service on Sunday. These customs are admirably described by the superior as "usages consacrés par des siècles, fondés sur des croyances réligieuses, et soutenus par un puissante hiérarchie— d'imposteurs." On the other hand, the number of victims is ridiculously estimated to be 3000, from which at least one 0 ought to be struck off.

* The King's sons, in African parlance, probably means some of his slavelings. In Europe they will doubtless become "African princes" by the blessings of the black skin. The "princess" is also an institution on this coast : two friends of mine have married princesses.

capturer of Abomey, who loved the senior as little as such junior usually does. It is distinctly despotic, orderly, and subordinate, even when surrounded by the turbulent semi-republics of Lagos, Badagry, and others. The people prostrate themselves in the streets when the messenger, bearing the king's cane, passes. The land is of fine soil, rich, loamy, and well filled for agriculture, and the natives are fond of fishing and trade. The population is estimated at 12,000 to 20,000. It was attacked by Abeokuta in 1839; and in 1840 the Eglas again assaulted Adu, a Popo town, tributary to Porto Novo, and lying on the road between the two capitals. Hence the old enmity between Dahomey and Abeokuta, which ten years afterwards resulted in the destruction of Ishagga, and in the crucifixion of the S'a Leone missionary Doherty.

The coast about Porto Novo showed a strip of land, backed by a thick bush. A single house or barracoon, with a flag flying, against the higher lands, marks the situation; and the town, which is some distance from the beach, is denoted by a grove of tall trees, appearing through an opening in the foreground.

It is said that Great Britain is never without her little war; as far as West Africa is concerned, this dictum is certainly true. And why not? She can no more expect to be at peace with her thousand neighbours, than a man of 50,000*l.* per annum in landed property, to be without a dispute or lawsuit. These little wars cost less than Aldershotts, and are ten times better schools for soldiering; the military nations of Europe, France and Russia, always keep up their tilting-lists, Africa and the Caucasus. These considerations arise from the view of a place where lately was fought the battle of Porto Novo. It happened after this wise: —

The late lamented Mr. Foote, Her Majesty's consul at Lagos, in February, 1861, visited, in H.M.'s S. tender "Brune," Lieutenant Stokes, R.N., commanding, the town of Porto Novo, where oil belonging to British subjects had been seized. The object of the consul was to add a few more stringent clauses to the already-existing treaty of 1852; but the King "Soji," backed, it is supposed, by Dahomey, behaved with great insolence, refusing to come on board or to treat upon the subject of slavery, which ten years before he had stipulated to abolish. After some *va-et-vient*, "Brune" fired a shot, first over, then into, the town. The people replying with energy, the crew of Krumen sensibly betook themselves to the coal-bunks and behind the paddle-boxes, whence they were with difficulty removed by their energetic commander Lieutenant Stokes. The gun-boat found it necessary to retire upon Badagry. The Porto Novians, after African fashion, danced, drank, sang out their "strong names," and swore that if she ever appeared again, they would convert her into a war-canoe for their king. The European population of Lagos, mostly veteran slave-traders, condemned by hard times to such grovelling work as selling palm-oil, exulted over our retreat, and fondly hoped to see the operation repeated.

From Badagry, Mr. Consul Foote, who could obtain no concessions from the king, applied for assistance to a "big brother," and this time things were better arranged. On the 26th April, Commodore Edmonstone, of H.M.S. "Arrogant," then commanding the West African squadron, accompanied by Mr. Foote in the "Brune," and followed by the hired steamer "Fideliter"—the "Bloodhound," drawing too much water, found herself aground—proceeded with two divisions, of five boats each, armed with howitzers and rockets, up the Ossa River, or Victoria Lagoon, whose mouth is nearly opposite Lagos! Above Badagry they were stopped by a barrier composed of two rows of stakes and floating green islets between—showing that the Porto Novians had not been idle. The work of six weeks, however, was demolished by the "Fideliter" and the boats in two hours and a half, and the fragments threatened to injure the navigation of the lagoon. Then appeared the vaunted Isso canoes, and their fighting owners, who, according to the croakers of Lagos, were to eat up the Englishmen for breakfast. Each long, narrow, and shallow barque carries two fellows, one paddling or poling with a spear, the other occupied with a bunch of shillelaghs and javelins, that are placed at his feet. They hurl the club, and when the adversary "ducks" his head, he is then transfixed with the assagai. The Isso are a tribe subject to Dahomey, and are located to the west of Porto Novo. They acted as a contingent against Badagry in 1851—1854. They are a fierce and lawless brood, originally, it is said, fugitives from Dahomey, and joined by kindred ruffians, the kidnappers and pirates of the coast. Their villages, which are mostly on the sea-side of the Lagoon, are described as embryo Venices, huts of bamboo and grass thatch, perched upon poles four to five feet above the level of the tide, and forming a boat-house below. They are remarkable for nothing but their teeth, blackened with snuff. They act as fishermen in peaceful times, and, like the Arabs of maritime Oman, they plunder when they can. A few rockets easily dispersed these braves, who preferred paddling into the rushy shore to standing up in the open.

At 7 A.M. on the next day the flotilla reached Porto Novo, which had never seen such an armada before. After a hot, but harmless, shower of balls, which all dropped short, both divisions replied with shot, shell, and rocket, doing awful damage. The Porto Novians, especially the Moslems, were no cowards; there were men in white turbans—here called " white-cap chiefs "— but I believe no Russians amongst them; they fought only too well, willing to be slain in the vain hope of killing some whites. The brave Isso retired beyond gunshot, and philosophically contemplated the disasters of their friends. After an hour or so, the town and the king's palace were on fire, the flames rising high. Captain Raby, V.C., of H.M.S. "Alecto," and commanding one of the boat divisions, landed in his gig, with two men, and spiking a gun, caused it to explode, singeing his face. It is curious how often experienced men will try this green trick: when you nail up a gun, please do not place your nose within a few inches of the touch-hole. The Commodore then sent, under command of Captain M'Arthur, of the Marines, and A. T. Jones, of the "2nd West"— a promising young officer, now, unhappily, deceased— some fifty blue-jackets and small-arms men, to fire the well-built houses which were still standing. This proceeding, on his part, won for Captain Edmonstone the lasting resentment of certain Europeans at Lagos, who deferred a proposed picnic, because they wanted no such smashing guest.

After this harmless little brush, the heroes, fasting, re-embarked at 11.30 A.M., to became heroes full. Dinner being over, at the German hour of 1 P.M., and fresh ammunition having been served out to all hands, Captain Raby's division formed in line within twenty yards and abreast of a point where the natives had made an ambuscade. These negro strategists expected us to land, another verdant trick, often tried by Englishmen, even where guns can be brought to bear. An action which begins with artillery, which proceeds with infantry charges, and which ends with a rush of cavalry, has never been unsuccessful in India. Victory under such circumstances being inevitable, we can hardly wonder that the plan has not been universally adopted, common sense being uncommon. Finding themselves discovered, the natives, who were in force, kept up a brisk fire from the reeds and rushes. They were soon mowed down by a *feu d'enfer* of grape and musketry, case and canister, rockets and howitzer-shells, and many fugitives were killed whilst retreating. Captains Raby, M'Arthur, and Jones then landed, spiked another gun, carried off a white flag; and the West Indian shot with his revolver the only man killed in the hand-to-hand fight. The firing afterwards became desultory, and when the place was destroyed,—even the metal heads of the king's canes were melted,—the flotilla disappeared, and the men rejoined their ships outside Lagos bar. Thus ended the battle of Porto Novo, in which we lost but one seaman, of the "Alecto," killed by a shot through the brain, and had five or six others slightly wounded. The number of the enemy was estimated at 10,000 well-armed soldiery, and their casualties, which were ridiculously exaggerated, were doubtless numerous: an officer present in the action old me that he had counted twenty bodies lying within a few yards. It was rumoured that a white man was found amongst the slain, and that another had been seen directing the operations of the enemy. Perhaps these might have been Brazilian mulattos, whom the King of Dahomey—it will be observed, that this great bugbear never killed a white man, nor did his father—occasionally orders to his capital rolled up like cigars, or, if recalcitrant, walking barefooted. But there is no folly which excited eyes will not see, and cause others to see, and of late years it has been the fashion to report the presence of hostile white men from China to Morocco. On the 13th June the king reluctantly signed the treaty permitting to all Porto Novians free trade with the

British. The town people were, as usual, middlemen between the merchant and the producer, consequently they are ever opposed to extension of traffic. Old Soji's palace had suffered the most, and all his property was lost. His people confessed to having had a bellyful,—the African, unlike the Asiatic, will own to a "thrashing,"—although he says, with some truth, that the English cannot fight on shore, and promised to be for the future a good boy.' Mr. M'Coskry, Acting-Governor of Lagos, kindly promised to procure for him new sticks. The destruction of this noted slave depôt has already borne fruit. Other towns—for instance, Adu—wavering between Dahomey and Lagos—they are all nests of slavery—now request permission to "come in," and treaties are being prepared for them. Thus, by degrees, the black Spartans of "Dah's Belly" will be shut out from the sea,—the greatest calamity that can befal an African power,—and will be broken up by foreign attack, or will abandon their annual breaches of the peace. Finally, the gallant members of the little expedition had the high honour of being grossly abused by a portion of the Manchester press, from which officers and gentlemen have nought to fear save praise.

Mr. Consul Foote died before he heard of this "crowning mercy." A most energetic and useful officer, he had seen long and hard service in the tropics, India, China, the Mosquito Coast, Greytown; and Salvador. After passing—

" Per varios casus, par tot discrimina rerum,"—

he was appointed to the Slave Coast in September, 1860, on the death of Mr. Consul Brand. Lagos seems to claim a good man and true every year. Like many others that have passed safely through pestilential lands, he imagined himself fever-proof. He who wants to live, so far from waxing careless, will gain at every step increased respect for the sun, the dews, and the night breeze. Mr. Foote entered without delay upon a course of bodily and mental work, most trying to new comers in these regions. The "Brune" grounding in the lagoon above Lagos, he set out, though unwell, in an open canoe to reach his post in time for writing by mail, exposed himself to the night air and the rain, and sank under a complication of fever and dysentery on the 17th May, 1861.

Mr. Foote was presently followed by Captain Jones, of whom more at a future time.

Along the straight dull coast we steamed eighteen miles, from Porto Novo to Badagry. By lagoon it is reckoned forty, and may be done in six to eight hours. Travellers usually avoid the sun by starting at night, and thus lose the beautiful scenery of the Ossa River, or Victoria Lagoon. This breakwater is one of the many that extend from the Volta, the westerly end of the Bight of Benin, to the Bonny River, in the Bight of Biafra. They form a huge reservoir, into which the streams from the upper country discharge themselves, and during the rains they burst through the sand embankments, which at other seasons defend them from the Atlantic. As a rule, they are river-like streams, rather brackish, and therefore garnished with mangroves. In places there are depressions in the land, causing widenings of the bed, with larger lakes; such are, beginning from the west, the Avon waters, the Denham waters,* and the Ikoradu, so called from a mart north of Lagos, and by us corrupted into Cradoo. I reserve a more particular description of these lagoon streams till we find ourselves upon one of them.

There is no landmark to show the position of Badagry save the mound which appears as a pyramidal clump of bushy trees. There were but three canoes and three merchant ships lying off this once lively, now dull and deserted place, where the landing is detestable and where the surf never seems to rest. It was founded by refugee Popos in 1727, when the King of Dahomey had conquered Whydah. It is therefore not directly mentioned by Bosman, who also ignores Dahomey,† whilst he dwells at length upon Fida, our Whydah, and upon Ardra, which Mr. Lamb calls Ardah. It was the landing-

---

* Captain Denham, who gave his name to one lagoon, in chart xv. places on it " City of Styche," probably a mistake, or a misprint for Stakes (fishing).

† In Letter twenty, however, Bosman speaks of a "potent kingdom farther inland," which uses certain customs of war well-known in Abyssinia, and "strikes such a terror into all the circumjacent negroes, that they can scarcely hear it mentioned without trembling; and they tell a thousand strange things of them." This must be Dahomey, whose king Takudumu, Chief of Fohi, captured the present capital about A.D. 1700. The intercourse between the Dahomians and Europeans is supposed to have begun in 1724.

place of the two Landers, who, in 1830, made their celebrated discovery of the Niger's true mouth. The picturesque narrative of what reception they met there, of King Adooly, of the tetrarchy of Mr. Hutton of Cape Coast Castle, and of the terrible Fetish tree, which caused the traveller to fall senseless into the arms of "Jowdie, his faithful slave," are fresh in the memory of this generation. Presently Badagry became so unsafe for Europeans, and kidnapping in the sandy streets,—when the victim was noiselessly seized, gagged, or garotted, and carried off to the canoe,—became so common, that in 1843 Mr. President Maclean and Commodore Foote thought right to hoist the British flag for the protection of the English. About that time Badagry became a large missionary establishment; and in 1861 it underwent the fate of Lagos at the hands of

The web-footed lion that swims ev'ry sea.

* * * * *

Evening placed us in the roads of Lagos. A mild evening: the wind was hushed, and the heat oppressive. It is said to average 10° Fah. hotter at this place than in Lagos town. Against the purple-black surface of the eastern sky the bar was smoking forth a white vapour, as if afraid to break, and we could hear from afar the muffled roar of the sullen surf. We and our fellow-sufferers, six or seven merchantmen, lay broadside on, with a monotonous ceaseless roll, which seems to drive comfort out of a ship. Many must pass months in this most unpleasant swing-swong till they have taken in cargo. We are lying in the French roads,* four miles eastward of the entrance or English roads. As night was near, not a canoe would put off from the shore. I spent my *soirée* in the study of bars.

The bar is a notable formation in Western, as in Eastern Africa. It seems placed by Nature—one of her many contrivances—to favour the pristine barbarity of the people. Many rivers are provided with one, the chief exceptions being the Gambia, the Rokel, the Cacheo, the Rio Grande, and the Kongo. A majestic stream like the latter will not tolerate such puny obstacles; others, on the other hand, like all the rivers between the Brass and the New Calabar branches of the Niger, are rendered useless by them. In riverless places, like Cape Coast Castle and Accra, the surf is sometimes dreadful as the upright walls of water on the Cornish coast, but it will not pile up a bar.

The favourite seat of a bar is at the mouth of a river or an outfall which is liable to be much swollen by the rains. From the inland comes a mass of matter mechanically suspended, and sometimes floating islets, which will trip vessels from their anchors; when the emission meets the tide, deposition takes place, and goes on increasing. Some bars are therefore of mud; others, where the sea has greater power, are sand hard as stone. The heaviness of the ocean swell is attributed by certain writers to distant storms; others, especially Captain Fish-

---

* These names are now obsolete on the coast.

bourne, to a "want of hydrostatic equilibrium." As the sun shifts its place, the rarefaction of the atmosphere produces an ascending and relieving movement, inducing "a wave from the point of greatest to that of least pressure." This hypothesis is favoured by the general belief in the exceptional warmth of the air about Lagos roadstead, but it is hardly borne out by the generality of the coast. The seas at S'a Leone are worst between December and April; in the Bights of Benin and Biafra, from April or May to October or November; and in Ascension from February till June; at the latter place the rollers cease in September, and in December they come from the north.

Lagos bar—or rather bars, for, as usual, there are two, an outer and an inner, the latter of which is little feared—is the best study on this part of the coast, with the exception, perhaps, of Benin. It is the bugbear of the Bights, and really dangerous. The average deaths, not including whites, are fourteen per annum; in 1858 there were forty-five casualties. This year nine were drowned in three months; amongst them, an Englishwoman, the wife of a merchant-captain, who preferred risking his life to paying a few dollars by steamer. Escapes are rare, and yet the Acting-Governor has been capsized in it three times. The principal danger to a strong swimmer is the shark. It is not every squalus nor every tiger that will attack a man. I have seen a sailor picked up unhurt from amongst a school of them in Suez harbour. This plague is not—others say rarely

—found in the waters off Badagry and Porto Novo. But in places like the sacred Dwarka in Western India, where dead Hindu pilgrims are cast into the bay, and at Lagos, where the corpses of slaves are allowed to float down the river, the shark never hesitates to seize a live man. The crocodile and alligator are to be beaten off by gouging or "purring," as the Lancashire inventors of a practice, supposed to be purely Transatlantic, call the operation. The shark, here at least, is far more terrible; even when he wriggles himself up to the beach sand, apparently for the purpose of scratching off parasites, all the people run away from the glare of his dull, ferocious, pale-blue eye, whilst the beast, as if conscious of power, never thinks of retiring till the desideratum has been leisurely completed. Few men survive a shark bite, and when seized, they usually lose their hands by snatching mechanically at the limb first hurt. I spare the reader some horrid cases which have come under my immediate notice. There is a small blue shark, which, when young, is eaten by the people. They do not, however, like the Arabs of Sur and Maskat, relish a tough old patriarch, whose taste is something between bull beef and tunny. To end with the shark, this evil might be diminished by spearing and poisoning the animals, and especially by rendering it penal to throw a corpse—night is the favourite time—into the Ossa. And the little "Advance" has already, it is said, done much towards frightening them from their haunts.

Lagos is the largest permanent break in the long line

of coast between the Volta and the Benin Rivers, and the greater part of the waters collected during the rains find their way in a tumultuous current through the sand-spit that parts the lagoon from the Atlantic. The safest months are December, January, and February, when at times it is smooth as glass. The most dangerous are those of the rainy season—it begins to be bad in March, and it wages war from May to October. The epochs of the vernal and autumnal equinoxes according to some, the days when the mail arrives according to others, are the worst; some declare that the new moon, others that the moon at her full and change, exasperates the bar. One may always expect bad bars during the violent rains in June, July, and August, when the struggle between the inner inundation and the outer surf is tremendous, closing ingress and egress sometimes, though rarely, for a fortnight. High tide is the safest time for attempting passage; then half-tide; and the worst of all is low water. "The African Pilot"* reckons the rise of the tide five to six feet at the full and change on the bar, and says that within the river one foot must be allowed in the dry and three in the rainy season. The people of Lagos assert that three to four feet is nearer the truth, and that there is little difference between the inside and the outside of the bar. The capricious and treacherous rollers will curl in five fathoms and break in three, and even four fathoms, on

* P. 175.

the radius of a mile from the middle of the entrance. The height of the wave may be fifteen feet when the surf is bad, and it breaks when perhaps you least expect it. The shifting sand of the bar is ever changing place and dimensions. On the 26th July H.M.S. "Prometheus" found but eleven feet under her bow off the eastern spit, where she had most unadvisedly been run: to-day we hear that there are eighteen feet, and that the spit has been nearly washed away; and this time next year there will be a hollow, bounded by a dwarf sandbank upon the place where the good old ship was reported to have broken her back. For the same reason the breadth of the entrance is ever varying; the "African Directory (1855)" gives it from 500 to 600 yards; the "African Pilot (1856)," half a mile from point to point. When I first saw it the width was not more than half a mile, but soon afterwards it greatly increased. The length is calculated to be 300 yards. The outer or sea bar is separated from the inner by a distance of six cables; both are of the hardest sand.

Across this pleasant formation there are three high ways:—the canoe passage, which hugs Le Greslie or the eastern point; it is very dangerous, but sometimes practicable when the other entrances are not. The perils of the Calemars or Raz de Marée, however, are greatly increased by the strong easterly current, which often carries small craft down the dangerous and inhospitable coast. The boat or central passage comes next: many accidents have happened from the use of gigs manned by Krumen, who drop their oars and are ready to spring on board the moment there is a chance of swamping. Why the Masoolah surf-boats used at Madras are not introduced here I puzzle my brains to conceive. Large ships lay at Beecroft or the western point abreast, and then turning to the north-north-east, make for the entrance. The landmarks, however, of course change with the bar every year, and without a pilot no one but a madman or those interested in barratry would attempt to run in. Usually the entrances are two, the ship or western, and the canoe or eastern passage.

No one seems to visit Lagos for the first time without planning a breakwater. About three years ago an American company proposed to make floating breakwaters, upon the condition of receiving the harbour dues for twenty years; Jonathan, however, was refused. But as from Ningo on the Gold Coast to Camaroons, there is hardly a pebble upon the loose sands, and no stone for many miles inland, the construction will probably keep till the wealth of the place enables it to afford a floating work. It is dangerous to meddle with such formations. About 1856, a little iron steamer from Benin sank whilst attempting to raise the guns which had been thrown overboard by Her Majesty's steam-sloop "Hecate;" and the bar, it is said, became worse in consequence. Walling the sides, especially the eastern, with a small "stone fleet," might be tried, but the measure would probably do no good; the outpour, strengthened by narrowing the mouth, would soon cut a new channel. The experiment, tried at Charleston, is said to have improved the passages there: here there are other forces at work. Some have tried landing upon other parts of the coast, but they have generally fared worse from the heavy breakers on the shore; consequently, the bar has become a necessary calamity. The merchants of Lagos were much pleased when they heard that a harbour-master had been appointed, expecting to see buoys laid down; at the end of the year, however, they had to congratulate themselves only upon a perch stuck in the sands of Beecroft Point. Loath, however, to break through a time-honoured custom, I venture to propose a system of "camels," by which the violence of the breakers would be greatly broken. We turned in early, hoping that the morrow would not prove a rainy day.

Betimes on Sunday morning we were visited by the "Advance," an iron steamer owned by Mr. McCoskry, now acting as Governor. Built as a tug for the Clyde, her tonnage is 120 tons, she draws six feet, with horse power variously estimated at 80 to 100, and her cost was 6000*l*. The mails no longer require to be headed up, an operation which recalls to mind the now classical English pipe-office. She is nearly lost about once a year, and the engineers cannot be kept alive even by drink. Still she makes shift to ply for papers and cargo whilst other vessels cannot. The tender "Brune" lost her funnel shortly after our departure; the "Handy" is pronounced unhandy to cross the bar; and the "Investigator" does not appear to relish the process of investigating. Besides which, the former is a "screw," and when these craft show their stern keels to the sky, the violent jerk almost always injures the gear. So the stout "Advance" is really in advance of Admiralty ships, and is a great boon to those who visit Lagos.

After breakfast the consul and I prepared to land by the ship passage. The "Advance" steamed steadily on, under the hands of two helmsmen; the wheel is on the bridge, the favourite station for travellers who do not like the look of the sea from the quarter deck. After getting the direction and breasting the smooth waters outside, we prepared for the run in. This time the much-dreaded bar disappointed me; on certain subsequent occasions it did not. The rapids of the St. Lawrence must be grand enough in an Indian "birch," which shows the wonderful ridge of waters cylindrically piled up in the centre of the stream. Nothing can be tamer when looked down upon from the first floor of a large floating-house river-steamer. I can imagine their emotion—men with a triple coat of brass round their præcordia—who first attempted this bar in the dingy of a caravel or in a wretched cutter. Indeed, even from the vantage ground of the bridge, where we stood high raised to see and sketch, we looked up as it were at the light-green foam-fringed waves swelling, rising, and towering like a concave wall about to tumble in and poop us, whilst the send of the break drove us forward as if lifted in strong men's arms, and required all the force of the helmsmen to prevent, as the seas combed under the quarter, the little steamer broaching broadside on—the great danger when crossing a bar. The background to this fierce ocean was a black and lowering surface of younger breakers, the nearer rushing like the waters above Niagara to the fray, and the more distant subsiding into the surface .of a horizon where the slaty heavens mingled with the leaden-coloured sea.

After shuddering and staggering over the first bar, which is about 900 feet long, and enduring the normal break of three—which may be thirty—seas, the brave little "Advance" fell into deep water, four fathoms or so, and I did not condescend to sketch the second or inner, which outlies the entrance. And now the settlement, before veiled by smokes, as fogs in these regions are called, began to appear. Upon Le Greslie, or Eastern Point, a low sandy formation, capped with stunted bush and bearing a few palms, stood a few out factories, looking very like negro barracoons. Twenty years ago boats floated over this Clifton of the Slave Coast. A flag was hoisted to inform the town that the bar was practicable. Two tide gauges had been set up, one at Le Greslie Point, the other inside the river, opposite the house of a M. Carrena, that the maximum rise might be indicated by signal. As we passed Beecroft Point, where curlews and plovers rose screaming wildly, and passed alongside of the shrimp stakes, the town came up to full view. It was a striking illustration of the difference between the pro-pyroskaphian and the epipyroskaphian settlement; no fort, no gothic hall, no big house, nothing but the plain bungalow built for an inn, not for a house. Here, as at Zanzibar, flagging appeared to be the custom; every factory flies a bit of bunting, and some fly two.

The site of the town, four miles from the entrance, is detestable; unfortunately, there is no better within many a league. It occupies the western side of an islet about three miles and a half long from north-east to south-west, by one broad from north to south; it is formed by two offsets from the Ikoradu (Cradoo) coast, namely, the Ossa River, opposite, and Five Cowrie Creek behind the settlement.

The first aspect is as if a hole had been hollowed out in the original mangrove forest that skirts the waters, where bush and dense jungle, garnished with many a spreading tree, tall palms, and matted mass of fetid verdure rise in terrible profusion around. The soil is sandy, and in parts there are depressions which the rains convert into black and muddy ponds; the ground, however, is somewhat higher in the interior, where the race-course lies. The gap of the Ossa or Badagry Lagoon, is nearly opposite the town; and on the other side there is low, swampy ground, a clay formation, which retains the water, and which adds something more to the evils of the place. The thin line of European buildings that occupy the best sites, fronting the water, are, first, the French *comptoir*, prettily surrounded with gardens; then a large pretentious building, white and light yellow, lately raised by M. Carrena, a Sardinian merchant—it is said to be already decaying; then the Wesleyan Mission-house; the Hamburghers' factory; the Wesleyan chapel, with about five times its fair amount of ground; the British Consulate, like that at Fernando Po, a corrugated iron coffin or plank-lined morgue, containing a dead consul once a year; the Church Mission-house, whose overgrown compound caused such pretty squabbles in days gone by, and which, between whiles, served as a church; another Sardinian factory; a tall whitewashed and slated house, built by Mr. McCoskry; and at the furthest end, another establishment of Hamburghers, who at present have more than their share of the local commerce: these are the only salient points of the scene. They are interspersed with tenements of less pretensions, "*suam quisque domum spatio circumdat*," a custom derived by the Anglo-Indians through the England and the Germany of Tacitus's day; and the thin line is backed by a large native town, imperceptible from the sea, and mainly fronting the Ikoradu Lake. Some of the houses extend their grounds to the back, and the cumbered sands are alive with impurities; the Acting Governor, however, has wisely determined to have one decent walk. He persevered in clearing a broad line along the water, fitted for riding or driving, despite the insolent opposition of sundry liberated or rather licensed Africans. One fellow who calls himself Captain, upon the strength of having bought a condemned hull, has gone so far as to drive away the workmen : he has been threatened with a special constable, in the shape of a fighting doctor, and as usual with these people, who have got to produce their John Hampden, he subsided. The only ships inside the bar are H.M.S. "Prometheus,"— *Prometheus Vinctus* now—the tender, " Brune," and a small Hanoverian steamer. The two former are required to defend the new occupants, and the town is in a considerable state of excitement.

For Lagos was born in the British family, the youngest member of her colonies, on the 6th day of August, A.D. 1861. Commander Bedingfeld, R.N., after a hard bumping on the bar off the east spit, had by high direction entered into a palaver with Docemo, King of Lagos, and after " jamming heads"—excuse the phrase, but the " Captain," as the earnest and Rev. M. Monk* insists upon calling him *usque ad nauseam*, piques himself exceedingly upon a very moderate knowledge of the coast—informed him that permanent occupation (a nicer word than annexation) was determined upon, and that he, Docemo, was to be pensioned, and become one of the many kings lately "retired from business." That barbarous person, curious to say, was not delighted by the intelligence. In fact, he made some difficulties. He proposed to meet Her Majesty's consul, " the Captain," and all the British merchants at Palma, a French station some thirty miles east of Lagos, where

* See prolegomena to Dr. Livingstone's letters, and ask " the Captain " what he thinks of them.

he probably intended to give them something more than a bit of his mind. They politely declined a trip so far out of the range of the Promethean fire. The caboceers and chiefs also demurred, and foreseeing an embargo upon their bribes and presents, waxed surly. At the bottom of the discontent were the liberated Africans,—

"Sharp rogues all, both great and small,"—

as the Cape Coast Castle song hath it. The worst by far were the S'a Leonites; they were in debt to the natives, and debt under English is a very different thing from debt under native rule. Besides which, all of them had slaves, and most of them, when occasion served, were slave-dealers. Mr. Consul Foote, shortly after his arrival, had summoned before him some of these pets of philanthropy. When the nice point of domestic slavery was mooted, and they were asked touching their nationality, the popular answer declared King Docemo of Lagos and the Alake of Abeokuta to be their sovereigns. They at once began to make mischief at another of our pets, Abeokuta—how can learned Professor Kingsley in "Westward Ho!" call it "Christian Abeokuta," when it numbers barely one "professor" to 500 heathen? They hinted, not obscurely, that wherever an Englishman plants his foot—the people of Scinde said the same when they pelted off Sir Alexander Burnes—he makes the land his own. Abeokuta took the hint with all the readiness of the suspicious African. Distant but sixty miles from the sea, she once wanted a road; presently she became curiously incurious about any communication more direct than the winding but defensible river; and she ended next year by violently expelling a British vice-consul, threatening if he followed the example of "Monsieur Qui-se-Leve," that they would "burn the house about his ears," or its African equivalent.

So matters ran till the 5th of August, when a flag-staff was slipped and rigged near the British consulate, and Commander Bedingfield landed with his marines. A crowd of people and some chiefs were assembled at the palaver-house. The king, when civilly asked to sign away his kingdom, consented and refused, as the negro will, in the same breath. On the next day he affixed his mark, for of course he cannot write; and there is no African king who will not, in full view of a gallon of rum, "put his name for book," no matter what that book may be, provided that he ignores its contents. In so doing he of course concludes that a bit of paper so easily cut through with a pair of scissors can have no binding force, and a few hours afterwards he will tell you that he can tear it to pieces. Without awaiting, however, the ceremony of signature, possession, nine-tenths of the law, was at once entered upon. The "Captain" read out an English proclamation, very intelligible to the natives, confirming "the cession of Lagos and its dependencies"—a pleasantly vague frontier. Then followed a touching scene. One Union Jack was hoisted in the town, another on the beach. 'Prometheus Vinctus" saluted with twenty-one guns.

The marines presented arms, three hundred fetish, or sanctified boys, as the convert people call them, sang a hymn, headed by their missionaries. It was not

"Dies iræ, dies illa, &c."

And as we Englishmen must celebrate every event with a dinner—I believe that if London were to follow Lisbon's suit, Londoners would dine together amongst the ruins of "Willis's" or the "Tavern"—forty-four Oyibos, Europeans, and Africo-Europeans, officials and merchants, sat down to meat upon the quarter-deck of the "Prometheus," and by their brilliant speeches and loyal toasts added, as the phrase is, *éclat* to the great event. Thus Lagos—rose.*

---

* The following is the official announcement of

THE CESSION OF LAGOS.

"Foreign-Office, Sept. 19.

"Earl Russell, Her Majesty's Principal Secretary of State for Foreign Affairs, has received a despatch from Mr. McCoskry, the Acting British Consul at Lagos, dated the 7th of August, enclosing a treaty concluded by him and Commander Bedingfeld, R.N., commanding Her Majesty's sloop 'Prometheus,' with Docemo, King of Lagos, for the cession of the isle and port of Lagos to Her Majesty. The treaty is as follows:—

"'Treaty between Norman H. Bedingfeld, Commander of Her Majesty's sloop "Prometheus," and senior officer of the Bights Division, and William McCoskry, Esq., Her Britannic Majesty's Acting Consul, on the part of Her Majesty the Queen of Great Britain, and Docemo, King of Lagos, on the part of himself and chiefs.

"'ARTICLE I.

"'In order that the Queen of England may be the better enabled to assist, defend, and protect the inhabitants of Lagos, and to put an end to the slave-trade in this and the neighbouring countries, and to prevent the destructive wars so frequently undertaken by Dahomey and

King Docemo was persuaded, on the next day, by a guard of marines, who grounded arms with a most ominous rattling in his presence, to be duly mediatised. He was also assured of a pension amounting to something less than 2000*l.* per annum. This sum is

others for the capture of slaves, I, Docemo, do, with the consent and advice of my council, give, transfer, and by these presents grant and confirm, unto the Queen of Great Britain, her heirs and successors, for ever, the port and island of Lagos, with all the rights, profits, territories, and appurtenances whatsoever thereunto belonging, and as well the profits and revenue, as the direct, full, and absolute dominion and sovereignty of the said port, island, and premises, with all the royalties thereof, freely, fully, entirely, and absolutely. I do also covenant and grant that the quiet and peaceable possession thereof shall, with all possible speed, be freely and effectually delivered to the Queen of Great Britain, or such person as Her Majesty shall thereunto appoint, for her use in the performance of this grant; the inhabitants of the said island and territories, as the Queen's subjects, and under her sovereignty, crown, jurisdiction, and government, being still suffered to live there.

"'ARTICLE II.

"'Docemo will be allowed the use of the title of king, in its usual African signification, and will be permitted to decide disputes between natives of Lagos, with their consent, subject to appeal to British laws.

"'ARTICLE III.

"'In the transfer of lands the stamp of Docemo affixed to the document will be proof that there are no other native claims upon it; and for this purpose he will be permitted to use it as hitherto.

"'In consideration of the cession, as before mentioned, of the port and island and territories of Lagos, the representatives of the Queen of Great Britain do promise, subject to the approval of Her Majesty, that Docemo shall receive an annual pension from the Queen of Great Britain equal to the net revenue hitherto annually received by him: such pension to be paid at such periods and in such mode as may hereafter be determined.

[Here follow the signatures.]

"'Lagos, Aug. 6.'"

equivalent to his annual revenue, but it is subject to revision. He ungratefully forwarded, *on dit*, an expostulation to Europe; so did his chiefs. On the other hand, the merchants of all nations were highly pleased with the result. Thirteen of them, foreigners as well as Britishers, signed a petition praying the "Prometheus" to remain inside the bar, for the protection of English life and property. She was nothing loath: her copper had been scraped off, her deck had an interesting but suspicious convexity about the middle region, and the divers brought up some tubes nearly sixteen inches long, with which the *Teredo navalis* had lined his dwelling-place. She was subsequently reported not seaworthy; an obstinate man, Mr. Master Scudamore, thought otherwise, and she reached home safely, where she will die of a respectable old age. The "Captain" took a lively interest in the baby colony, and perhaps cherished an idea that his various merits might promote him to the proud position of being its nurse. Calumny declared him guilty of a plebiscite, but I can hardly believe this. He was disappointed in this *coup d'état*, but he was duly promoted, as every man who loses, or who nearly loses, his ship ought to be. A French naval officer presently entered the harbour, and when he heard of the cession, departed in a pet, which was not *raisonnable*. The decennial treaty with our old rivals, in which the "high contracting powers" pledged themselves to refrain from picking and stealing further territory in Africa, expired in 1855. The Gaul will, it is reported, lay *main forte* upon the Benin River. *Tant mieux!* The civilisation of the coast, or rather its redemption from a worse state than the merest savagery, can be effected only by its passing into the hands of Europe. Japhet must not only live in the huts of Ham, he must gird his loins for a harder task than he has ever dreamed of in the idle tents of his brother Shem.

Before landing at the dwarf pier in front of the Consulate—no mean precaution where the crocodiles are so uncommonly "spry,"—we accompanied poor Hollingworth on board the "Prometheus," for a visit of ceremony. We were received with that condescension which sits so gracefully upon the shoulders of Greatness, and hurried off to the shore. The ship had enjoyed remarkably good health under an experienced and active surgeon; only three men out of her hundred whites had died during the last year. We little guessed, however, that of those sturdy fellows only sixteen would be left— all the rest had been carried off by fever (twenty actual deaths), or had been sent sick to Ascension—at the end of March, in four months. Thus, after long indemnity, she eventually found herself no exception to the rule of the Coffin squadron. Mr. McCoskry was fortunately at home, and I had the pleasure of making an acquaintance which I hope may become a friendship.

After an excellent dinner, in which the presence of palm-oil chop argued the old "African," I was shown a symbolical letter, which, on August 24th, had found its way from Dr. Baikie's camp at Mount Patta, near Laird's Town, and opposite Igbebe, at the confluence of the Kwara and the Binue.* This style of writing has been described by Mr. Crowther as being common on the Lower Niger, and Miss Barber, of the "Coral Fund," has obliged the public with a sketch of it. It is inferior to the Mexican symbols, the rudest form of correspondence, showing a great gulf between the African mind and that of the lowest Asiatic. The "letter" consisted of two pockets from an old pair of Calico pantaloons, and a "flap," from which the buttons had been removed; it was empty, and significant enough. There was a little bundle of twine, European and native wound together, to show that white and black, even in their poverty, were not divided. An Arab Taawiz, or talisman—here barbarously called Grigri,— hinted that the bearer was a Moslem, and little pellets of paper containing writing, and whipped round with

---

* I would propose to brother Fellows that the river below the confluence retain the classical name, Niger—Joliba is Park's name for the upper waters, and its extension; that the western influent be called, as by the Kanuri named, Kwara; and the eastern, Binue, a term well known to the Haussas. "Chadda," founded only upon the misconception that the stream drains Lake Chad, should be formally dismissed from our vocabulary. Lake Chad, like the Tanganyika, the Caspian, and many others, receives many tributaries, and sends forth none—evaporation does all the work of drainage. This is hard to instil into the mind of the theorist, who determines, despite the direct evidence of Lake Chad, that all such formations, if undrained, must be salt. The natives have, of course, no general name for the stream, save Water, or Great Water, which, as usual in such cases, varies with every dialect.

string, showed that the path was dangerous. Three broken cowries, loose and scattered, insinuated that the sooner a fresh supply was sent the better; half a Malaguetta pepper, or Cardamom, gave comfort, showing that the traveller's heart was still warm. The thing had all the savage ingenuity that goes to making an assagai and a war-club. Whilst upon this subject it may be as well to state that the confluence of the Kwara and the Binue is distant only twenty days of quiet marching from Lagos, without running the risk of climate and the now hostile villages that fringe the banks below the apex of the Delta. It will be the favourite route of explorers. At present the Egbas are fighting one of those ridiculous fights—they almost put to shame the earlier Yankee battles—with the Ibadans, their northern neighbours.

The afternoon was devoted to inspecting the town, which is native to the last degree. Is is said to be five miles in circumference, and containing 30,000 inhabitants, of whom 700 to 800 are Moslems. Like the people of Badagry and Porto Novo, the Lagosans are of Popo race, and many of them are originally Beninese. The eastern is here the "west end," and there have been the usual quarrels for frontage, each factory and mission-house wishing to secure for itself as much, and to leave its neighbour as little, as possible. The native town, which is divided into sundry quarters, Okofája, Obebowo, Offí, and Eggá, which contains the palace of the now destitute Docemo, is to the west of the

"Garden Reach," and stretches over the interior of the island. The streets want only straightening, widening, draining, and cleaning. Ibrahim Pasha's excellent means of confiscating a house that would not keep its environs clean should be applied here at once. There are irregular buildings—intended for market-places, and called, I suppose, squares,—into which the narrow lanes abut; they are dotted with giant heaps of muck and mixen, and in hot weather wooden pattens are required. The houses, not the factories, are of switch or puddled clay, built in courses, and fished-out of the river: apparently they are all roof, a monstrous thatch, like that of Madagascar, making, as it were, the brim too broad for the face. These things burn like tinder when Shango the fire-god pays a visit to Lagos; so fast, in fact, that little harm is done to the interior. Europeans prefer, for the same reason, slates and tiles. Even the garden-walls must be protected by a weather-thatch of palm-leaves, or they would be washed away. Everything has the squalid, unclean look of an idle people, and what can be expected from men to whom Pomona has been so indecently kind, whose bread and butter, whose wine and oil, grow for them in the trees around? The redeeming feature was the mixture of country with town, the *vestigia ruris*, which all admire. Like Jericho, it is a city of palms: the cocoa grows almost in the salt water; the broad-leaved bread-fruit, introduced from the far Polynesian lands, has taken root like an indigen; and in the branches of the papaw nestle amadavats, orioles, and brilliant palm-birds. The people struck me as being of a lower caste than those of the Gold Coast, more approaching the typical genuine nigger of the Southern republic. They suffer much from cutaneous complaints, krakra, yaws (*frambœsia*), lepra, elephantiasis, and a phagœdenic ulcer common at Fernando Po, and from which even Europeans have no immunity.* The other diseases are fever, dysentery and dracunculus; they have not yet had an attack of true vomito, but it is gradually on its way down from S'a Leone. This yellow fever differs but little in quality from a violent bilious remittent, and the peculiar feature from which it derives its Spanish name, seldom appears till dissolution approaches : the course is rapid, fever, delirium, cramp, convulsions, emetism, death. At times the place becomes a charnel-house. This mangy people appeared to me a merry race of pagans; even at this early hour I saw a man sitting upon the little raised step of clay, the East Indian chabutarah, and shamelessly making himself drunk with "hashish." The instrument is a calabash with tubes and clay chillam or head, and, as usual, the leaf is inhaled through water. This smoking Diamba or Liamba, as the local European name is, is a practice which has probably spread from the East — Egypt and her neighbours. There are travellers who contend that in Western Africa cannabis,

---

* It is often fatal. Amputation must be resorted to, and the patient, who has probably suffered from dysentery and other debilitating diseases, cannot support the shock : sometimes there is an oozing of blood from the cut bone.

or bhang, never grows wild, and that, like the lotus, it is an exotic which, without much care, would die out. This may be true touching the lands about the Gaboon River's mouth; the plant, however, is certainly an indigene of the African continent,—the Moroccans have their fasukh, the Hottentots their dakha, the Eastern people, mbangí, and the Western, diámbá.

An unexpected pleasure was in store for me. Lagos contains, as has been said, some 800 Moslems, though not yet 2000, as it is reported. Though few, they have already risen to political importance; in 1851 our bravest and most active opponents were those wearing turbans. Among these are occasionally found "white Arabs." One had lately died at Ekpe, a village on the "Cradoo waters," where the ex-king Kosoko, lives, and, though a pagan, affects the faith. I was presently visited by the Shaykh Ali bin Mohammed El Mekkáwi. The reverend man was fair of face, but no Meccan; he called himself a Maliki, as indeed are most Moslems in this part of El Islam, and I guessed him to be a Morocco pilgrim, travelling in the odour of sanctity. He was accompanied by the Kazi Mohammed Ghana, a tall and sturdy Hausa negro, with his soot-black face curiously gashed and scarred: he appeared to me an honest man and good Moslem. The dignitaries were accompanied by a mob of men in loose trousers, which distinguished them from the pagan crowd; one of them, by trade a tailor, had learned to speak Portuguese in the Brazils.

Very delightful was this meeting of Moslem brethren,

and we took "sweet counsel" together, as the missionaries say. The Shaykh Ali had wandered from Tripoli southwards, knew Bornu, Sokotu, Hausa, and Adamáwá— the latter only by name, and he seemed to have suffered but little from a long journey, of which he spoke favourably. He wished me to return with him, and promised me safe conduct. I refused, with a tightening of the heart, a little alleviated, however, by the hope that Fate may spare me to march at some future day through Central Africa homewards. And in that hope I purified my property by giving the Zakat, or legal alms, to the holy man, who palpably could not read nor write, but who audibly informed his followers that "this bondsman" is intimately acquainted with *kull' ilm—omnis res scibilis.*

The Shaykh then presented me with a handful of kola nuts,* which have been called the African coffee. They are the local "chaw," the succedaneum for tobacco, betel nut, mastick, and sweet earth. The tree, which grows everywhere in the damp and wooded regions of the tropical seaboard, and on the islands of West Africa (where, however, the people ignore its use), is a kind of sterculia, in leaf not unlike the magnolia, but a stunted scrubby tree; the flower is small and white, with a polypetalous corolla, and the fruit is a large pod, like a mis-shapen cucumber. The edible parts are the five or six beans, which are compared to Brazilian nuts, and to horse

* The Kola (Sterculia acuminata) is written in many ways—Cola, Colat, Khola, Gura, Goora, and Gooroo; the latter three are the names given by the older travellers.

chestnuts; they are covered with a pure white placenta, which must be removed with the finger-nails, and then appears the rosy pink skin—some varieties are yellow—which gradually becomes rusty by exposure to the air. The nut is easily divided into several, generally four sections, of which one is eaten at a time. The taste is a pleasant bitter, and somewhat astringent. Water drunk "upon it," as the phrase is, becomes, even if before offensive, exceptionally sweet. It must be a fine tonic in these relaxing climates. I am not aware of an extract having been made from it: if not, it would be as well to try. Travellers use it to quiet the sensation of hunger and to obviate thirst. In native courts eating kola nuts forms part of the ceremony of welcoming strangers, and the Yorubas have a proverb: "Anger draweth arrows from the quiver: good words draw kolas from the bag." It is held to be aphrodisiac—of these half the African, like the Asiatic, pharmacopeia is composed—and like the betel to be

"A detergent, and a kindler of Love's flame that lieth dead."

A powder, or an infusion of the bark and leaves, promptly administered, is used on the Gold Coast as a cure of snake bites. There, also, kola powders finely ground are drunk in a wineglassful of limejuice by those who do not wish to become mothers. And a decoction of the leaves, like the terebinthinate palm vine, acts as a substitute for copaiba.

On the morning of the 23d September the fair-weather flag was not hoisted at the beach: to go or to lose one's passage became the serious question. In due time, however, the bit of bunting flew up, and the "Tender Brune," Lieut. Forrest, R.N., was under steam. After taking a temporary leave of our kind host, we transferred ourselves on board, and ran merrily down the Lagos waters, past the tide-rip of the influent Badagry Lagoon, and past the three salient points—Bruce, Beecroft, and Le Greslie. The bar was like that of yesterday, half angry, but it is easier, methinks, and safer to front these formations than to turn back upon them. Although the wind was dead ahead we shipped only four seas, of moderate dimensions—the danger is of their putting out the fires —and the soundings were never less than eleven feet.

At Lagos we dropped our Frenchman—a typical Frenchman in all points but one, he avoided all mention of the fair sex. A Gascon and a Jesuit, bound for the Whydah mission, he represented himself, for what reason beyond "keeping his hand in" no one knows, as a clerk in the establishment of Messrs. Regis & Co., Marseille. A thorough miso-Albion, he was our favourite butt. Being of a serious turn of mind he dwelt long and loudly upon the revolting selfishness of the British Government; the unscrupulousness with which it carries out even its plans of philanthropy, and the grinding tyranny inflicted upon the wretched Roman "Cats." He said it was a horror that priests were not paid like *les ministres Protestants*, by *le Government*, and that Ireland is not permitted to send members to *le Parlament*. French tobacco was superior to English, French manufactures beat the world; *la France* was the cream of creation, and Paris was the cream's cream. *Monsieur* had travelled *beaucoup* and knew the world; he had even visited Switzerland, and therefore, as in the case of the "Fall of Kars," he could tell you all about China. *Londres* was *le plus sale endroit* that he had ever seen, and as for *Liverrepoule*—he would only exclaim with M. de P——, "Ah! bah! poof!" He wore one shirt *apparament* from Madeira to Lagos; he never removed his hat or cap in the *salon*—probably to show his contempt for *ces Anglais*—and he walked the quarter-deck bareheaded. We parted, however, on the best of terms; he promised me *un diner* in case of my visiting Whydah, and I, as the Yankee saith, "re-ciprocated."

At Lagos, too, we parted with another queer lot—our slavers. They are dark, but European or Brazilian; they speak Portuguese, travel under *aliases*—to-day Soarez, to-morrow Pieri—and they herd together. One claims to have been a lieutenant in some royal navy. They have visited England to lay in a further stock of money for the next cargo of *casimir noir*, and with a view to medical assistance. They are worn out by excessive devotions at the shrine of Venus, and they seem to live chiefly on tobacco smoke. Part of their game is to supply naval officers with champagne and excellent cigars; to ask them to dinner, and to affect equality with them, as if both were of the same trade. The new comer on the coast sometimes associates with them, thinking he will discern their secret, whilst they are reading his, and are persuading the natives that he is in league with them. I should strongly exhort officers to be very wary of such society, and certainly not to trust themselves to a dinner on shore, where a cup of coffee would materially assist the departure of a cargo. As for the fiction that they are to be treated like gentlemen, whilst plying a trade which our law makes felony, it is easily disposed of. The pickpocket or the burglar might, with equal reason, claim equal respect for his "profession."

About midday we found ourselves on board the "Blackland," and we entered slowly upon the short stage of about 100 miles which separated us from our next station, the Benin river.

Lagos, according to native tradition, was founded by a body of Beninese warriors, sent by their king, who claimed suzerainty over these parts, to reduce the rebels of Ogulata, or Abulata, a place on the mainland north of the islet. Their leader—whose name is not quoted—having failed in his enterprise, and fearing to return, settled upon the then desert bit of sand, made friends with European travellers, and rejected all promises of pardon. Islands in Western, as in Eastern, Africa are ever the favourite places of settlements; they are defended by the sea, and the habit of fishing raises a generation of canoe-men who have many advantages over the inland peoples. Presently the Ogulata people recognised the chief, and the King of Benin made Lagos a dependency, with annual tribute, which ceased when the slave dealers had strengthened it to resist the mother city. Hence the island's native name, Aonin, or Awáni, corrupted to Oni by Europeans, alluding to its connection with Ini, Bini, Ibini, or Benin. There is another name, Daghoh, mentioned by the slave Abubeko; but is probably a native corruption of "Lagos"—the Lakes—a name given by the Portuguese, probably in memoriam of their Lusitanian home. The old chart-names for the islands Curamo and Ikbekou are not to be met with here. The town is known to its population and throughout Yoruba as Eko, of which some make Ichoo. The settlement must be modern: it is not mentioned by Bosman in 1700.

The great development of the slave trade at Lagos took place about the beginning of the present century. In 1839-41, emigrants to Abeokuta, 265 in number, were plundered and maltreated by the people. In August, 1845, Kosoko (Coçioco), cousin of the King, a powerful slave-trading chief, after twenty-four days' fighting, drove out the liege lord Akitoye, who favoured the English, and murdered, in the market place, his brother Letida and two of the Chief Aduli's sons. Akitoye, a weak man and a foolish, fled to Abeokuta, but the great warrior Shodeke was dead, and the encampment at the town of Adú was broken up. Several missionaries remained at Badagry, the road to Abeokuta, their destination, being unsafe. The first who entered "Understone" was the Rev. T. B. Freeman, on Sunday, the 11th December, 1842, and he was not followed until the 27th July, 1846, when Messrs. Townsend and

Crowther were enabled to reach it. A coalition between Lagos and Porto Novo, backed by Dahomey, threatened the British establishments at Badagry. Under Kosoko, who ruled at Lagos for six years, an attack was actually made upon the place; it was, however, beaten back by the Egbas and their General Shomeye, who afterwards became principal captain of war at Abeokuta. This outrage, which took place in June and July of 1851, led to reprisals.

On the 25th November of the same year, a force of 260 men, in twenty-three boats, under the command of the late Commander Forbes, Her Majesty's ship "Philomel," preceded by the late Mr. Beecroft, carrying a flag of truce, entered the river. About 5000 armed men were assembled, they kept up a sharp fire from behind the houses and trees. Our men landed; but they were soon compelled to retreat, with the loss of two killed and several wounded. The Rev. Mr. Bowen ("Central Africa"), who was near the scene, and shows scant regret at the English being "whipped,"—we were risking our lives for the pretection of him and his,— describes it as a pretty considerable (John) Bull's run.

Being somewhat more enthusiastic about slave-trade matters in those days, we determined effectually to scotch the serpent at Lagos. On the 26th and 27th December, 400 men, from four ships, and headed by the commodore, Captain R. W. Bruce, Her Majesty's ship "Penelope,"—his name is preserved in Bruce Island (Iddo), a green spot in the "Cradoo Waters" to the north of the town,—attacked the place. Kosoko had prepared it with stockades, cannon, and all the material for a determined resistance. The principal fighting was a little beyond the house occupied by Mr. M'Coskry; here the walls of vegetation enabled the defenders to fire unseen upon the assailants. We lost sixteen men killed and seventy-one wounded, a fair proportion out of 400; the destruction of the natives was much greater. Kosoko and his party, after doing their best to no purpose, fled to Ijebu, where he remained four years, and his cousin Akitoye was reinstated. The latter was not fated to live without troubles. In July, 1853, two slave chiefs—Aginia and Pellu—rebelled, and joined their master Kosoko; and on the 5th of August was fought a drawn battle, during which the English Branch Mission and School House was burned. In September of the same year Akitoye poisoned himself at midnight, in the presence of two slave boys—the local custom when the King ceases to give satisfaction to his subjects.

Through the influence of the late Mr. Campbell, Her Majesty's Consul, Docemo succeeded his father in 1853, to the prejudice of Kosoko. This fine old chief eventually took up his abode at Ekpe, upon the Ikoradu Lagoon, and at periods filled the mind of Lagos with a panic. In 1852, the English residents at Badagry, conquering their alarm, visited Lagos, and were followed in a few weeks by the Church and the Wesleyan Missions, the Baptists remaining to till the field. In 1855, most Europeans believed that a plot had been made to murder the Consul and all opposed to the slave trade. Docemo, however, proved himself superior to his father, and not unfriendly to the stranger. But the wheel of Fate revolves at Lagos as elsewhere; kings' heads, according to the Arab saying, now touch the stars, then are under the stones. Docemo was dethroned on the 6th of August, 1861, and Kosoko, for years the horror and *bête noire* of Consul Campbell and the missionaries, is again growing into favour; it has even been thought of readmitting him to his country.

As late as the year of grace 1851, when Mr. M'Coskry first came to Lagos, there were thirty Portuguese, and but four English: not one of the whole number, save himself, survives, or at least has remained here. Those were merry days; the slavers had nothing to do but sleep and smoke, with an occasional champagne tiffin on the beach. The trade-man made all the bargains; the doctor examined the "contrabands;" they were shipped off by the captain and crew, and in due time came a golden return. Then followed, in 1851, the palmy days of palm-oil. Ten gallons were then bought for two and a half heads of cowries=five shillings, and sold per ton of 300 gallons at 40*l*. Every year the price has increased, owing to concurrence, jealousy, and want of combination among the traders, who enjoy "cutting one another's throats," as the phrase is. The oil has now risen from 2·5 to 10 heads, and threatens to rise still higher.* The Lagos oil

* The cowrie currency, assuming the dollar at 4*s*. 6*d*., its normal price in these regions, is as follows:—

is celebrated as the best and clearest upon the West African coast, and the tree extends to at least sixty miles in the interior. The "puncheon" is not, as in the "Oil Rivers," of a fixed size; it may be anything, from a breaker upwards. The amount of oil exported from Lagos this year is about 3,800 tons, worth (at 40*l.* per ton) some 152,000*l.*, and here, as elsewhere, the trade is only in its fitful infancy.

Lagos is a young and thriving place. Its position points it out as the natural key of this part of Africa, and the future emporium of all Yoruba, between the Niger and the sea. It cannot help commanding commerce: even under the wretched management of the native princes, it attracted the whole trade of the Benin country. In proper hands it will be the sole outlet of trade from Central Guinea and the Sudan,* lands teeming with various wealth—palm-oil, cotton, shea-butter, metals, native cloths, sugar, indigo, tobacco of good quality, and ivory; in the neighbourhood of Ilorin, about eight days' journey north of Abeokuta, it is not worth their while, on account of the heavy tolls, to export their tusks. At present the bar is an obstacle to im-

```
40 cowries   = 1 string = 3 farthings to 1d.
5 strings    = 1 bunch  = 3d. to 6d.
10 bunches   = 1 head   = 1s. 9¼d. to 2s.
10 heads     = 1 bag    = 18s. to $4 = 16s. 8d.
```
The bag contains 20,000 cowries, and the rates are exceedingly various.

* Sudan properly means negroes : it is an ellipsis for Bilád el Súdán, *i.e.*, negroland. Moslem nations call the negroes of the interior, the Sudan : thus the negroland of Egypt lies south, and that of Lagos north.

provement; time, however, will remedy that. The roads require attention, but they are hardly so important to Africa as people at home suppose. In these prairie lands a path is easily cut, and soon becomes a rut impracticable to an Englishman or a horse, but perfectly fitted for the African. Were you to give him the finest highway in Europe, after a year he would have worn a deep track by marching in Indian file, and the rest would be a bright expanse of verdure. These remarks will apply to the special fund of £200, of which an advertisement, " Aquapem Mountain Road," appears once per month in the " African Times," a methodistical publication, whose tone and spirit, venerable cant, and worn-out declamation, take us back to the days of A.D. 1800.

I should like to see, but have very little chance of seeing, Lagos (now that she has become part and parcel of the empire upon which Dan Phœbus must be somewhat weary of gazing) become a model colony. We have learned "what to avoid" in West Africa: as the subjoined extract from the returns of expenditure for the year ending December 31, proves, S'a Leone barely pays itself, whilst Gambia shows a deficit of one-third, and the Gold Coast of nearly half.

PAYMENTS FOR SLAVE AND TONNAGE BOUNTIES.

			£	s.	d.	£	s.	d.
To officers and crew of H.M.S. Viper	-	4,223	10	0			
,,	,,	Spitfire -	2,574	10	0			
,,	,,	Pluto -	4,382	0	0			
		Carried forward -	-	-	-	11,180	0	0

		£	s.	d.	£	s.	d.
Brought forward					11,180	0	0
To officers and crew of H.M.S. Archer		2,007	10	0			
,, ,, Triton		5,609	10	0			
,, ,, Arrogant		946	0	0			
,, ,, Alecto		1,375	0	0			
To Colonel Hill, Sierra Leone		1,610	0	0			
To Mr. Pike, harbour master, Ditto		170	0	0			
Transferred to Civil Contingencies in repayment of advances on account of votes for the service		8,698	10	0			
					20,416	10	0
					31,596	10	0
Paid for support and conveyance of captured negroes					19,388	18	11
Paid to Commissioners for suppression of the slave trade, including Commissioner at Loando, 1,300*l.*; arbitrator, 800*l.*; clerk, 400*l.*					10,750	0	0
Total expenses of slave suppression					£61,735	8	11

COLONIAL REVENUE AND EXPENDITURE, 1860.

	£	s.	d.	£	s.	d.
Sierra Leone—Expenditure	29,146	0	0			
,, Revenue	29,912	0	0			
Gambia—Expenditure	15,273	0	0			
,, Revenue	10,190	0	0			
Gold Coast—Expenditure	9,558	0	0			
,, Revenue	5,004	0	0			
Total expenditure over revenue				8,871	0	0

SPECIAL SERVICE.

	£	s.	d.	£	s.	d.
Niger—Dr. Baikie, salary	500	0	0			
Expenses at the Confluence	1,000	0	0			
				1,500	0	0

ESTIMATE OF CONSULS' SALARIES, &c., FOR THE YEAR, 1862.

	£	s.	d.	£	s.	d.
Lagos—Consul (allowance, 200*l.*)	500	0	0			
Abeokuta—Consul (allowance, 100*l.*)	400	0	0			
Fernando Po—Consul (allowance, 20*Cl.*)	500	0	0			
Sherbro—Consular agent	250	0	0			
Quillimane—Consul	500	0	0			
				2,650	0	0
Grand Total				£74,756	8	11

It wants a Civil Governor, who should be a military or a naval man; a secretary ditto, ready to act as principal when necessary; a staff surgeon, with a relief ready at home when required; a harbour-master—a lieutenant R.N., if possible; a surveyor; and, without ambition of shining as a politician, a civil engineer to lay out the town; three police magistrates; but, in the name of all that is nameable, no civil courts, no courts of appeal, no "regular lawyers," no lawyers' clerks. The one thing needful is a military force, sufficiently strong, not for offence, but to back our authority, and to keep the peace amongst a number of petty, quarrelsome tribes around. A force of 200 men has been proposed; it is about one-third of what is required. Some have advocated Sepoys, who would not live here a month; what is unhealthy to the European would be doubly so to them. Hindus of caste would die on the voyage; Moslems shortly after arrival. Chinese would be excellent, but their day on this coast has not yet come; we are only beginning to learn their value as soldiers in their own land. Others advocate West Indians, the refuse of Jamaica and S'a Leone, fellows little calculated to resist climate, and despised by the black people because of themselves; their conduct in camp is complained of, and only the bravery of their officers enables them to behave even tolerably in the field. The Hottentots might be tried, but, as Captain Speke's imprudent example shows, they are not to be relied upon out of their own country, and little even there. The best men would be from the Gold Coast mixed with Moslems from the north, Ilorins, Fulas, and Gambari, or Hausamen: the greater the mixture and the further the soldier's country, the better. The military establishment requires one small troop of horse artillery, armed with rockets and Blakeley's guns; another troop of eighty cavalry, and a weak regiment of 400 infantry. The latter would be divided into half companies, and besides mere drilling and parading, should fortify the place and make military roads; so shall we escape the sight of those soldier-drones that now infest the colonies. The error to be avoided lies in the multitude of officers: the forces should be irregulars, with a commandant, a second in command, an adjutant, a quartermaster, a full surgeon, and an assistant surgeon—no captains, lieutenants, nor ensigns; if these are wanted they might be kept at home as duplicates.

The custom-house officers would be two in number and the taxes at once changed. To the present time the only impost levied by the King has been export duty of 2·5 per cent. on ivory and oil; and of these the place, probably never exported more than 180,000*l.* per annum, whilst now, in consequence of the protracted war, it exports still less. This is a truly suicidal proceeding: the only possible tax for the present is 2·5 per cent. on imports, which, assuming them at 190,000*l.* per annum, already realises 4797*l.* a year,* without causing the

---

* Mr. Consul Campbell reported in 1858 that Lagos exported 4,612 tons of palm oil (184,480*l.*), 5,776 lbs. of ivory (1,500*l.*), and 2,103

natives to feel it. The Gold Coast has warned us against a poll-tax, and though the whole seaboard is virtually in our hands, it would hardly be prudent as yet to lay a duty of fifty per cent. on arms, ammunition, and alcohol, a consummation which I most devoutly desire may become universal in Western Africa. We might, however, begin with ten per cent.

The town of Lagos is certainly one of the most unhealthy spots on these malarious shores, but the climate may be mitigated. As the people do not bury in their ground-floors, it is here easy to remove a house. Broad streets, admitting free currents of air, and perfectly drained, should run the whole length of the settlement parallel with the Lagoon, and at right angles to these, cross ways from the water side to the interior would supply ample ventilation. The site has a good slope towards the flowing stream which is a ready-made *cloaca maxima*, and very little cutting would draw off the rains, which now stand long upon the stiff hardened sand. Another abuse calls loudly for correction. The town is filled with deep holes, from which the sand mixed with swish for walls has been dug —Clapperton found Sokotu in the same state; these become favourite stores for offal and rubbish, and the

bales—weighing 263,500 lbs.—of cotton (5,912*l*. 10*s*.) The total of export in that year was, therefore, 191,892*l*. 10*s*. Although sheabutter had appeared in the market, the native chiefs had organised a powerful opposition to the palm-oil trade, hoping a return to the old state of things. In 1859 the deficiency in the whole export trade of palm oil from the Bight of Benin was expected to reach at least 10,000 tons.

hot weather fills them with putrefaction. And, finally, the natives should be taught, or rather forced, to learn something like purity in their habits.

With this little establishment, and with such simple precautions, I am certain that Lagos, when ten years old, will be able to provide for itself, and that in ten more it would become the emporium of the great and rich Yoruba and Dahomian countries, whose natural adit and issue it is.

CHAPTER XI.

BENIN—NUN—BONNY RIVER TO FERNANDO PO.

"Ye banks and braes o' Bonny ——"
Burns.

24TH SEPTEMBER, 186—.

IT is September, and one whole month from home—how short a time, and how great a change! Within that limited period we have passed through summer, autumn, winter, and spring, and now we are in the brumal season once more. A cold and drizzling Irish rain, driven by the wind across decks, makes everything comfortless. As yet, however, we have been unable to complain of heat. The "unapparent fount of glory" is shorn of his beams by the gaseous steamy air, which fends off the heat from earth. So different is radiation in the dry air of the desert, that, after an experience of Scinde and Aden, the consul declared he had not yet felt a hot day; the climate is that of Naples during the sirocco. Touching the four seasons which we have endured within the last thirty days, it is usual to make in West Africa a very different distribution of the year, little intelligible to the pure European, *e. g.*, the dries, the tornadoes, the early rains, the little dries, the later rains, the later tornadoes, and the smokes. Yet, by minute inspection, he can discover something of the mechanism of the European year. The decay of old, and the substitution of new growths, even in a land of evergreens, show a distinct demarcation. Spring opens with its thunder-storms in October and November; the hot dry summer lasts till May; and from June till late in September, autumn and winter fill up the year.

At 8 P.M. on Tuesday, the 24th September, we find our pop-guns off the mouth of the Benin river, or Great Rio Formoso, conspicuous by its high north-western bank. The vessels were rolling in the long surf, which is here worse than even at Lagos. We took in two passengers, Doctor and Mrs. Henry—little thought we at that time that she was destined to an untimely death! As the steamer never touches here on her way home, passengers from Benin must perforce endure a long and dangerous week's trip round the "Oil Rivers." Benin assumes the dignity of almost classic ground. It was visited in 1485 by the Portuguese Affonso de Aviro, who returned home, bearing a demand for Christian missionaries on the part of the King. Fernão de Poo, after discovering the "Beautiful island" which has taken his name, sailed up the "Great River Beautiful," which he probably so named from the family likeness of the scenery: he founded a settlement at Gwato, and it speedily numbered one thousand converts. According to Barbot, who takes, as will be seen, the story from Merolla, the King of Great Benin City offered, for the very small consideration of a white wife, to drive all his subjects into the pale of the Church. At the island of San Thomè, "a strong appeal," to use Mr. Wilson's words,* "was made to the Christian feeling of the sisterhood, one of whom had the courage to look the matter in the face, and actually accepted the hand of his sable Majesty. She ought to have been canonized, but it is not known that this deed of self-sacrifice ever received any special notice from the Father of the Church." I may add, that if the then King was as fine-looking a negro as the present occupant of the "Stool," which here is synonymous with the "Throne," the young lady lost little by exchanging him for an ex-sanguined white of San Thomè.† Here, however, the matter ended, the country was found unwholesome, and at last, after many a struggle, Christianity died out. Benin was visited by Captain Thomas Wyndham in 1553, and in 1823,

* "Western Africa," p. 192.
† Bosman, Letter XX., calls San Thomè the Dutch churchyard, and attributes the excessive mortality to three causes : the scorching heat, the "thick and stinking mists," and, thirdly, the "excessive phlebotomy of the Portuguese ;" adding, "they have recourse to this on the very least occasion, some of them letting blood above five times in a year, and this it is which I believe makes them look more like walking ghosts than men ; and this practice, the longer continued, must necessarily the more weaken the constitution, for the nature of the country is not such as to supply them with hasty recruits of new blood." Captain Owen ("Narrative of Voyages," Vol. II. p. 383) asserts that during his whole experience on the African coast, there was not one instance of perfect recovery after a liberal application either of the lancet or of calomel—"decidedly the most deadly enemies in a tropical climate." And yet, in the same page, he recommends these two destroyers, the one as a preventative, and the other as a restorative. "I pray you avoid them."

Belzoni of the Pyramids left his bones near its banks. The lowlands are rich in palm-oil; a little gold is found in the uplands, despite the theory which limits the precious metal to the Secoom river, west of Accra, and the interior exports a few ivories; piper cubebs and Malaguetta pepper grow wild, and the soil might be taught to bear coffee and cocoa, indigo, sugar, and cotton. At present it is a mere waste.

I had no opportunity of entering the Benin river. At the time piracy and murder had been reported, the people of Fishtown had slaughtered a Kruboy or two, belonging to the Messrs. Harrison. A cruizer was hourly expected by the natives to "break town," and they had prepared for it by running all their valuables into the bush. The fault, as usual, lies with the traders, who will not " pull together." There is no "king"— Africanicè for "head native"—in the lower river. Benin was in old times divided into two separate states, Benin Proper and Wari (Warree). The royal family of the former place becoming too numerous, divided, and settled at the latter, which was of course tributary and dependent, till the Portuguese persuaded it to throw off the yoke. Some years afterwards, one of the Wari family, or according to others, a slave of the King of Benin, founded a town on the Jakwa (Jackwaw) creek, which also, in due time, became independent. Alusa, the King of Wari, died in 1848; Jambrá, the present sovereign of Benin, has little power, and "Governor Jerry," of Jakwa, is an effete old man. The state of the river is that of perfect anarchy. Some Europeans sigh for the order and the responsibility of a single ruler—others, and they are in the majority, prefer not to pay the comeys or customs which royalty would demand and enforce.

I inquired of an intelligent fellow-passenger concerning the Joemen, or Ijomen, to whom Mr. Consul Hutchinson has given, by hearsay, so vile a reputation. Next to the tribes of Fernando Po, they are the best abused race in this part of Africa, and both deserve a better fate. Lieut. Forbes* calls them the Joh pirates, and makes them the chief carriers of the human cargoes exported from the Beninese interior to Lagos. A reference to Mr. Henry, of Benin, enables me to deny that Mr. Henry had ever asserted that the "Ejoemen" had eaten two Kruboys, that had deserted from a Liverpool ship. It has not been proved that the Ijos ate the two young officers of Captain Denham's ship, who imprudently boated up the river without sufficient force. Nor can it be established that the West Indian, Carr, who in 1841 (Second Niger Expedition) was returning to Aboh, on the Niger, viâ Bonny, was "killed by these people, or King Boy, an Ejoeman."† He was most probably murdered by the Ibos, at the suggestion of some Christian trader.

Cannibalism is an interesting, though somewhat morbid subject. Once, all anthropophagous tales were greedily swallowed; they are now fastidiously rejected. The pages

---

* "Dahomey and the Dahomians," chap. 1.
† "Ten Years' Wanderings among the Ethiopians," chap. 5.

of many African travellers show so much hearsay and little eye-sight, they supply, moreover, such ridiculous details, that the public is justified in doubting anything but personal evidence. But to deny, as some very silly philanthropists of the Ethnological Society have denied, its existence in West Africa, is to maintain, like the old African, the impossibility of water becoming hard because he had never seen it so.

After leaving Lagos, the low lands become a "false coast," the gift of the Niger, whose western branches extend as far as our new colony. Eastward, the furthest limit is the Bonny, and possibly its eastern neighbour the Andoni River, and the Ahombola (Humballah) creek, an inlet not named, though placed, in our charts.* Nothing is more simple than to sketch the view as seen from the sea. Above, an azure space based upon a band of dull and bright greens, resting upon a thin line of golden sand, and in the foreground a little deeper ultramarine than in the air. In the rainy season, change the blue above to a heavy mass of clouds, reposing upon the land, and the blue below to a brown olive. Where a river gap exists it will be denoted by an uneven notch in the land, and as a rule the proper right point, that is to say, the western, will be somewhat higher than the other. The apparent continent will be found divided into islands, and sub-divided into islets, by river-like

* The direct connection of the Bonny River with the true Niger is still a subject of geographical speculation : I hope to solve the problem, despite all its difficulties.

mangrove-haunted creeks, which I prefer to describe when upon them.

About noon, on the 24th of September, we were off the "Escravos," Slave river, corrupted to "Escrados," the first stream lying southward of the Benin: it has a bad bar, and is shallow, fit only for the humbler sort of slavers. Next to it is the Rio dos Forcados "of Galley-Slaves,"*—a bathos—it is called by our pilots, with scanty reason, the "Warree river." With a bar that carries thirteen feet at low water, some say twenty feet, and with a very narrow slope, this noble estuary is wholly neglected. Its next neighbour is the Ramos, or Bough river, which has twelve to fifteen feet on the bar. Up this stream there are fine clay banks, raised twenty to twenty-five yards above the water, and bearing noble trees; the people, contrary to the usual habits of the "Creekmen," cultivate the ground. Of the Dodo I could hear nothing, and will not quote the Directory. Next in order is the Pennington river, so called from the young officer of Her Majesty's ship "Avon," surveying the coast under Captain Denham, in 1846, who was treacherously murdered by the aforesaid Creekmen. The Middleton is as unimportant and little known as the Dodo; it was christened after the assistant-surgeon of the "Avon." The next is the Winstanley outfalls, so called from another murdered man—here, as in the prairies of North America, death·

---

* These descriptions, as far as the Niger, are mere hearsay: I have not visited the mouths of the above-mentioned streams.

seems to be the only thing that can be recorded of localities—belonging to the "Avon": the people probably supposed her to be a slaver, awaiting opportunities of capture, and fought accordingly. It was too late for vision when we were off the Sengana, or Sengma, the westernmost direct outlet of the Niger, and it was midnight before we steamed across the mouth of "Blacklands' Nile."

The obvious projection of the land at the base of the immediate delta, has been called by old travellers, whose eye for beauty appears to have been keen, "Cabo Formoso;" with us it is "Cape Formosa," upon the principle that the *prima donna* is ever saluted with Bravo, and geographers differ as to whether it is to the east or to the west of the river's mouth. The Nun, or Non, was possibly so called by the Portuguese, who seem to have denoted by a negative the several *ne plus ultras* of their course from Lisbon to Australia.* It was promoted to the dignity of principal outlet within our memory; the last century and the first quarter of the present, held four theories touching the course and issue of the mighty Niger.

1. The ancients,† who, unlike the moderns, made their chief explorations by land, and not by sea, held

---

* Cape Non, in Morocco, may be derived from the Arabic Ras Nun —of Fish—as Jonah is called Zu'l Nún, master of the fish.

† Pliny shows a certain knowledge of the Nigir, Nigeir, or Nigris, its divergence into many streams (ἐκτοπας, as Ptolemy says), and its rise, like the Nile, after tropical rains. Ptolemy adds some remarkable details, which, if mere coincidences, deserve to be considered marvellous.

that the Niger flowed from past the centre of the continent to the eastward, losing itself in a great central reservoir, like the Caspian Sea, called Wangara, or Ghana,* where it was lost in the sands or evaporated by the sun. This theory became popular after the first journey of Mungo Park, whose very short experience had only taught him that the course of the Niger was easterly. This theory had one merit, it anticipated the discovery of the Lake Regions of Central Equatorial Africa, concerning which the geographical world is now so curious.

2. Others opined that the Niger terminates in the White Nile, which D'Anville had then traced to the south-south-west of Senaar. Mr. Grey Jackson, of Moroccan celebrity, published the interesting fact, that in 1780, seventeen native travellers from Tinbuktu reached Cairo by water the whole way in eighteen months, passing 1200 towns and cities. Major Rennell, by a comparison of Mr. (Darfur) Browne's altitudes, found this to be physically impossible.

3. Mr. George Maxwell, an experienced African trader, who had lived long at the mouth of the Kongo, and who had planned a boat exploration of the river, persuaded Mr. Park—contrary to his better judgment, we must hope —that the Zaire, or Kongo river, is the mouth of the Niger.† Many objections were raised to this theory, e. g., that it would make the stream cut the "Kong Moun-

---

* In Captain Tuckey's map the Zaire, or Kongo, is also made to issue from a great marsh.

† Park, writing to Sir Joseph Banks, makes his Kasson guide state

tains "—which it does—and give the Niger a course of 4000 miles, or 500 longer than the Amazon. The theory, however, led to the fatal expeditions of Park and Tuckey.

4. The two latter were pre-eminently English and erroneous opinions; the fourth was French, and correct. M. Reichard ("Ephémerides Géographiques," Weimar, 1808) was sanctioned in 1813 by the great Malte-Brun ("Précis de la Géographie Universelle," vol. 4, p. 635), in opining that the Niger falls into the Gulf of Guinea by a great delta, the Rio del Rey being the eastern, and the Great Rio Formoso, or Benin,* being its western, limits. This remarkable hypothesis, right in the main, whilst wrong in detail, and characterised at the time as "hazardous and uncertain," was probably suggested by native testimony, the coasts of the Gulf of Guinea being well known to French traders. It is hard indeed to comprehend how an intelligent sailor could pass by these shores without suspecting them to be the delta of some great stream. Caillié, the much-abused discoverer of Timbuktu, wrote in 1828 these remarkable words—" If I may be permitted to hazard an opinion as to the course of the River Dhioliba, I should say that it

that the Niger, after passing Kashna, runs directly to the right hand, or southwards, and that he was certain that it did not end anywhere near Kashna or Bornu. This shows a glimmering of light.

* I quote the above memoriter. If correct, the limits of the Nigrotic delta thus given are totally incorrect. The Rio del Rey is wholly unconnected with the Niger; even the nearer Calabar and Cross rivers do not flow from it. The same is the case with the Benin river: its source was placed by Mr. Beecroft in the highlands to the westward of the Niger.

empties itself by several mouths into the Gulf of Benin." In 1829—*longo intervallo*—Mr. Macqueen, after collecting a large amount of evidence on the subject, recommended a careful examination of the rivers between the Rio Formoso and Old Calabar, neither of which, by the bye, are directly connected with the Niger. I have given below* a summary of northern West

* In 1553, Capt. Thomas Wyndham, the Portuguese Anes Pinteado, entered the Benin river.
In 1558, Mr. Thompson reached Tenda by the Gambia, and was followed there in 1620 by Robert Jobson.
In 1637, Jannequin ascended the Senegal.
In 1670, Paul Imbart attempted Tinbuktu *viâ* Morocco.
In 1698, the Sieur de Brue visited Galam on the Senegal.
In 1715, M. Compagnon reached Bambûk *viâ* St. Louis de Senegal.
In 1723, Stables reached Bambûk *viâ* the Gambia; the same journey was repeated by Moore in 1731.
In 1742, M. de Flandre reached Bambûk by St. Louis, and he was followed in 1749 by the celebrated M. Adanson.
In 1748, M. Follier reached Bambûk by the Cape Nun Coast.
In 1785, MM. Sanguier and Brisson made the same journey.
In 1786, M. Ruband reached Galam *viâ* St. Louis.
In 1786-7, M. de Beauvois explored Benin and Wari.
In 1787, M. Picard struck Futa Toro *viâ* St. Louis.
In 1791, Major Houghton ascended the Gambia river, and died at Jarra in Ludamar.
In 1794, Messrs. Yates and Winterbottom reached Timbo by the Rio Nunez.
In 1795-7, Mungo Park's first journey to Silla on the Joliba or Kwara river.
In 1804, Mr. Nicholls died in the interior of Old Calabar.
In 1805, Mungo Park's second expedition : all his 44 companions, including Lieut. Martyn, and Messrs. Anderson and Scott, died.
In 1809, M. Roentgen reached Busa *viâ* Mogador.
In 1810, Robert Adams, *alias* Benjamin Rose, an American, was carried prisoner to Tinbuktu.

African, including Nigritic, exploration, brought down to the present date. The reader may see, by casting his

In 1815, Mr. James Riley, another American, master and supercargo of the brig "Commerce," reached Tinbuktu by the western coast.

In 1816, Capt. Tuckey, R.N., accompanied by Lieut. Hawkins, Mr. Fitzmaurice, master and surveyor, Dr. McKerrow, with petty officers and marines, besides supernumeraries; Professor Smith, botanist; Mr. Cranch, zoologist; Mr. Tudor, anatomist; and Mr. Lockhart, gardener; visited the lower Kongo; of his 54 white men, a party of 30 set out on the land journey beyond the cataracts, and of these only nine returned home.

In 1817, Major Peddie and Capt. Campbell reached Kakondi *viâ* the Nunez river.

In 1817, M. Bandia reached Panjikot *viâ* Egypt.

In 1817, P. Rouzié travelled into the interior.

In 1818, M. Mollien reached Timbo *viâ* St. Louis.

In 1818-19, Capt. Gray, Royal African Corps, reached Bulibani, the capital of Bondu.

In 1819, M. Dochard reached Yamina *viâ* the Gambia.

In 1819, Mr. Bowdich visited Kumasi in Ashantee.

In 1820, M. Cachelot reached Wad Nun by the west coast of Africa.

In 1822, Major Laing reached Falaba *viâ* Sierra Leone.

In 1822-5, Major Denham and Lieut. Clapperton explored Mandara and Sokotu of the Sudan, losing Dr. Oudney and other Europeans.

In 1825-6, Captains Clapperton and Peace and Dr. Morrison lost their lives in penetrating from the Bight of Benin; Richard Lander being the sole white survivor.

In 1827-8, Réné Caillié visited Tinbuktu and returned *viâ* Morocco, and in the same year Major Laing was murdered on his way from Tinbuktu.

In 1830-1, Richard and John Lander entered Africa *viâ* Badagry, and discovered the embouchure of the Niger.

In 1832-4, the first, or Liverpool merchants' expedition, under the late Messrs. Laird and Oldfield, and accompanied by Richard Lander, ascended the Kwara to Rabba, and the Binue (Chadda) to Dagbo. Of the 49 European crew in the steamers Qworra and Alberkah—the latter is Anglo-Arabic for a blessing—only nine lived to return. Richard Lander was shot with a bullet in the groin, by some people of Anjama,

eye upon the map, that discovery has but begun. At present, as in Arctic travelling, there is a lull, but it cer-

in the Oru country, as he was descending the river in a canoe full of cowries, and died at Clarence, Fernando Po.

In 1836, 1840, and 1845, the late Mr. Beecroft, under Mr. Jamieson of Liverpool, ascended in the "Ethiope" the Benin, Wari, Niger, Old Calabar, and Cross rivers : he reached within 30 miles of this side of Busa.

In 1841, the Government expedition under Captain the late Admiral H. D. Trotter, in the "Albert," and Commander W. Allen in the "Wilberforce," accompanied by the "Soudan," Commander B. Allen, ascended to Egga, 150 miles above the confluence, losing in 64 days (the "Soudan" remained only 40) 48 out of 145 white men. The late Mr. Consul Beecroft ran up the river in the "Ethiope," and succeeded in saving the "Albert," conveying her to Fernando Po.

In 1845, the late Mr. Duncan visited Abomey.

In 1852, the African Steam-Ship Company was formed, and in 1856-57 an intercolonial steamer was sent to promote the establishment of a regular steam communication between Fernando Po and the confluence of the Kwara and Binue rivers.

In 1854, the Chadda mixed expedition, sent by the late Mr. M. Laird, who received 5000*l*. from the Admiralty for the expenses of the voyage, under Dr. Baikie, R.N., the senior Government officer after the death of Mr. Consul Beecroft, Mr. D. J. May, master R.N., Dr. Hutchinson, Mr. Taylor, afterwards vice-consul at Abeokuta, representing Mr. Laird (the reader has probably perused Dr. Baikie's "Journal"), explored — in the little steamer "Pleiad," built by Mr. J. Laird, on the lines of the yacht "America"—150 miles of virgin ground, and remained in the river 118 days, with 54 Europeans, of whom not a man died ; a new era in African exploration.

In August, 1857, the Niger mixed expedition,—missionary, scientific, naval, and commercial,—began under Dr. Baikie, Mr. D. J. May, master, Lieut. Glover, Dr. Davis, Mr. Barter, botanist (dead), and Mr. Dalton, zoologist. In opposition to this Government party was Mr. Laird's commercial venture, Captain Alexander Grant (died at Benin), supercargo, Mr. Howard (dead), purser, and Dr. Berwick. The "Day Spring," which carried them, was lost on a ledge near the Jebba rock, 16 miles above Rabba. Her commander, by means of his steward,

tainly will not last. The Niger, as has been well observed, is not a lottery in which men may win for-

Selim Agha, returned overland to Lagos in February, 1858, recruited outfit, and once more made the camp.

In 1858, the African Steam-Ship Company's ship "Sunbeam," Capt. Fairweather, went to Fernando Po. Lieut. Glover made a second overland journey to Lagos, and finding the ship to draw nine feet of water, despaired, and once more returned to the camp. The "Sunbeam" was successfully taken up to Rabba, in July, 1858, by Capt. Fairweather and Mr. May, master R.N., an excellent officer. At the end of September, 1858, came out the African Steam-Ship "Rainbow," Capt. M'Nivan, and the latter returning home, she was commanded by Capt. Walker, whose interesting narrative may be found in the Blue Book of 1861.

In April, 1859, Dr. Baikie and Mr. Barter, followed during the next month by Mr. Dalton, Lieut. Glover, and Selim Agha, rode up to Rabba, and descended the Niger in the "Rainbow" and the "Sunbeam" to the Confluence, where Dr. Baikie has remained ever since.

In Nov. 1859, Lieut. Glover, during the "battle of the departments," left the Niger, having "differed in opinion" with, or been differed with by, every other in the river.

In 1860, Mr. Macgregor Laird, the main-spring of the Niger movement, died; he had not reaped where he had sown, and his executors have, it is said, resolved to end the present expedition before the spring of the year 1862. Meanwhile there is little doing. Dr. Baikie is still at the confluence, and his only white companion, Mr. Dalton, was preparing to return to England; the "Sunbeam," Capt. Walker, was also about to leave; H.M.S. "Espoir," Commander Douglas, is said to be hard and fast near Tuesday Island, about 80 miles from the mouth, and *on dit* H.M.S. "Bloodhound," Lieut.-Commanding Dolben, though drawing 10 feet of water, will be sent up with supplies for her.

It is to be hoped that Dr. Baikie will not remain unsupported. Knowingly or unknowingly he has adopted the true plan of civilising Africa, by abandoning the deleterious and impracticable coast to missionaries, and by settling in the interior. He has collected a large town around him, and with a constitution which seems proof against any hardship, privation, or fatigue, he remains there, maturing fresh plans for opening up the African interior.

Without entering into lengthy details touching the produce of the

tunes, but a field of labour in which they may earn them. It is directly connected with the twenty or thirty Nigerian regions, I may be allowed to quote the following list of the Central and Western African articles sent by him and others to the Exhibition of 1862, extracted from the Catalogue :—

AFRICA, CENTRAL.
Under Staircase, near Central Entrance to Horticultural Gardens.
Baikie, Dr. W. Balfour, R.N.—

1, 2. Striped men's cloth, from Hausa.
3, 4. Cloth made of fibres of the wine-palm and cotton, from the right bank of Kwarra.
5. A tobe, poorest quality, made in Nupe.
6. A tobe of finer quality.
7. A white tobe with plaits, from Nupe.
8. Striped trowsers, Nupe or Hausa make.
9, 10. Common cloth, for women from Bonu.
11. A woman's wrapper, made in Nupe.
12. A woman's wrapper, from Nupe.
13. A woman's wrapper, not made up, called "Locust's tooth."
14. A wrapper containing red silk, called Maizha'n baki, or "red mouth."
15. An inferior wrapper, from Nupe.
16. Blue and white cloth, from Nupe.
17, 18. Cloth made in Yoruba.
19, 20. Cloths from Nupe.
21—25. Cloths from Yoruba.
26. Small cloth for girls, from Nupe.
27. Bag from Onitsha.
28. Mat, from right bank of Kwarra.
29. Tozoli (sulphuret of lead), applied to the eyelids.
30. Man's wrapper, from Ki, in Bonu.
32. Woman's head-tie, or alfuta, from Nupe.
33. Bags for gunpowder, from Onitsha.
34, 35. A calabash and ladle.
37. Red silk, or "Al harini," of Hausa.
38. Sword hangings, or "Amila," made at Kano, in Hausa.
39. Siliya, or red silk cord, from Kano.
40. Rope, from Onitsha.
41, 42. Bags.

millions of people in the Sudan; the centres of trade are upon the stream, yet the long and terrible caravan

43. White cloth, or fari, made in Nupe and Hausa.
44. White cloth, from below the confluence.
45. A white tobe, from Nupe.
46. Four calabashes, for pepper, &c.
47. A small calabash and lid, for food.
48, 49. Pinnæ of leaves of the wine-palm, dried and used for thatching.
50. Fruit of a leguminous plant, which buries its fruit like *Arachis hypogæa*.
51. Grass cloth, of wine palm.
52. Two cloths, from Okwani.
53. White cloth, from below the confluence.
54. White perforated cloth, from the Ibo country.
55. Mats from Onitsha.
56. Large man's wrapper, from Nupe.
1. A white mat of leaves of the fan-palm, from Bonu.
2. Mats of the fan-palm, from Bonu. Fan-palm mats, called guva, or, "Elephant mats."
3. Fine mats and hats, of leaves of the *Phœnix spinosa*, dyed. Circular mats of the same material, used by chiefs, from Nupe.

AFRICA, WESTERN.
Northern Courts, under Staircase, near Central Entrance to Horticultural Gardens.
Commercial Association of Abeokuta.

1. Oils: Of beni seed, obtained by fermentation and boiling. 2. Of Egusi, from wild melon seed. 3. Of palm, for home consumption; 4. for exportation, obtained by beating, pressing, and boiling the fruit. 5, 7. Of palm nut, for home consumption; 6. for exportation. 11. Shea butter. 10. Egusi, or wild melon, fruit. 8. Beni seed. 9. Fruit of the Shea butter tree.

1. White cotton thread; 2. Dyed; 3. Blue. 4. Fine spun cotton. 5. Coarse strong spun cotton, called "Akase." 6. Akase cotton, cleaned and bowed; 7. In seed. 8. Seed itself of Akase cotton. 9, 10. Ordinary native cotton. 11, 12, 13. Ordinary green, black, and brown seeded cottons. 14. Silk cotton. 16. Country rope of bark.

march of four months still supplies articles more cheaply than we can afford to sell them, *viâ* the Niger. Hitherto all has been mismanagement. Government favoured the African Steam-ship Company, which excited the jealousy

17. Palm fibre. 18. Red dyed native silk, from Illorin. 20. Fibre used for native sponge. 23, 24, 25. Native silk, from a hairy silk-worm at Abeokuta. 26. Leaves of the cotton tree. 27. Pine-apple fibre. 29. Bow-string fibre. 30. Jute.

15. Long black pepper. 22. Senna. 21. A sample of native antimony, from Illorin.

Sundry native manufactures.

N.B.—Cotton is obtainable in any quantity, and is now grown extensively throughout the Yoruba country, especially to the east and north. Great quantities of cotton cloths, of a strong texture, are annually made, finding their way to the Brazils, and into the far interior. To obtain a largely increased supply of cotton, it is only necessary to open roads, and bring money to the market. Upwards of 2000 bales have been exported this year, and the quantity would have been doubled or trebled if the country had been at peace. The present price is 4½d. per lb. The other fibres are not at present made for exportation, though, doubtless, some of them—jute, for instance—would be, if in demand. Of the native manufacture, the grass cloths, made from palm fibre, and the cotton cloths, are most prominent. Very nice leather work is done. The art of dyeing Morocco leather different colours has been introduced from the interior. Indigo is almost the only dye which can be obtained in considerable quantities. The natives manufacture all their own iron implements, and the quality of the metal is considered good.

2. McWilliam, the late Dr. C. B.—1. Cloth, from the Confluence of the Niger and Tchadda. 2. Raw silk from Egga. 3. Cotton from the confluence. 4. Fishing spear, used by the natives of Kakunda. 5. Spoons, from Gori market. 6. A curved horn for holding galena, used to paint the eyelids. 7. Cloths, from towns on the Gambia. 8. Grass mat, from Angola. 9. Grass mat, from Binguela.

3. Walker, R. B. *Gaboon.*—A collection of mats, fibres, commercial products, skins, native arms, musical instruments, &c., of the Ba Fan tribes.

of others, especially the traders of the Brass river, who urged the villagers in the lower course to acts of direct hostility. The last 4000*l.* a year, however, have been granted, and a much larger subsidy, say 9000*l.* or 10,000*l.*, should take its place. Mixed expeditions have been sent out only to fail: where naval officers, missionaries, and mercantile men are all urging their several interests, success can hardly be expected. The quarrels between the members of the last expedition completely crippled it: moreover, it was managed on Exeter Hall principles. Captain Trotter frightened his sailors to death by chalking up, it is said, "PREPARE TO MEET THY GOD," and similar consolatory recipes, in the largest letters, all about the ship. The next exploration allowed the Krumen to rob what they pleased, and the lieutenant who managed naval matters is said to have encouraged slaves to desert from their masters—a proceeding sufficient to account for any failure.

We shall never drop the Niger: the main artery of Western Africa north of the Line must not be neglected. All agree that it will pay pounds, where pence are now collected, though people differ as to the means of making it pay. After many a long "talk" with those whose opinions are worth most, I propound the following as the directest way of opening up the stream. A large armed hulk, manned by Krumen, under military or naval law, and carrying an outfit like that sent to the Brass river, would be stationed at Akassa, within the Nun bar. The next measure would be to make treaties with the hostile chiefs of the delta, settling a certain Comey upon them: the want of this is the principal cause of disturbances. The great requisite would be a commander ready to act with energy, and not "mickonary;" two gunboats would be safer, in case of grounding, than one, and they should not enter the river later than the first of June. After making or forcing a peace, postal and intercolonial steamers might begin plying; they should visit the river every month or six weeks, and steam as high as the Confluence, where they could run all the year round, if built after the American fashion, flat-bottomed, drawing two to three feet, with stern wheels, and with walking-beam engines; the furnaces should be able to burn wood, the bulwarks high and musket-proof, and the armament wall-pieces, and a few culverins. After the steamers would come depots and trading-houses, at the five following points :—

1. Anjámá, at the head of the lower delta.
2. Aboh, at the head of the upper delta.
3. Oricha, midway between the sea and the Confluence.
4. Idda, between the Onicha and the Confluence.
5. Ibegbe, or the Confluence of the Kwara and Binue.

Thus, and thus only, can considerable collections of cotton be made upon the Niger; and thus the traffic of the Great Artery, which injured, it is to be feared, the fortunes of the intrepid explorer, will, after a few years, become of importance to England.

On the morning of the 25th September I inspected, *en passant*, what is supposed to be the "Beautiful Cape."

To the leeward, or eastward, is "Cape Filana," by the English called Palm Point, a fine clump of feathery trees springing from a thin line of the blondest sand. Here was the old Portuguese town of Akassa, long since in ruins: it is said that a tomb was lately found there, bearing the date A.D. 1635. If this be the case, the Portuguese must have known the upper Niger centuries before we did, and must have kept it a mystery as profound as the Kongo is in the year of grace 1861. Point Trotter, a blue line of tree-clad bluff, rises within Filana, and opposite the latter, or to the westward, is Cape Nun, which we know as "West Point." The bar is said to be one of the best on this coast: it has shifted, however, since the date of the last chart.

We are now fairly inside the Bight of Biafra, or Biaffra, an English corruption from the Portuguese Rio de Maffras, a name which they gave to one of the rivers. It is the innermost part of the Guinea Gulf, extending from Cape Formoso, or the Delta of the Niger, in N. lat. 4° 16' 17" to Cape St. John, in N. lat. 1° 9' 7". A straight line, uniting both these promontories, and passing near Prince's Island, would measure about 450 miles; along the coast about 650. It is divided into two very distinct sections by the mass of mountains called the Camaroons. The country to the north of that glorious pile is a false coast, a succession of continental islands and land in a state of formation. The expanse of mud and mangrove forms a fit habitation for the iguana and crocodile, with flats and fetid lagoons haunted by crabs and craw-fish; whilst a few villages, at long intervals, lurk at the bottom of blind channels and tidal inlets, where they can preserve themselves by fight or flight. The creeks and rivers, outspread as a network over the mass of dense and rotten vegetation, are kept *in loco* by the strong and steady tides which dredge the beds without sweeping away the mangroves that hedge them in. A glance shows you that all around is literally a young country, which, perhaps, in ages to be may constitute a Nigrotic empire. To the south, beginning even at the Camaroons river, there is a change: the banks are high and clayey, the palm-oil tree (Elæis Guineensis) becomes rarer, yielding in traffic to ivory, and the people are, though wilder, a finer race than those of the Delta. This gradual improvement continues through the Gaboon river to Angola, where provisions are procurable, horses will live, and human life has some enjoyment. The southern section of the Bight of Biafra contains, also, two little coves, known in charts as the Bights of Pannavia and Bata; the words, however, are now little used. Pannavia lies to the north of the Batanga country, whose river, the Elobe, forms its southern extremity. The Bight of Bata is between the Campo and the Benito rivers; it is the seat of those remarkable foundations—the Seven Hills or Sisters.

Of the twenty-five streams which discharge themselves into this great Bight, there are six Oil Rivers—viz., the Nun, or Niger, the New Calabar, Bonny, Old Calabar, Camaroons, and Malimba: those to the south are visited for ivory, gum-elastic, and timber, especially ebony, African cedar, and mahogany, cam-wood and dye-wood. As yet nothing is known of the interior.

At 7 A.M. on the 25th September we found ourselves off the Brass river.* In this part of the coast every stream appears to have received, from its christeners—Diego Cam, or Fernão de Poo—as many names as that Portuguese hidalgo to whom, as the old Spanish story relates, the innkeeper refused to open his gates, stating that he could not accommodate so many people. The Brass is called Second River, because in old times ships bound for the New Calabar and Bonny estuary used to coast down the six rivers, along the 60 to 70 miles eastward from the Nun or Niger. It is also known to the English as St. John; to the Portuguese as Rio Bento; and some books call it the Oddy, Fonsoady, and Malfonsa.

The land is mangrove, the sky cloudy—nimbus and cumulus disposed meridionally, as they love to be in the tropics, flecking patches of a pale milk-and-water blue—and the dangerous bar chafes and seethes across a dwarf indent, whose bluff and wooded banks open like portals into the azure region within. The next, passed at almost an equal distance—ten to eleven miles—with surprising regularity of shelve, one fathom of depth representing one mile of distance off shore, is the St. Nicholas, Filana or Tilana, Sempta or Lempta,† Juan Diaz, or Third

---

* It was so called from the then favourite object of traffic—"Neptunes" or brass pans.

† Some apply the last two names to the Fourth River, the Santa Barbara.

River; its double bar, which breaks right across, was afterwards crossed by the Consul and Lieutenant Dolben, H.M.S. "Bloodhound," under direction of the late Captain Alexander Grant; they found this stream to be a branch of the Brass river, and there is a well-known creek which threading the "Mosquito Country," as it is called, leads into the New Calabar. Leaving the St. Nicholas, whose coast projects somewhat seawards, we made the broad Santa Barbara, Meas, or Fourth River, another fine study of a bar. The Consul and Lieutenant Dolben were nearly swamped in an attempt to cross it, but escaped, much to the regret of certain gentry on board H. M. S. "Bloodhound," who would willingly have quitted the Bights and the Oil Rivers for the "South Coast Station."

It was almost too far to distinguish the gap of the half-way stream, Rio San Bartolomeo, or the Fifth River. The glass, however, showed us from the southwards an island in mid-channel, formed by two narrow arms; and the bar was seen bursting with rollers, whose "wall-like sides and hairy heads" looked peculiarly unprepossessing. Then came the Rio Sombreiro, also called the Rio dos Tres Irmãos,—of the Three Brothers— and Sixth River: the first name is derived from a patch of trees on the bluff western entrance, resembling a priest's shovel-hat; they have of course disappeared long ago. Another seven miles took us to our present destination, the broad estuary of the New Calabar, or Kalabar, *alias* Rio Real, *alias* Calbarine, *alias* Neue Calborgh, *alias*

Calbary.* The brother stream, Bonny, or Grand Bonny, is at least as rich in nomenclature.† Its present popular English name is doubtless derived through the native word "Obani." The contrast between name and nature must have rendered the easy corruption a fashionable pleasantry—nothing can be more categorically unbonny —and possibly the foul sky, fouler water, and foulest land, may have reminded some irate Scotchman of Bonny Dundee, thereby giving so *débonnaire* a sound to so ungodly a hole. "Grand" it is—in abominations, moral and physical.

The approach to the Bonny from the west is denoted by Fouché, or Foché, Gap, a deep indentation in the wooded seabank, three miles to westward of the estuary. Then comes the village and the Point Fouché. Barbot calls the former Foko, and says that the Dutch named it "Wyndorp," on account of its abundance of palm wine: he places it on an island and numbers 309 houses. Dr. Daniell reckons above 300 souls, pilots and fishermen. They are under King Amakree, of New Calabar (from

---

* The name is said to date from almost two centuries back, when one of the Ephraim Duke family from old Calabar settled here.

† Barbot, 1678-1706, calls it Bandy, or Great Bandy river. The people's own word is Okoloma; the Ibos call it Obani, Ibani, and Okoloba; and the Abo tribe of Ibos call it Osiminika.

All is changed since 1826, when H. M. S. "Barracouta" surveyed it. Sualo Island, east of New Calabar mouth, is now covered with trees, and is growing to be part of the main land. Monkey Creek and Young Town are not laid down at all; Breaker Island is laid down as a mere shoal—it is now overgrown with vegetation, and is rapidly rising from the sea.

whose rule, however, they would willingly escape), and they want a lesson, as do most of the negroes in these parts; but, ten to fifteen years ago, the "Juju-king" Awanta was deported to Ascension Island for firing upon ships' boats. We passed the mouth of the New Calabar, about one mile broad, and divided from the Bonny by the Middle Bank, or Calabar Flat. We then crossed over, passing by Breaker Island in the centre to near Rough Corner, the east end of the estuary: Barbot places his Bandy Point four leagues east of Fouché Point; it is usually reckoned seven miles across.

The proper Bonny mouth is two to three miles broad, bounded by Rough Corner, which from its clump of trees the Portuguese called Fanal, or the Lighthouse, and Breaker Island, a low sandy bushy patch, distinctly above high water, and commanding a fine view of the outer bar. Portuguese Channel and Man-of-War Channel being unbuoyed, are left to starboard; they are never used by the mail steamers. There are three chief banks, the Western, the Balcur, connected by a sandpit with the former, and separated by deep water from the third or Portuguese Bank. The shifting of the swashways and channels makes this river, even with the best of lead and look-out, a place of cold perspiration to shipowners; and so it will remain, until some acute official fines the negroes 100 puncheons, and buoys the entrance. The A. S. S. Company is most unwise in stationing its large steamers within this river, whose adit presents more dangers than all the rest of the voyage together, whilst the salt water affects the ships' bottoms, and materially interferes with their rate of progress.

At 1 P.M., when we prepared to run in, the amphitheatre of bar and breakers—roaring, foaming, and bursting everywhere ahead of us, and on both sides—looked uncommonly threatening. We followed, however, the usual rule, avoided the Baleur bank, by keeping Peter Fortis, or Peterside, a village on the river's right bank, a sail's breadth open from Juju Point, a projection of the left shore. The buoys were in good order; we left the outer one on our left, the "Red Nun" and the "Black Can" —a little bucket-like affair—on our right, and we looked vainly for the Black Beacon of the charts. We carried five feet of water clear over the outer bar, which is not so long as that of Lagos; and the inner, here, as in all other African rivers, presents no terrors. Rough Corner is known by an unwhitewashed framework, representing the fanal. A native house or two subsequently added represent embryo defences against possible Yankee pirates. When troubles with America were expected, the supercargoes proposed raising a battery at Rough Corner, to command the run in; the clear way was, however, nearly three miles broad, and would require at least a floating battery. The bar was not unduly violent: perhaps the annual little girl had just been sacrificed to it.*
Behind the low, jagged line of trees, called Breaker Island,

---

* According to Dr. Madden (Parliamentary Report, 1842), this barbarous custom was kept up as late as 1840, and it is more than probable that the sacrifice is still privately performed.

a giant cloud, purple with wrath, usurped one quarter of the heavens, and threatened trouble.

The Bonny fleet then drew in sight, tall ships that are pleasant to look at—little profitable, however—and seventeen in number. There were seven or eight hulks, four of them beached, all whitewashed and thickly thatched over; the most conspicuous was the "William Money," an old Indiaman, teak-built and Dutch-like; she is about seventy years old, and now acts coal-hulk to the A. S. S. Company. The merchantmen rode high up the stream; lower down, in the men-of-war anchorage, lay a single paddle-wheel, which proved to be H. M. S. "Bloodhound," Lieut.-Commanding Dolben, bound for the Niger, with a cargo of two score black missionaries, male and female, who managed to oust him from his cabin, and to beg provisions till he had not the heart to refuse. As we passed Rough Corner on our starboard side we remarked the excessive denseness of the bush; near the framework of whitewashed scantling that acts landmark, is a small platform, where it is said sporting skippers have spent the night, waiting for leopards, here called "tigers." European sailors were seen perambulating the sands; it was low tide then; at the flow this "marine parade" is under water, and decks form the only promenade. Within Rough Corner, and separated by a mile of bend, or baylet, lies Juju Point—the white man's grave before the cemetery was removed to the former place: now it is occupied by witch houses and holy trees. From this point three giants of the forest, rising side by side, mark the site of Bonny Town—one smells it, however. Traces of old barracoons are shown on the other side of the creek, which leads up to Juju Town; occasionally a ship's gig, with a white face in the stern, and six Krumen rowing, may be seen stealing along like cat on housetop that way. "The sex" is not fetish at Juju Town, and King Jack is a *bon enfant*, a *Gunjisk i tildi*, or "Golden Sparrow," as the Persians call it. A little beyond this lies Smoke Town, so called from the curls of vapour that alone denote its existence; there were, however, sundry palms, everywhere in Africa the symbol of population. On the other side of the broad channel is a low dark bank of vegetation, " Deadman's Island," thus grimly called from the feud between the Bonny people and the New Calabars. We pass in succession Tallifer (1000 souls), half hidden by bush; Fishtown, and the village of Peter Fortis, the latter opposite the Bonny creek. But, where is Bonny itself? The experts reply by pointing to a few rugged wash-houses on the beach, and by telling you that the town, being in a hollow, shows only the top of its smoke to the river.

From the sixteenth century almost to the present day, Bonny was the great slave market of the Bights, seldom exporting less than 16,000 souls a year. According to the philanthropic Clarkson ("History of the Abolition of the Slave-Trade"), this river and Old Calabar exported as many " contrabands " as all the rest of the coast together. Hence the "Eboe" (Ibo) woman of the United States. This lasted till 1832, when it came abruptly to an end; from 1825 it had begun to decline. There are still men on the river who can remember the blockade of boats at the mouth, and tell with gusto how the jolly slavers often managed to make a run. The fate of Bonny is now changed. The old slave river has now become the great centre of the palm-oil trade, seldom exporting less than 16,000, and sometimes 18,000, tons per annum, or nearly three-quarters of a million of pounds sterling, to be divided amongst ten or twelve houses.*

An old collier-like craft, painfully bluff, looked sadly misplaced near the noble Bonny fleet. She proved to be the brig "Bewley," Captain Le Marquand (Jersey man), of 184 tons new register, twenty-eight years old, and hardly worth £400. Messrs. Gammon, Sons, and Carter, coal merchants at Ratcliffe, chartered her, with a crew of twelve articled seamen, for the snug sum of £200 per mensem—receiving £900 in advance—to the King Pimento of these Cannibal Lands, who has come to his own again. On the 18th August, 1861, his Majesty reached the river, without a poet-laureate, but accompanied by nine men—a premier, a secretary, an assistant-secretary, three clerks, and one doctor,—who, before leaving home, expressly stipulated that he was to "hold his proper position at court,"—a farmer to trim mangroves, and a valet for the royal person. The salaries varied from £600 a-year, plus £15 for naval

* The Bonny puncheon is thirty-eight inches in head, and forty-two in stern, and contains 240 gallons.

uniforms, to £60, and some of these imprudent greenhorns were men with families at home, and perhaps in want. I regret to say that there were two Englishwomen,—Mrs. Wood, the gardener's wife, who was to act schoolmistress, and "Miss Mary," a servant girl, who became maid-of-honour to Eleanor, *alias* Allaputa Queen Pimento. The *suite*, on seeing the real state of affairs, became highly indignant; they were half-starved on board, and when they reached the unbonny river, the store of doubloons, supposed to be concealed, was not forthcoming; nor was the sum of £12,000, owed by the King of Calabar, paid. One of them was too glad to compromise a debt of £120 on the receipt of half-a-sovereign, the only specie in the royal exchequer. The captain wanted £1829, arrears of pay, and retained the king's kit, which royalty valued at £1676,—the last figure removed would probably be nearer truth. Meanwhile there was a scene on board the "Bewley" that would hardly bear describing; the less said about the "inner life of an African king," and his *suite* also, the better.

About eighty or ninety years ago, an Ibo chief settled with his slaves on the Bonny river. This Opubo, or Obullo, the "Great Man," was grandfather of the present chief: his son took the name of Pepper, which he now spells with a change, and married a woman from the Abilli (Billa) country, west of the New Calabar river. Their progeny, the "king," in the African acceptation of the word, also espoused a bush-woman. He is one of the three free men in this part of the river, the others being Ben Pepple, a half-idiot, and our friend Jack Brown, of Juju Town; this is a small proportion to about 9000 serviles, of whom some few are "Bonny free," but none "proper free."* This population of Ibo slaves speaks the Okoloma, or Bonny language; but all the slave "gentlemen" know a kind of English. On the 21st November, 1848, he made a treaty for the suppression of slavery with Captain Eden, of Her Majesty's ship "Amphitrite," for an annual present of $2000 till 1854. In 1853 a stroke of paralysis, induced by over-indulgence, crippled King Pimento's right side, and from this hemiplegia he has never recovered. Two of his men, Ishakko, *alias* Fred Pepple, and Yanibu, were then appointed as chiefs and regents. On the 23rd January, 1854, Mr. Consul Beecroft, at the request of all the native chiefs and traders, deposed his Majesty, who was ruining the river by his wars with Calabar, and substituted for him Prince Dappa, or Dapho, son of Pimento's elder brother, and therefore rightful heir to the stool. Pepple was carried to Fernando Po, and his protector died there. At last it was resolved by Commodore Adams and Mr. Acting-Consul Lynslager to send the king, with Allaputa, his wife, and his family, to Ascension Island. On the 7th of December, however, he fled into the bush

* The population of Bonny is calculated to be 5000 to 6000; of Juju Town, 1500; Tallifer, 1000; and the rest are less. New Calabar numbers some 4000.

à la Charles, and sat under two large trees surrounded by bushwood. The royal oak, however, was not here, and Pimento was sent off the next day on board Her Majesty's ship "Pluto," Commander Clavering, begging hard that if he died his body might be headed up in a cask of rum, and sent to lie near his fathers. Since that time he has enjoyed the memory of Ascension, which he has learned to call his St. Helena.

Prince Dapho died 13th August, 1855, surgeons say of inter-susceptio, others of poison, administered by friends of the ex-king. Fred Pepple and Yanibu were saved with difficulty from the fury of the mob by Captain Witt, of the "Ferozepore," when a shocking massacre commenced; 600 to 700 friends of the "king" were murdered; many blew themselves up; the white man's house—used by the court of equity, and also as a chapel—was razed to the ground, and trade was stopped by the people, because the supposed poisoners were carried by Mr. Acting-Consul Lynslager to Fernando Po. On the 1st September, 1855, the same official visiting the river in Her Majesty's ship "Philomel," Commander Skene, appointed four regents, viz., Annie (*alias* Ilola) Pepple, Captain Hart (*alias* Affo Dappa?), Ada Allison,* and Manilla Pepple.

* These ridiculous names are taken from English ships. The slave chiefs have all their own native names, *e.g.*, Manilla Pepple is known as Erinashaboo. All were the property of old King Pepple, who, when dying, appointed Annie Pepple as guardian of his son's wealth. He fought with Manilla Pepple, was beaten, took to drink, and died. His son is the present Annie Pepple.

Meanwhile, King Pimento was so persevering a petitioner that he was allowed, in November, 1855, to quit Ascension for S'a Leone, where he arrived some time in 1856. After another bout of correspondence he reached London in 1857; there he resided four years, was baptised, and became a temperance man, sitting under the great George Cruikshank. He abandoned his favourite dish, a boy's hand-palms, and was admitted to the Upper House, where doubtless he graced *les nobles lords* as much as Sir Jung Bahadur does the Christian Knights of the Bath. He became very pious; he begged £20,000 to raise a missionary establishment —the traders declare it is the one thing wanted for total ruin to the river,—and he roughed it in champagne and sherry. The application for a mission was celebrated by a missionary periodical in some fearful verse, beginning with—

"Oh, who shall succour Bonny's King!"

He seemed to me, however, to have a little neglected his English. The answer to my question touching her sable majesty's health, was "He lib!" meaning thank you, she is quite well.

Pimento, permitted to return home, arrived in the Bonny river on the 18th of August. Instead of landing at once, as expected, he lingered coward-like on board till the 15th of October, although several of the supercargoes had offered to accompany him. Instead of going to the Juju-House,—it fell, by-the-by, a terrible bad omen, on the day of his disembarkation—he used to send for supercargoes to read the Scriptures to him. By way of contrast, he despatched his assistant-secretary and chief clerk, in naval uniforms, swords included, to invite the four regents and chiefs on board the "Bewley." The influential slave, Ilola, *alias* Annie Pepple, whose father was a confidential chattel of the former king, whose body is buried in his house, and Affo Dappa, head slave to the late Prince Dapho, and one of the four regents, steadily refused.

After two or three meetings, King Pimento sent his ship's captain, with the same gentlemen—one of these had been twenty-eight days in Paris, vainly trying to negotiate a French treaty—armed with revolvers, to fetch Ilola by force, if necessary. Seven of the Manillas were combined against Pimento, about seventeen for him, and by striking this blow at Ilola, all would have been brought round. The white men went to the black man's house, and offered a document for signature, which was refused. Presently a pistol dropped out of a certain pocket. About fifty negroes had assembled, but Ilola quietly promising to return, left the house and quitted the town. He had hemiplegia of the left side shortly afterwards, and died, probably poisoned.

When King Pimento landed, all his whites were dismissed. The unhappy doctor, who had stipulated about his "position at Court," was only too glad to take a free passage to Fernando Po, and his majesty was with difficulty persuaded to pay the fare. The supercargoes most kindly contributed 10*l.* to remove the unfortunate

Englishwomen from the pollution of such a position. "Miss Mary" left in October, on board the "Golden Age." Mr. Wood and his wife followed a month afterwards, in the "Star of the Sea," and the premier, the head secretary, and the last of the clerks disappeared in December. The wretched valet was the only one permanently left, a rosy-faced English William; he had died of semi-starvation and discomfort. Yet Pimento has done nothing towards recovering power. Perhaps it is better he should not; he has learned a trick or two in Europe, and he only awaits his opportunity; he threatens with the lawyer or the missionary on all occasions. He lately asked permission to establish a consul for Bonny in London, at a salary of 500*l.*: and he gave as a reason for the indulgence, that he had always permitted Her British Majesty's consul to visit his dominions in the Bights of Benin and Biafra. This is not bad for an individual who dares not stir a cannon shot from his townlet, and whose name and fame amongst his fellow chiefs are about equal to the area of his territories. Of course the strings of this poor old black puppet are pulled by gentlemen "*qui font l'industrie*" nearer home.

The African Steam Ship "Blackland," was to remain two days at Grand Bonny, we therefore took the opportunity of visiting its celebrated Juju House. Taking heart of grace, and stuffing our noses with camphored cotton, we rowed up the river; it was neap tide, and the waters had left a terrible sight of bare mud and naked slime. The stream runs apparently north and south; it is foul and feculent as Father Thames of the Tom cats, and the atmosphere around it forms a *bouquet d'Afrique,* worse than that of a London ball-room, which I had hitherto believed to be the *ne plus ultra* of supportable decomposition, animal and vegetable. Reaching a creek about four miles from the mouth, and connected with the Andoni, corrupted from San Antonio, and the Kom Toro, or Kom river, whose place is marked in our hydrographic charts, but remains nameless,* returned to the east, and fronted the town of Bonny, or as the people call it, Kalomi. It was rising from its ashes, having been burned down about one month before. This is the north or west end, the site is best described by a former observer to be "all water, mud banks, and mangroves—mangroves, mud banks, and water." The houses are Africanised models of the Swiss cottage, the sharpest gables, the most acutangular ridge roofs, with all the exaggerated goniology of the last Neo-Gothic. The roofs are of dirty thatch, sometimes with a misplaced glass window half way up, and the sides are smeared with a sickly yellow clay taken from the creek. There were some fine canoes, matted over against the sea and rain, and provided with a sand hearth for fire, when cold is felt. Some of them are sixty to seventy feet long, and easily carry twelve puncheons of palm oil; there may be 100 pull-a-boys, or paddlers, of whom fifty will be fighting men, and the sides bristle

* In old maps the Andoni is called Rio de San Domingo, Loitomba, or Laitomba: the Kom Toro (or Kan Toro) is called Rio.

with swords, falconets, and wall pieces, whilst a long carronade is lashed to strong cross-pieces in the bow. We turned into a much smaller back-water, which leads a few yards to the south; at low water it will be a sheet of putrifying slime, in which a man would sink knee deep, and in places women and boys were washing themselves with their waist clothes, which they will presently wring out and restore. It was the most squalid of sights; no relieving feature but a few large cotton-trees and masses of parasites, which hem in the other side of Bonny. Nothing easier than to find a better site for Bonny, but it is "Bonny fash" to stick to Bonny. We forced the boat upon this sewer, and soon reached the landing-place, a rude scaffold of rough round tree-trunks lashed to uprights, and leading up the slippery clay embankment. After this spectacle of filth, I resolved to avoid even the 'Nda, or Bonny salmon, of which writers speak so highly.

Landing, we observed the effects of the fire, which has been highly beneficial in removing scorpions, centipedes, and whip-snakes, the myriads of mosquitoes and sand-flies, which, too minute almost to be seen, cannot be guarded against. The houses were rising rapidly. The chiefs collect, on such occasions, their families and dependents, and dividing them into companies, apply them to different work in rebuilding. Some cut stakes in the bush, others sharpen and plait them with withies and wattles, others apply the dab, whilst the rest prepare beams and thatching for the roof, or break up old boxes to make doors and shutters. The floor is of tamped earth. Small houses have but three compartments, kitchen, salon, and Juju-room, or private chapel. Great men have most intricate establishments, all a congeries of rooms, *oubliettes*, *culs de sac*, and passages, more like a labyrinth than a dwelling-house. The outer entrances and the interior doors—which must serve as chimneys—are fortified with strong staked thresholds, eighteen inches high. They are possibly intended to keep out animals; the "housemaster" is fond of sitting there, and if you cross the step whilst he is so doing, he will have a sickness, and complain of "poison for eye," that is, you have bewitched him. The women's and the men's apartments are distinct, and furniture, such as it is, is always either of the commonest kind or broken by the awkward slaves. The wealthy make their houses Old Curiosity Shops, everything, in fact, from gold cloth to a penny print. The greater part of their wealth, however, is packed up in boxes, huddled into a lumber room, or buried, so that it never lasts long. The bed is a grass mat, and a fire of embers enables men to dispense with bedding. Every gentleman must have his "Juju-room," and every little *rentier* his altar. The Lares and Penates are anything between a sheet of Punch and a tobacco pipe. This private chapel is a favourite place for stowing away things, especially rum, as no one will then steal it. Kings and chiefs are buried in the grand Juju-houses.

After walking through the rising town, we pursued

our way towards the "Grand Juju." Nothing worse than the streets, narrow, filthy, pool-dotted paths, that wound between the houses and the remnants of rank bush. Some of the people there met, were curiously fair, when compared with the coal-black Ejo men, and all were scantily clad, even adult girls had not a trace of clothing. The slaves wore a truly miserable appearance, lean and deformed, with krakra lepra and fearful ulcerations. It is in these places that one begins to feel a doubt touching the total suppression of slavery. The chiefs openly beg that the rules may be relaxed, in order that they may get rid of their criminals. This is at present impossible, and the effects are a reduplication of misery—we pamper our convicts, Africans torture them to death. Cheapness of the human article is another cause of immense misery to it. In some rivers a canoe crew never lasts three years. Pilfering—"Show me a black man and I will show you a thief," say the traders—and debauchery, are natural to the slave, and they must be repressed by abominable cruelties. The master thinks nothing of nailing their hands to a water-cask, of mutilating them in various ways—many lose their eyes by being peppered, after the East Indian fashion, with coarsely powdered cayenne—their ears are cut off, or they are flogged. The whip is composed of a twisted bullock's or hippopotamus's hide, sun-dried, with sharp edges at the turns, and often wrapped with copper wire; it is less merciful even than the knout, now historical. The operation may be prolonged for hours or for a whole day, the culprit's arms being tied to a rafter, which keeps them at full stretch, and every fifteen minutes or so, a whack that cuts away the flesh like a knife, is administered. This is a favourite treatment for guilty wives, who are also ripped up, cut to pieces, or thrown to the sharks. If a woman has twins, or becomes mother of more than four, the parent is banished, and the children are destroyed. The greatest insult is to point at a man with arm and two fingers extended, saying at the same, *Nama Shubra, i.e.,* one of wins, or a son of some lower animal. When a great man dies, all kinds of barbarities are committed, slaves are buried, or floated down the river bound to bamboo sticks and mats, till eaten piecemeal by sharks.

The slave, as might be expected, is not less brutal than his lord. It amazes me to hear Englishmen plead that there is moral degradation to a negro bought by a white man, and none when serving under a black man. The philanthropists, doubtless, think how our poorer classes at home, in the nineteenth century, would feel if hurried from liberty to eternal servitude by some nefarious African. But can any civilised sentiments belong to the miserable half-starved being, whose one scanty meal of vegetable per day is eked out with monkey and snake, cat and dog, maggot and grub; whose life is ceaseless toil, varied only by torture, and who may be destroyed at any moment by a nod from his owner? When the slave has once surmounted his dread of being shipped by the white man, nothing under the sun would, I believe, induce him willingly to return to what he should call his home. And as they were, our West Indian colonies were lands of happiness compared with the Oil Rivers; as for the "Southern States," the slave's lot is paradise when succeeding what he endures on the west coast of Africa. I believe these to be facts, but *tant pis pour les faits*. Presently, however, the philanthropic theory shall fall, and shall be replaced by a new fabric built upon a more solid foundation.

The Juju-house, now a heap of ruins, was a wattle and dab oblong of 30 to 40 feet. At the head of the room rose a kind of altar, with mat eaves to throw off the rain, and concave, bulging out behind. Across the front, underneath the roofing, in lines impaled together, were fleshless human skulls, often painted and decorated: one had a thick black imitation beard, doubtless a copy of life. Between these two rows were lines of goat's heads, also streaked with red and white, whilst an old bar shot, probably used as a club for felling the victims, hung from a corner. Near the ground there was a horizontal board, striped like the relics, and a sweep of loose thatch from below it formed a base to the altar, and left a central space in which was a round hole, with a raised rim of clay, to receive libations and the blood of victims. There were scattered skulls and spare rows of crania, impaled like Kababs, and planted with their stakes against the wall. As there had been no prisoners of late, I saw none of those trunkless heads "which placed on their necks, with their faces towards the Juju-house, present a dreadful and appalling appearance, as of men rising from the ground." To a small framework of sticks outside, were nailed those relics which the Abyssinians prefer as trophies. The foul iguana, as appropriate to this land as is the shark to these waters, crawled about all this wreck of humanity with perfect fearlessness. Some years ago the monkey was Juju, but he was degraded for theft, a battue took place, and all were "chopped." So these people not only eat each other's gods, but, like certain Christians, their own god. The iguana has since been in favour, and the stranger who maltreats one would be roughly handled. White cloth is also Juju, and the Fetishman's caprice can invent as many other such ordinances as the religion of the place may require.

There is apparently in this people a physical delight in cruelty to beast as well as to man. The sight of suffering seems to bring them an enjoyment without which the world is tame; probably the wholesale murderers and torturers of history, from Phalaris and Nero downwards, took an animal and sensual pleasure—all the passions are sisters—in the look of blood and in the inspection of mortal agonies. I can see no other explanation of the phenomena which meet my eye in Africa. In almost all the towns on the Oil Rivers, you see dead or dying animals fastened in some agonising position. Poultry is most common, because cheapest—eggs and milk are Juju to slaves here—they are tied by the legs head downwards, or lashed round the body to a stake or a tree, where they remain till they fall in fragments. If a man be unwell, he hangs a live chicken round his throat, expecting that its pain will abstract from his sufferings. Goats are lashed head downwards tightly to wooden pillars, and are allowed to die a lingering death; even the harmless tortoise cannot escape impalement. Blood seems to be the favourite ornament for a man's face, as pattern-painting with some dark colour like indigo is the proper decoration for a woman. At funerals numbers of goats and poultry are sacrificed for the benefit of the deceased, and the corpse is sprinkled with the warm blood. The headless trunks are laid upon the body, and if the fowls flap their wings, which they will do for some seconds after decapitation, it is a good omen for the dead man. When male prisoners of war are taken, they are brought home for sacrifice and food, whilst their infants and children are sometimes supported by the middle from poles planted in the canoe. The priest decapitates the men—for ordinary executions each chief has his own headsman—and no one doubts that the bodies are eaten. Mr. Smith and Dr. Hutchinson both aver that they witnessed actual cases. The former declares that when old Pepple, father of the present man, took captive king Amakree, of New Calabar, he gave a large feast to the European slave-traders on the river; all was on a grand scale, but the reader might perhaps find some difficulty in guessing the name of the dish placed before his Majesty at the head of the table. It was the bloody heart of the King of Calabar, just as it had been torn from the body. He took it in his hand and devoured it with the greatest apparent gusto, remarking, " This is the way I serve my enemies!"

Shortly after my first visit, five prisoners of war were brought in from the eastern country. I saw in the Juju-house their skulls, which were suspiciously white and clean, as if boiled, and not a white man doubted that they had been eaten. The fact is that they cannot afford to reject any kind of provisions, and after a year or two amongst the people, even a European would, I suspect, look somewhat queerly upon a fat little black boy. Living at Bonny is exceedingly expensive, and at the end of the season a cloth worth 3s. has been known to fetch only three small yams. Of course if a stranger asks about their anthropophagy they will invariably reply *anemea*—I don't know!

The climate of the Bonny is exceedingly debilitating; like that of Baghdad and Zanzibar, it is celebrated for developing latent diseases. The Harmattan, or dry season, locally called *Ikringa,* begins in early December, and lasts three months; old stagers usually find it the most unhealthy; it is invigorating, however, to the stranger, who admires the cool grey look of the sky, and the sensation of dry cold which reminds him of the north. March, April, and May are the healthiest months, calm and serene, with pleasant breezes, and highly fitted for travelling. The rainy season sets in about latter May, and continues till the end of September; during July and August it rains almost incessantly, except for an hour or two in the middle of the day. September is a fine month, and in October and November begin the tornadoes, which continue till the Harmattan sets in.

The Bonny, like all regions on this coast, is subject to periodical epidemics, which clear off almost all the white population. Such a year has just happened. The tornadoes had been scanty, and it was observed that the land wind had taken the place of the sea breeze. A typhus, which was rather a yellow fever, soon developed itself. The first case happened on the 14th March, 1862, and was speedily followed by a crisis in May. The last cannot be said to have occurred. Yet, between the middle of March and July, out of a total of 278 to 300 Europeans, there died six supercargoes, five doctors, five clerks, and 146 men, a total of 162. One ship, the "Osprey," lost all her crew—sixteen to seventeen men—except the master. During that fatal year the vomito, of late confined to Northern Guinea, Gambia, and Sierra Leone, descended the West African coast as far as Fernando Po, and extended northwards to Tenerife. It was not confined to Europeans, the Bonny men died by hundreds. The "coffee-grounds" and the yellow colour of the corpse showed what the disease was. And in some places it was followed by a typhus of exaggerated type, the patient sinking at once, and dying after a few hours of low muttering delirium.

The usual Bonny working day is simple. The "gentleman" comes on board as early as possible after daylight, and begins the usual process of "round trade," chaffering and dodging with all his might, now "ryling up" the agent, then sawdering him down, but never going to extremes. He breaks his fast when he can, lounges about, sitting as if at home, using tobacco, and occasionally begging for this, that, and the other thing. After the forenoon thus profitably and energetically spent, he disappears about midday, and is seen no more till the morrow.

The holiday is one of unmixed laziness: the gentleman dozes till late in front of the dead fire that went out before "Cockerappeak." Sending back his night companion to the women's apartments, he passes into a court, sits upon the high threshold and enjoys an air bath, chewing the while pieces of fibrous wood or the plantain fibres, called sápo in the dialect of the Gold Coast. This is followed by the tooth stick, now becoming used in England; it has the advantage over the brush that every separate tooth obtains a careful attention, inside as well as outside. Whilst thus cleansing mouth and throat from the hesternal fumes of tobacco and palm wine, he cracks his joints and—equivalent to European stretching—he twists his neck as much as possible without dislocation.

The whole fabric of society is naturally founded on polygamy. Some of the head chiefs have as many as fifty wives—all, as usual, under the head wife or queen, who is usually the daughter of some great house. There is the customary anxiety for a numerous offspring; yet, contradictorily enough, there are many ways of limiting propagation, such as for instance the destruction of twins, and the banishment of the too prolific mother.

The gentleman presently steps into his bathing room, and undergoes, in the hands of his favourite wives, a thorough soaping from head to foot. The apartment has usually a strong floor of raised rafters, which allow the water to drain off, and the seat is an empty box or a block of wood. There are neither baths nor tubs; calabashes of cold water are poured upon the head, after the fashion of the East Indian "Ghara," and hands are used as flesh brushes to rub the back. He then indulges in a practice popularly known as "wash um belly." During these operations audiences are given to favourites and other persons coming on business.

After being duly scrubbed the gentleman proceeds to his robing court, where sundry large boxes, like sea chests, contain his dresses and ornaments. He is extremely fastidious about the choice of his toilette, opening, and perhaps tying on, a dozen cloths before one suits his fancy. He will kiss it in token of admiration or respect if it has belonged to his ancestors. A silk pocket handkerchief is then folded triangularly and passed through a loop in the knife scabbard—like the British sailor they are abandoning the clasp knife for the bowie form—which is thus attached to the right side. His skin is then polished up with a little palm oil, and his neck, wrists and ankles are adorned with strings of coral or beads, and substantial metal or ivory rings, sometimes decorated with his English name cut out, or "fixed" in various coloured tacks. Finally, his wool is carded, with a comb made of bamboo, whose three or four long prongs are fit only for a horse's mane, and a casquette of broadcloth supplants the scarlet night-cap, fashionable in former days. The kerchief intended for hand use is hung, cravat or scarf-like, round the neck or wrist. Here, as in the Highlands, pockets are wanting.

The toilette being thus finished, breakfast is served. It is a little dinner, ordinarily consisting of obeoka, nda, fufu, fulu and tomeneru,—*Anglicè*, fowl, fish, mashed yam, soup *i.e.* (the liquid in which the stews have been boiled), and tombo, or palm-wine, the latter, however, hard, tasting like soapsuds, and very intoxicating. The cooking is excellent, when English dishes are not attempted. All families have some forbidden meat,—which Captain Owen and Dr. Livingstone call motupo and Boleo ki bo,—such as fowl or fresh beef. The race, however, is carnivorous, eating, when wealthy, fish, poultry, goats, deer, elephant, tortoise and crocodile, the two latter of which are said to be not unlike turtle. Most of the dishes are boiled, and copiously peppered with cayenne and green chili pods to induce thirst. There are many savoury messes of heterogeneous compounds, fish, fresh and dried, oysters, clams, and cockles, poultry, goat and deer, salt beef or ship's pork, yams, plantains, and palm oil. Smoked shrimps are pounded in a wooden pestle and mortar, with mashed yam for consistency, and are put into the soup like forcemeat balls.

The meal always concludes with an external application of soap and water.

After the breakfast tombo is drunk, the warm and savoury nature of the food requiring copious draughts. It is a diuretic, and promotes perspiration, so many a gallon will disappear in the course of a day. When the natural appetite fails, they suck slices of the acid lime, or chew kola nut, or eat ossessossa, a tasteless yellow berry, with a large stone and little pulp, which is said to increase intoxication. When half-drunk the gentleman retires to a cool room, where, fanned by young girls in a state of nature, he sleeps away the sultry hours of noon.

After the siesta he receives or pays visits to his friends, being careful not to appear without armed slaves carrying his large Juju and his snuff-box. He does not dip finger and thumb into the latter, but pours it into the palm of the hand, and leisurely makes up a pinch. Whenever he meets a white man he shakes hands, or rather cracks fingers, holding the crackee's index between the forefinger and thumb of the right hand,—the left is devoted to another purpose,—and loosing snaps them together. It is a knack somewhat difficult to acquire properly. The inferior chiefs and upper slaves are devoted to gambling; all cheat when they can, and a man after losing his supplies, which represent coin, will part with his beads, armlets, and anklets, next follow his knife, red nightcap, and loin cloth, and lastly his wives, relations, and himself. Some of them have proved adepts at European games, especially draughts. When the gentleman stays at home, he performs upon some native instrument, grinds a barrel organ, or enjoys a musical box, a throng of his wives and children peeping through the doorway. Or he looks at conjuring tricks, and perchance jokes with his jester, some slave, whose dry humour, sharp tongue, salt wit, and power of mimicry have made him a favourite. Africans are uncommonly keen in perceiving and in caricaturing any ridicule; they have never, however, attained the dizzy height of Art in the days of Thespis.

A dinner similar to breakfast is eaten at 4 to 5 P.M. Soup and stews are the favourite *ménu*, and mashed yam acts substitute for bread. It is also made into a spoon by a deep impression of the thumb, and thus it carries a thimblefull of soup with every mouthful of yam. The evening is passed by the aid of music, chatting with the women, and playing with the children. It is wound up by smoking and drinking tombo, to which, however, at this hour, the "damned distillation" is preferred, and the gentleman turns in drunk at midnight.

The women and children pass their day in a far humbler manner: they begin at dawn by washing in the creek; they then repair to the artistess who performs the mysteries of body painting. The favourite colour is blue, red, however, is also used. The tints are the indigenous indigo and dye wood, laid on with a hard, flat, sharp-pointed stick. They do not, as our sailors do, depict ships, animals, or figures; they prefer the chequer pattern, and the arabesque, curves and scrolls, beginning and ending with the finest hair strokes, and swelling out, leech-like, to half an inch in the middle. The head woman, whose face and body, arms and legs, have thus been decorated, dresses herself in beads and shawls, or fine cloths, and sallies out after breakfast to see her friends. Sometimes she is received with a nautch, than which no cancan can be grosser: the more literal it is, the more she enjoys it. Men and women prance promiscuously, and the children look on with uncontrollable delight.

Women of the poorer sort pass their time in making nets, hats, fishing-lines, and little mats. During the greater part of the forenoon, and again in the afternoon, they sit in the market-place, selling rum, yams, and plantains. Those who are trusted by their husbands are put in charge of the villages on the banks of the river, and of the " small countries," eight to ten miles in the interior, where superfluous goods and valuables are kept, beyond the reach of bombardment or fire. Sometimes the King invites white traders to his " seat," for the purpose of shooting bullocks that have run wild. The sport is exciting, but as there are no riding animals over-fatigue will probably induce fever. There are, it is said, horses a few days' journey in the interior, and beyond that point they are used as beasts of burthen.

Once a year every great house with its chief repairs to the bush, and makes a surround of men and boys to trap gazelles and antelopes; at times they catch a tartar, in the shape of a leopard, and as few are armed with anything but clubs, a hole is opened in the human ring-fence, allowing it to pass. The evening of the *battue* is spent in devouring its proceeds and in hard striving with strong drinks.

Ladies who are not favourites with the lords their husbands, and all wives of poor men, perform servile work, fetching water, cutting and carrying fuel, fishing with seines, and smoking and drying the proceeds. The younger children are kept at home; after a certain age they resort for education to the streets, or accompany their fathers on business, and when ten years old they are as wise, touching most things and one thing in particular, as their parents.

After this hurried but by no means exaggerated sketch of Bonny Town and the Bonnymen, the reader will perhaps join me in admiring the 'cuteness (Dred, p. 17) which has laid open " the wonderful and beautiful development locked up in the Ethiopian race."

* * * * *

The A. S. S. "Blackland," left this African Styx precisely at her contract time, 4 P.M. on the 26th September. Early on the next morning, when we appeared on deck, all eyes were turning towards the beautiful Peak of Fernando Po, which, after the dull swampy scenery through which we had passed, appeared of giant dimensions. Separated by a narrow channel of nineteen miles from its still more glorious sister, the Camaroons, or, as the savages more poetically call it, the "Mountain of Heaven," it forms the western staple of a Gate that stunts to a nothing the columns of Hercules. The distance-dwarfed grassy cone, superimposed upon the huge shaggy shoulders of the towering ridge, glowed sweetly rosy in the morning sun, and night still brooded in the black Caldera, or chauldron, which, sheer falling for thousands of feet, breaks the regularity of the ascent on the north-eastern side. Upon the flanks, where dark and umbrella-shaped trees rose tier by tier in uninterrupted succession from the base to the foot of the highest crater-cone, heavy white mists, gently rising in the morning air, clung like flocks of cotton to a quickset hedge. We are now entering the tornado season, when the views are almost without atmosphere, and consequently without distance; one supposes the Peak three or four miles off; by directest route it is a good dozen.

I had eyes for little else that morning. The "Blackland" lay in Clarence Cove, a small semicircular bight, with a brace of islets at the mouth, and a perpendicular seabank of stiff yellow clay, ninety-eight feet, ascended by a double and diverging Jacob's ladder, and showing to the sea front a scattered line of about a dozen whitewashed and thatched bungalows. The background was a glorious host of palms, with cotton woods and African cedars, the noblest of their noble family.

Enfin we are here. This is our destination; the Ilha

Formosa, or Beautiful Island, afterwards called after its Portuguese discoverer, Fernão de Poo, and lately known as the "Madeira of the Gulf of Guinea," or the "Foreign Office Grave." It is vain to attempt fixing its locality in the public brain. The secretary of the Hakluyt Society is perhaps capable of telling you that it is a modern discovery. Sundry friends asked the new Consul how he liked the prospect of the Pacific Coast of South America; he was puzzled, till he remembered that as all have read Robinson Crusoe so all must have heard of Juan Fernandez. I may add that the name is infamous in civil and military examinations; when a *coup de grace* has to be administered, young Bœoticus is questioned touching Fernando Po. He returns "plucked" to his papa, who, equally perplexed, employs himself for that day in asking his friends, "Who the deuce is Fernando Po?" to which the natural answer comes—"How the devil should *I* know?"

So closed my voyage outward-bound. Arriving in these outer places is the very abomination of desolation. I drop for a time my pen, in the distinct memory of our having felt uncommonly suicidal through that first night on Fernando Po. And so, probably, did the Consul.

THE END.

www.ingramcontent.com/pod-product-compliance
Lightning Source LLC
Chambersburg PA
CBHW022118230426
43672CB00008B/1422